The Radical in Performance

D0217736

The Radical in Performance interrogates the crisis in contemporary theatre and celebrates the subversive in performance. It is the first full-length study to explore the link between a Western theatre culture, which, says Kershaw, is largely 'past its sell-by date', and the blossoming of performance in the post-modern, much of which has a genuinely radical and democratic edge.

In staying determinedly poised between Brecht and Baudrillard, modernity and post-modernity, Baz Kershaw identifies crucial resources for the revitalisation of the radical across a wide spectrum of cultural practices. He asks 'what next?', once political theatre is all but dead, smothered by the promiscuity of the political in post-modern culture.

This is a timely, necessary and rigorous book. It will be compelling reading for anyone searching for a critical catalyst for new ways of viewing and doing cultural politics.

Baz Kershaw is Professor of Drama at the Department of Drama, University of Bristol. He is the author of *The Politics of Performance* (Routledge 1992).

The Radical in Performance

Between Brecht and Baudrillard

Baz Kershaw

London and New York

First published 1999
by Routledge
11 New Fetter Lane, London EC4P 4EE

Simultaneously published in the USA and Canada
by Routledge
29 West 35th Street, New York, NY 10001

Routledge is an imprint of the Taylor & Francis Group

Typeset in Baskerville by Routledge
Printed and bound in Great Britain by TJ International Ltd,
Padstow, Cornwall

British Library Cataloguing in Publication Data
A catalogue record for this book is available from the British
Library

Library of Congress Cataloguing in Publication Data
Kershaw, Baz.
    The radical in performance: between Brecht and Baudrillard /
Baz Kershaw.
    Includes bibliographical references and index.
    1. Theatre – political aspects. I. Title.
    PN1643.K47   1999   98-55479
    792'.0904–dc21   CIP

ISBN 0–415–18667–6 (hbk)
ISBN 0–415–18668–4 (pbk)

For

Francis Cammaerts,
freedom fighter, world union leader, teacher

and to the memory of

David Sample, 1944–96,
champion of justice

Just because everything is different, doesn't mean anything has changed.
Southern Californian Oracle

Contents

Illustrations

Acknowledgements

This book has had a long and somewhat secretive gestation, even for its author, which means it is inevitable that some people who deserve thanks will not receive them. I am sorry for this because I'm sure the net of collaboration was often stretched for my benefit by colleagues and friends well beyond the call of duty or pleasures of mutual entertainment. So thanks to those of you who had a now invisible influence on what follows.

I owe specific debts of gratitude, great and small but never insignificant, for many different kinds of stimulation, encouragement and support from the following individuals who participated directly (though sometimes they may not have known it) in the evolution of this book: Nicholas Abercrombie, Michael Balfour, Martin Banham, Clive Barker, Herbert Blau, Patrick Campbell, Byron Eyre-Varnier, John Fox, Scott Fugate, Viv Gardner, Gabriella Giannachi, Sue Gill, Tracey Harding, Gerry Harris, Wallace Heim, Albert Hunt, Ann Jellicoe, Lloyd Johnston, Russell Keat, James Kelman, Richard Kimmel, Annette Kuhn, Mandla Langa, Gordon Langley, Francesca Leighton, Chris McCullough, Hugo Medina, Lindsay Newman, Lee Phillips, Malcolm Quainton, Andrew Quick, Frances Rifkin, Nick Sales, Wally Serota, Ted Shank, John Somers, Nigel Stewart, Alison Sutcliffe, Bron Szersynski, Peter Thomson, Jennifer Till, Simon Trussler, John Urry, Enrique Vargas, Jatinder Verma, Mick Wallis, Lois Weaver, Nigel Whiteley and Lynn Wilman.

Ten years of being quizzed, humoured and partied by Theatre Studies students at Lancaster University, particularly in the Radical Theatre and Research Issues courses, inform these pages like the ground swell of the sea. I also benefited greatly from the challenging thinking of many colleagues and friends in the University's Institute for Cultural Research and the Centre for the Study of Environmental Change. This was matched only by the waywardly creative adventures

I had with some of the performance companies that I write about in this book.

I am very grateful for financial support in the form of a Research Leave Award from the British Academy and for various grants from the Committee for Research at Lancaster University. At Routledge I have had sterling support and guidance from Talia Rodgers, while Jason Arthur provided an unassuming and impressively reassuring efficiency.

I am especially grateful to Jill Sample for agreeing to let me dedicate this book to the memory of Dave Sample, who, together with Francis Cammaerts, taught me more about humane politics than I can probably ever expect to achieve in practice.

This book could not have been written without Gill Hadley's always intelligent and empathic presence. Without Eleanor and Logan it would not have been half so much fun. To them I owe gratitude beyond measure.

Parts of this book have appeared elsewhere in print. I am grateful for permission to recycle this material from the following sources: *The Authority of the Consumer* (London: Routledge, 1994); *Analysing Performance: A Critical Reader* (Manchester: Manchester University Press, 1996); *New Theatre Quarterly*, *Theatre Forum*, *Research in Drama Education*. The C.P. Cavafy quotation from 'Ithaca' appears courtesy of the Estate of C.P. Cavafy, from *The Complete Poems of Cavafy*, trans. Rae Dalven, Hogarth Press, 1961 (© 1961 and renewed 1989 by Rae Dalven; reprinted by permission of Harcourt Brace & Company).

Every effort has been made to trace copyright holders of material used in this book; copyright holders not named should contact the publisher for inclusion in any further editions.

Of course, if there are any errors in this book they are entirely my responsibility.

Prologue
Radicalising performance

What happens to the hole when the cheese is gone?
Brecht

Dancing to the drill-bits

I left school at fifteen and started work as an apprentice: five years of hands-on training in a Manchester engineering works. For the first three months I was an office boy, learning how to make good tea and do technical filing, then I was transferred to my first shop-floor job. I'll never forget the morning switch-on in the machine shop: the long rows of lathes, grinders, planers and drills gradually start up and the noise builds into a deafening commotion of squealing, banging, thudding, shuddering and groaning that goes on for the whole day long. The factory air grows thick with vibration and I remember my boy's body being thrilled to be part of its amazing power.

On that first morning the foreman led me to a short row of pillar drills: five vertical motors that narrowed down to chucks that held five different sized drill-bits, the finest thinner than a match-stick. By each chuck there was a thin nozzle that spurted milky-coloured liquid to keep the drill-bit cool. A narrow grey metal table ran under the drills, scarred and polished by years of use and fringed by channelling through which the coolant drained back into an endless cycle. On the end of the table there was a three-inch cube of steel that hinged in half and had five small bobbins or bushes set into three sides, each with a hole the same size as the bits in the drills. Just by the jig was a small and oily card-board box, and in the box was 'the job': about 200 quarter-inch diameter, inch-and-a-half long shiny brass pins. Each pin had to be fastened into the jig, which was then moved along the table, stopping at each drill. A lever then had to be pulled down so that the bits went through the bushes to end up with the pin neatly drilled with five holes. After the last drill the jig was opened, the pin flipped into another cardboard box and the whole process started again.

It took the foreman just a minute or two to show me the routine. Then he stood by, watching closely as I slowly worked through the first few pins. To start with, it wasn't easy to clamp the jig without nipping your skin. Getting the jig into the right spot so that the drill-bits didn't skew to one side and break was harder than it looked. Pulling down on the lever with the exact pressure to get a clean cut and avoid jamming the drills was tricky. Even emptying the jig without burning your fingers on the hot metal needed a well-judged flick. So drilling the first few pins was really frightening, because it was obvious that the bits could break or you could easily put one through your finger. With the foreman peering at me I felt totally unco-ordinated: my hands trembled and it took a massive effort to move my arms – almost as if they didn't belong to me. I got through it, though, with only a shallow, nasty gouge in the back of my hand from where I had jagged it up against one of the nozzles. I remember the foreman smiling as I watched my blood leach into the white coolant dribbling across my knuckles. He winked at me and was on his way along the shop-floor without a word, satisfied I was safe enough. But I was shaking with tension and just wanted to run for it, to get out of there.

But by the thirtieth pin I'd got the hang of it and was shifting along the table fairly efficiently. By the sixtieth pin I was even beginning to enjoy myself as I found something of a rhythm. By about the hundredth pin I started to wonder if I could manage it with my eyes shut. Not long after that I was having a great time, feeling totally in control of the job with everything judged just right and moving so crisply it felt like I'd been doing it all my life. And soon I'd got into the whole swing of it so much that it was like dancing and I was exhilarated at having met that machine and learning so quickly how to make it work so smoothly. It was a brilliant feeling of dancing satisfaction at being a real apprentice as I worked through the last few pins in the cardboard box.

The foreman came back a few minutes after I'd finished the last pin. I was really excited by the idea of going on to a new job, perhaps on one of the roaring lathes. He looked at the drilled pins in the box and without a word nodded for me to follow him. We walked down the long lane between the machines and the working men towards his desk. I remember two or three of them grinning at me. When we got to the end of the shop the foreman pointed at a heavy trolley that was loaded up with big wooden ammunition boxes. I was so chuffed at what I'd done that I didn't catch on until he opened the top box and I saw it was filled with thousands and thousands of brass pins, just the same size as the ones I'd drilled. I helped the foreman drag the trolley back to the pillar drills, all the way fighting back tears. I was on that job for the next three months, cursing the factory nearly every day, even when I sometimes danced to its strengthening tunes.

Introduction
Pathologies of hope

All modern thought is permeated by the idea of thinking the unthinkable.

Foucault

A touch of the radical

This book is an investigation of the radical in performance. What makes a performance radical? How might performances cause people to become radical? Are there common sources for different kinds of radical performance? What are the conditions through which radical performance can thrive? Such questions, I think, are becoming more urgent as the world wakes up to the twenty-first century, because the processes of *performance* have become ever more crucial in the great cultural, social and political changes of our times. Simultaneously the place of *theatre* in post-industrial societies seems increasingly compromised, even by its success, and so its potential for radicalism has become subject to doubt. In the wake of the 'collapse of communism' in Russia and Eastern Europe old notions of political theatre are falling into intellectual disrepute, and as corporate capitalism spreads across the globe the established estate of theatre is transformed into a playground for the newly privileged, a quick stop-over site on the tourist and heritage map, an emporium in which the culturally curious can sample the latest short-lived life-styles. But while theatre mostly has become a marginal commodity in the capitalist cultural market-place, performance has emerged as central to the production of the new world disorder, a key process in virtually every socio-political domain of the mediatised globe. The *performative* quality of power is shaping the global future as it never has before.

The issues raised for *radical performance* in this turbulent context are, well, radical. For example, in the capitalist democracies, confidence in the legitimacy of established political processes is in a state of continual crisis, and that, paradoxically, undermines any performance that aims to be politically oppositional: if few people really believe in the State then it is hardly worth attacking. Simultaneously, the mediatisation of society disperses the theatrical by inserting performance into everyday life – every time we turn into the media we are confronted by the representational styles of a performative world – and in the process the ideological impact of performance becomes ever more diverse. Moreover, the globalisation of communications presents the life of other cultures performatively, as widening realms of human identity become object to the spectator's gaze, and the social and political resonance of terrible crises, such as the suffering of starving Somalians or the war in Bosnia, is absorbed by the relentless opacity of the electronic spectacle. As performance proliferates, the radical in performance becomes harder to pinpoint.

The new importance of performance is one of the key features of 'the condition of postmodernity' (Harvey 1990). Dick Hebdige has mordantly summarised some of its attributes:

> ...morbid projections of post-war generation baby boomers confronting disillusioned middle age...a proliferation of surfaces, a new phase in commodity fetishism, a fascination for images, codes and styles, a process of cultural, political or existential fragmentation, and/or crises, the 'decentring' of the subject, an 'incredulity towards metanarratives', the replacement of unitary power axes by a plurality of power/discourse formations, the 'implosion of meaning', the collapse of cultural hierarchies....
>
> (1993: 71)

Hence, post-modernity signals an acute destabilisation of the cultural climate throughout the world: an end to all the human certainties of the modernist past. There is a marvellous sense of liberation in this – at last the individual is free to construct him- or herself as he or she desires – but also an acute anxiety: on what are we to base our judgements? As a result, in writing about the post-modern and post-modernism critics and scholars have tended to become polarised, setting up conflicting critical camps. Historians and analysts of theatre and performance have not, of course, escaped this pathology. Particularly in Britain, but elsewhere as well, theatre scholars have embraced post-modernism as a major breakthrough to new kinds of knowledge, or rejected it as confused and contradictory: the product of passing fashion. Especially if you write about *contemporary* performance, either you are *with* the post-modern or you are not.

This kind of polarisation, in some respects, is entirely reasonable. If one accepts that the meta-narratives deriving from the Enlightenment must now be subject to intense incredulity because, for example, they led to the obscenities of the Nazi Holocaust or the absurdities of Soviet-style communism, then one is bound to be suspicious of anything that smacks of a rational, totalising explanation of the world. So even a rela-tively moderate generalised claim, say to a belief that democracy might be the best political system for every society, can look dangerously totali-tarian. At the same time, it looks odd to argue, on the one hand, for the universal progress of humankind towards democratic dispensations in which a fair measure of justice, equality and freedom will be available to all, *and*, on the other hand, to believe that the inescapable diversity of human identities undermines universals of any kind and so scuppers any notion of a progress that claims to include everybody. This type of logical polarity is rife in the debates stimulated by post-modernism. Ironically, it becomes very difficult to profess a *straightforward* reservation about the way the debates tend to produce exclusive critical camps. But this book aims to hold on to such a reservation, and to straddle some of the theoretical fences between the camps, in its attempt to throw some clarifying light on the confusions of an *actual* world of performance in which the great paradigms of post-modernism and modernism are not so much locked in logical opposition, but instead are intertwined like the lines of an unfinished mandala.

Contemporary live performance, especially outside theatre buildings, is a wonderfully energetic field to tap into in undertaking this task, because as a profoundly public genre it is inevitably thoroughly contam-inated by its wider cultural context. It follows that contemporary performances will be more or less *constituted* by the ways in which the paradigms are rubbing up across each other. This will be the case particularly for any performance identified as *radical*, because by defini-tion it will be deeply rooted in the conditions of the contemporary. So radical performance always participates in the most vital cultural, social and political tensions of its time. Currently, the greatest radical turbu-lence can be found in performance when modernist and post-modernist versions of the world collide.

This is why I invoke Brecht and Baudrillard in my sub-title, as they provide profoundly radical perspectives on the socio-political signifi-cance of performance, but from such contrasting points of view. They are my emblems for a way of exploring the radical in contemporary performance that aims ultimately to keep several analytical perspectives in play at once. My chief purpose in this is to give primacy to the practice of performance itself, even though in writing about performance we are always automatically subjecting it to theory. So while sometimes it will be very uncomfortable to hover between Brecht and Baudrillard, a straddling of the various theoretical fences may not be such an unsound stance if through it we can gain a clearer view of contemporary performance in practice. The strategy might even provide answers to the question at the heart of this book: if we stay resolutely astride the contemporary paradigms, if we perch on the cusp between Brecht, Baudrillard and the other great emblems of recent cultural change, what insights might be gained into the processes of the radical in performance, and what light will that throw on the great political, ethical, genetic and ecological issues confronting the world at the start of the twenty-first century?

Pathological hope

Four-hundred people crowd along the edge of the dockside. The Captain yells instructions through a megaphone to a minion in a dinghy in the middle of the dock. The great arm of a crane swings out over the water and moments later it is hauling up, from out of the oily depths, a seventy foot-long skeletal apparition, liquid pouring from masses of flapping seaweed as it is cranked up into a steep slant to tower above the heads of the amazed audience. It represents only the stern-end third of the great ship, but it is chillingly suggestive of much more hidden below the shimmering surface. The syncopic band strikes up a bouncy tune and the crowd retreats to the tiered seats set twenty metres back from the brink of the dock. As dusk falls, the show that calls up the dead to bear witness to the sickness of Western civilisation begins.

Raising the 'Titanic' was staged by Welfare State International at Limehouse Basin in the East End of London in 1983, as the only commission for the second London International Festival of Theatre. Besides the sixty-strong professional team of performers, makers, engineers, stage managers and community liaison workers, over 150 local people worked on the show. Many of them lived in the appallingly run-down blocks of 1960s high-rise flats that still make up much of nearby Tower Hamlets. From the site of the show they could also see the Thames-side Victorian warehouses that had been converted to gentrified bolt-holes for the metropolitan élite, including a couple of major celebrities of British theatre. Only three months after Thatcher's re-election to a second term of office in the triumphalist wake of the Falklands War, there were deeply ironic parallels between the current social context and the class-ridden subject of the show. To stage those ironies, *Raising the 'Titanic'* was designed unambiguously, in director John Fox's words, as 'an allegory about the state of Western Culture' (Fox 1988: 9; Coult and Kershaw 1990: 207–18).

The allegorical impulse to render symbolism transparent was apparent in virtually every aspect of the show's vaudeville format. In the opening scene at the 'Captain's Table', for example, the wealthiest passengers of the ship stage a song in celebration of culinary excess in which the 'food' is cleverly made from the detritus of contemporary consumerism – an old car inner-tube becomes a sumptuous salmon, bits of cast-off foam create a wondrous dessert – ironically indicating the depravity of their greed. More obviously, the vertical layers of the set, built from real ship-containers, are made to represent the class system, as in a later scene the black-faced stokers climb up in revolt from the ship's lower depths, only to be beaten down by rich and decadent fancy-dressers wearing death masks. Also, the variety-style structure conforms to a loose but clear narrative progression, from the musical 'launch' of the show as a metaphoric voyage to the achingly sad lament of the 'Survivors', who clamber on to dockside debris as the huge frame of the skeletal *Titanic* is set aflame and slowly lowered back down, sizzling into the black waters of the basin. This was agitprop on the grand scale, an attack on Western culture mounted through a fairly systematic symbolism, larded with dashes of surrealist imagery. As such, it could be seen to reach back through the great avant-garde traditions of twentieth-century Western theatre even to the medieval mystery and morality plays of the early modern world. In many respects *Raising the 'Titanic'* was certainly a modernist production.

Yet many post-modern tropes can be identified easily in both the detail and the total structure of the event. For example, even a brief scene that covers a complicated set change carries a deconstructive charge. Two 'cleaning ladies' sweep the concrete dock with a couple of anachron-istic and obviously knackered vacuum cleaners, raucously singing 'My bonny lies over the ocean' and finally confronting the audience side by side in choral extravagance.

BOTH: We are the clichéd cleaning ladies, the stereotypes to make you laugh. As far as I'm concerned they're all the same – owners, dealers, captains – same system, same organisation, same rotters.

Figure 1   The 'cleaning ladies' from *Raising the 'Titanic'*, 1983

Note: The stern-end of the skeletal *Titanic* can be seen to the left above the ship-container set, with its lifting crane to the right. Performers: Celia Gore-Booth and Val Levkovitz

Source: Welfare State International at LIFT (London International Festival of Theatre) (1983). Reproduced by kind permission of Welfare State International. Photograph: Vicki Carter

But they suddenly stop the choric parody, and speak plainly and simply as 'themselves'.

FIRST: I speak for a woman who lived in Southampton. Her man couldn't get work, so he went as a foreman aboard the Titanic. His pay was stopped the minute the ship went down. It didn't matter though – he drowned.

SECOND: I speak for a mother who lived in Portsmouth. Her son couldn't find work, so he enlisted as a cook on the 'Sheffield'. He died in the Falklands of really modern burns.

The simple switch of register problematises the subject – who is speaking? – and simultaneously reinforces the self-referentiality of the choric opening, ironically drawing further attention to its own construct-edness. In this, as well as in its use of 'personal' testimony or witness, the scene participates in the kinds of post-modern provocation staged by, say, Forced Entertainment in England or the Wooster Group in America.

In some ways, too, the structure of the whole event operated in a deconstructive realm. The show itself was preceded by a dockside market in which local groups sold home-made produce from stalls decked out as lifeboats, and it was followed by a barn-dance on the dockside that had the audience bopping to the Welfare State band until late into the night. The sandwiching of 'social' and 'artistic' forms blurred the difference between everyday and aesthetic experience, producing a hybrid genre that challenged the distinctions between the 'high' and 'popular' arts, between professional and non-professional cultural production, between International Festival triumph and local community celebration. In these ways and others, *Raising the 'Titanic'* – generated a 'collapse of cultural hierarchies' that tended to detach representation from the real – shifted everything it touched towards Baudrillardian simulation.

Yet, too, the show could be cited as a late example of the major twentieth-century theatrical genre that Elinor Fuchs calls the 'mysterium'. She identifies the mysterium in the work of Strindberg, Artaud, Brecht and Beckett, among many others, arguing that it 'evolved in part as a revival of allegorical methods, however dislocated by a self conscious, modernist irony' (1996: 37). Fuchs perceptively sees the mysterium as a singular force in an ongoing transition from moder-nity to post-modernity in Western cultures, as:

> …a station en route to the new allegorisis of postmodern 'concep-tual' performance, in which the spectator becomes the organiser and interpreter of patterns, but now without the mediation of a shared set of references, however fractured.
>
> (1996: 51)

The dislocation and fracturing of 'shared set[s] of references' (or mean-ings), especially when driven home by irony, is often identified as a key characteristic of post-modern performance (Kaye 1994: 22). Indeed, this privileging of the audience in the process of making meanings has become crucial to the construction of clear distinctions between mod-ernist and post-modernist aesthetic forms, the former working on the assumption of the possibility of stable meanings that can be 'shared' between author and reader, actor and audience, stage and auditorium, and the latter forever disrupting that assumption by deconstructing the process of meaning-making itself. From this perspective, the show's use of the *Titanic* as an over-riding metaphor for a corrupt Western civilisation creates stable meanings: in theory, every image and action could be significantly 'placed' as part of a coherent allegorical pattern. Moreover, the disruption of signification, the separation of sign from referent typical of post-modern theatre, is undermined by the clear parallels between the show's text and its social context. The corrupt and unfair hierarchy portrayed by the allegory had actual referents in the cityscape that was visible to the audience sitting in the outdoor auditorium. The spirit of Baudrillard may have (in)substantially informed the show, but Brecht's ghost was certainly making a challenge to gain the aesthetic and ideological upper hand.

So viewed through binocular theoretical lenses, the show was *both* modernist *and* post-modernist, a strongly allegorical mysterium and a pattern of signs that were forever slipping beyond shared sets of references, away from stable meaning. As a result, *Raising the 'Titanic'* can be seen as absolutely riddled with contradictions. For example, the allegory attacked consumerism yet consumed a great deal of materials in the process, and it advocated egalitarian and democratic ethics while being so logistically complex that it had to be organised like a military campaign. However, the event continually transformed these contradictions into paradoxes through a sustained reflexive irony that was produced through its double dealing across paradigms: even as the allegory assumed the possibility of stable meaning it was undermined by the incommensurability of its signs. So, for example, it demonstrated that disaster has to be courted in order to avoid it. And it showed that when extravagance attacks itself, excess advocates restraint. *Raising the 'Titanic'* became paradoxically illuminating in these and other ways, I think, because it participated in modernity *and* post-modernity, borrowing, in a sense, from both Brecht and Baudrillard to create a cultural hybrid that wonderfully celebrated new kinds of creativity. Despite its desperation about Western civilisation, then, the event was vitally inflected by a pathology of hope.

Theatre and performance

The debates about contemporary culture that have raged in the arts, humanities and social sciences for many years suggest a definition of the post-modern as primarily a zone of ideological contention and cultural tension. This definition is an enabling move for my overall argument here, because it positions current issues in the analysis of theatre and performance as symptomatic of wider instabilities in contemporary cultures, so the more vigorous the debates the more likely it is that they signal significant shifts in the broader scene of the social. Probably *the* major issue in the study of theatre in recent years, particularly in America but increasingly in Europe, has been about the nature of the relationships between theatre and performance.

The growing interest in performance can be traced in a wide range of books by theatre historians and scholars, from Raymond Williams's remarkably prescient *Drama in Performance* (1954) to Marvin Carlson's *Performance: A Critical Introduction* (1996), but, as Carlson points out, it is only relatively recently that performance has become an important idea in many other disciplines (1996: 1). A major part of the reason for this can be identified, I think, in widespread changes in the processes of the social, which are producing what I call the *performative society*. Performative societies in the contemporary world are found particularly where democracy and capitalism meet. In such societies performance has gained a new kind of potency because multi-party democracy weaves ideological conflict visibly into the very fabric of society. It follows that, especially in highly mediatised societies, the performative becomes a major element in the continuous negotiations of power and authority. So modern democracies, including the new ones thrown up in the wake of 1989, may be described with some accuracy as *performative democracies* in order to indicate how fully they rely upon various types of performance for the maintenance of their political processes and social structures. Moreover, late-capitalist liberal democracies reinforce this tendency by making the market so central to social organisation. Although the 'performance' of companies, firms, shares, employees, institutions, etc., may be measured primarily in mundane material and/or statistical ways, the notion that they are 'players' on an economic or industrial or civil 'stage' is always implied by the usage. Equally, how individuals fare in the competition between life-styles or the struggle for survival depends increasingly on their ability to 'perform'. Hence, late-capitalist multi-party democracies produce societies in which performance pervades cultural process; it becomes the *sine qua non* of human exchange in virtually all spheres of the social. It is hardly surprising, then, that conflicts among theatre scholars and historians should arise, as they have, about the proper object of study in their discipline: should it be theatre or performance, or both? And if it is both, how are their relationships best figured?

Typically, the performance theorist and director Richard Schechner framed the problem with provocative aplomb for the gathered ranks of the American Association for Theatre in Higher Education in 1992:

> The fact is that theatre as we have known and practiced it – the staging of written dramas – will be the string quartet of the twenty-first century: a beloved but extremely limited genre, a subdivision of performance.
>
> (1992: 8)

And he went on to list what he sees as the 'broad spectrum of entertainments, arts, rituals, politics, economics, and person-to-person interactions' that constitute performance. In the performative society the list can be extended easily, but it will not move us any closer to a better understanding of performance itself, nor of theatre's relationship to it, because the analytical method is crucially flawed. As David George points out in an excellent essay on 'Performance epistemology', the list produces a classic 'hermeneutic circle', because:

> Any list of items purporting to be 'performances' has been based in its selection on some implicit, latent definition of what performance is but the very definition has been derived from the list.
>
> (1996: 17)

George aims to break this vicious circle through a response informed by phenomenology. He argues for a recognition of the primacy of performance over representation, because performance:

> ...offers a rediscovery of the now...rediscovery that all knowledge exists on the threshold of and in the interaction between subject and object; a rediscovery of ambiguity, of contradiction, of difference....
>
> (1996: 25)

Readers alert to the drift of my argument will by now have spotted that the debate between these two positions shadows major themes to be found around the cusp of current paradigm shifts. But the problem of the relationships between theatre and performance cannot be solved simply by aligning 'theatre' with a sclerotic modernism – the string quartet syndrome – and celebrating 'performance' as a metaphorical key to the slippery delights of post-modernity. For performance and theatre participate crucially across the paradigms, because it is the performative society that is producing the lines of the unfinished mandala of contemporary change.

Nevertheless, the argument of this book follows some of the tendencies in the Schechner–George debate by picking up an underlying theme in the general critical realignment of theatre and performance. The theme has two dominant but wholly interdependent strains, the first worrying over the now manifest *limitations* of theatre and the second breathless about the unavoidable *limitlessness* of performance. My purpose here is to give due recognition to the ways in which the theme may be keyed to actual changes in contemporary cultures, while highlighting the conceptual usefulness of the two terms – theatre and performance – in relation to each other. Hence, I emphasise the pragmatic limits of 'theatre' by using it to refer mainly to the permanent buildings (and their institutional structures) that have been created specially for the housing of live performance; in this sense theatre is a tiny part of the burgeoning cultural industries of the performative society. But also I aim to side-step the theoretical abyss that opens up when 'performance' is attached to almost every human activity, by using it mainly to indicate cultural presentations that have recognisable theatrical components: namely, framing devices that alert the audience, spectators or participants to the reflexive structure of what is staged, drawing attention to its constructed nature, and more or less to the assumptions – social and/or political and/or cultural and/or philosophical, etc. – through which that construction is achieved. Not all performances in the performative society are 'performance' in this sense, but a good deal of what goes on outside 'theatre' (as well as some things that happen in it) is encompassed by this definition.

I am drawing the distinction between theatre and performance in this way partly because it can then be taken to exemplify major characteristics of the contemporary shift between paradigms: from fixity to flexibility, from cohesion to fragmentation, from hierarchy to equality, from unity to plurality, from culture to multi-cultures, and so on – but without falling into the trap of a wholesale binary opposition between the two. Hence, in Part I of this book, I aim to create a contrastive link between the 'limits of theatre' and the 'excesses of performance' that indicates the diminished role that I think theatre is likely to play in the making of a contemporary radical socio-political agenda for the future. This critical strategy then opens up grounds for the analysis of a wide range of performance types in Part II, including protest events, prison drama, blackface minstrelsy, heritage performance, reminiscence theatre and performative mazes. These examples are explored to test 'performance beyond theatre' as a more fruitful domain for radicalism than performance in theatre. I argue that performance beyond theatre provides powerful sources for the radical, paradoxically because its excesses are more directly shaped by the cultural pathologies that threaten radicalism in the theatre. Those pathologies ensue from the inevitable instabilities of any culture articulated to the cusp of a paradigm shift. For example, in capitalist democracies cultural tensions are generated between (a) the conformity forced on cultural production by capitalist consumerism and (b) the diversity of cultural differences fostered by liberal democracy. Performances beyond theatre may engage with such tensions in particularly telling ways, revealing how many established ideas, theories, traditions and practices have been shaken fundamentally by tectonic shifts in the cultural, social and political disorder of the late twentieth century. Hence, customary versions of the marriage between 'politics' and 'theatre' have been infected fatally by the new pathologies, threatening an end to conventional ideas about the political in theatre. But if 'political theatre' is dying, what might replace it?

Radicalism and its sources

For some time now the idea of 'political theatre' has been in crisis. Postmodernism and related theories have profoundly upset established notions of the 'political' in theatre, which were usually defined in relation to left-wing or socialist/Marxist ideologies. Right-wing theatre, by implication, was not political. The problem is now compounded because Left-progressive ideologies appear to be in decline, but more importantly also because of the new promiscuity of the political. Since the personal became political, in the 1960s, the political has found its way into almost every nook and cranny of culture. Identity politics, the politics of camp, body politics, sexual politics – the political is now ubiquitous and can be identified in all theatre and performance. Such promiscuity, though, breeds a new kind of uncertainty.

The critical sources of this destabilisation are not difficult to locate. So long as we accept the full force of the post-modern paradigm and allow that Barthes has finally done for the intentional fallacy by murdering the author, Foucault has incontrovertibly shown that power is everywhere, Derrida has uncoupled the signifier from the signified forever, Lyotard has raised incredulity about master narratives to a new order of intensity, Butler has demonstrated that even gender is a cultural construct, and Baudrillard has possibly capped it all by banishing the real, we will be plagued by an acute indecision about the politics of theatre and performance in the contemporary world. The anti-foundational theorists of post-modernism and its cousins, though offering an exhilarating release from oppressive systems of thought, also threaten to plunge us into a miasma of ideological relativity.

So how might we judge one aesthetic approach to be more politically promising than another? Is live art's deconstruction of the politics of representation, say, any more or less potent than community celebration's political reinforcement of collective identity? The difficulty of such questions then tends to reinforce the relativities that gave rise to them in the first place: it all depends just where you're standing when. A piece of performance may have tremendous political resonance for its audiences, but someone somewhere else is bound to find it ideologically vacuous. Whilst one might happily applaud the healthy celebration of difference implied by such relativism, clearly it also has the potential to impose a debilitating limitation on analysis. Any conclusions about the potential ideological efficacy of any particular approach to performance practice inevitably will be constrained in their scope. Most worrying of all, the general contribution of theatre and performance to social and political histories may become impossible to determine. The kind of vision projected by Brecht – which encompassed a world enjoying a growing measure of justice, equality and freedom – will forever be a thing of the past.

The argument of this book pursues the notion that 'radical performance' might usefully replace 'political theatre', not because it will enable us to somehow settle the issues raised by the promiscuity of the political in post-modernism, but rather because it will allow us to more directly encounter them. I have just suggested how a shift of focus between theatre and performance should provide more open grounds on which to encounter those issues. Similarly, a broadening of scope from the political to the radical should produce opportunities for a more thorough mapping of the territory gained from a fresh look at the politics of performance. This is chiefly because the radical is bound to be evoked vitally by any paradigm shift, as the old certainties are uprooted and the new dispensation scatters its seeds of hope for a rejuvenated future. But also the idea of the radical can encompass both the fundamental change and the uncertainty of outcome signalled by the post-modern and post-modernity. In this regard, Raymond Williams has framed one of the most acute definitions of the term:

Radical seemed to offer a way of avoiding dogmatic and factional association while reasserting the need for vigorous and fundamental change.

(1976: 210)

Clearly, in this definition the radical has no necessary ideological tendency; hence it may be claimed (as indeed it has been) by both Left and Right factions in contemporary politics. But by the same token it gestures beyond all forms of the dogmatic, towards kinds of freedom that currently cannot be envisaged. It is particularly this sense of the word that I wish to invoke in 'radical performance', because, as well as joining in the challenge to old ideas of 'political theatre', I want vigorously to interrogate the limits that post-modernism places on the potential of creative radicalism.

These limits are paradoxically produced by the liberation from the oppressions of modernism promised by post-modernity, and they create some of the major themes traversed in this book. Hence, on the cusp of the paradigm shift new freedoms are offered by post-modernism's celebration of human difference, by its reconstitution of the individual as a series of subject positions, by its recognition that all subject positions are equally 'valid', by the tolerance implied by its expansive embrace of pluralism, and so on. But the distaff side of this radical liberalism is the death of community, the loss of agency, the end of history, even the demise of meaning in the wholesale rejection of anything that smacks of ontological and epistemological certainty. So the chief challenge offered by the paradigm shift to the idea of the radical can be framed generally as follows: how to hold on to the healthy democratising pressures of the post-modern, without succumbing to the dangers embedded in its tendencies to ethical relativism, political pragmatism, genetic quietism and ecological pessimism?

My response to this challenge is an argument that claims for radical performance a potential to create various kinds of freedom that are not only resistant to dominant ideologies, but that also are sometimes transgressive, even transcendent, of ideology itself. In other words, the freedom that 'radical performance' invokes is not just freedom *from* oppression, repression, exploitation – the resistant sense of the radical – but also freedom *to reach beyond* existing systems of formalised power, freedom to create currently unimaginable forms of association and action – the transgressive or transcendent sense of the radical. What I am interested in centrally, then, is not the ways in which radical performance might *represent* such freedoms, but rather how radical performance can actually *produce* such freedoms, or at least a sense of them, for both performers and spectators, as it is happening.

This entails a search for convincing accounts of the *sources* of such freedoms in performance in order to fully realise the potential for radical cultural praxis on the cusp of the paradigm shift. Because if we can convincingly identify the possibility of sources of radical freedom as such, then we will be closer to answering my opening question about what makes a performance radical. I am aware, of course, that my choice of the word 'source' can be interpreted as begging the question of the doctrine of first causes that post-modernism healthily challenges; that there is, for example, an originative point to knowledge that would provide answers to all the mysteries of the world, if only we could find it. Keeping one foot in the post-modernist camp entails a rejection of that doctrine; but at the same time the modernist ambition to make generalisations that may help to transform the world into a better place informs the argument of this book. So I hope to maintain an admittedly precarious theoretical balance by speaking in the plural of 'sources' and by using the word transitively in the sense of 'fountain-head' or 'a work supplying information or evidence'; that is to say, 'sources' indicates points of process through which *new* energy and knowledge can be freely created. The sources of such freedom in performance *are* its radical potential, in that they give rise to the creation of new radical possibilities *in* performance.

To variously test these ideas to their limits, it makes sense to look for the sources of radicalism in performance where oppressions are at their most acute, where the threat of ideological incorporation and co-option is intense, and where tolerant repression offers its subtlest welcome. Accordingly, I write about performances in the contexts of the global media circus (protest events), in prisons (prison drama), in the colonial nexus (blackface minstrelsy), in the heritage industry (heritage performance), in the 'retreat' into old age (reminiscence theatre), and in the merry-go-round of international cultural festivals (performative mazes). Apart from the fun it provides, I chose such a wide spectrum of unlikely places because it enables a search for radicalism in performance in crucial features of contemporary social process. Thus, protest events are expressions of civil society; prison drama and blackface minstrelsy engage with ubiquitous systems of panoptic oppression; heritage performance and reminiscence theatre play in the realms of cultural memory; and performative mazes explore the potential of virtual community. If we can identify any common or overlapping features to the sources of radicalism in that variety then we might be able to spot them more easily elsewhere. More importantly, if radicalism can flourish through performance as part of *those* social processes, then it may potentially prosper in many others. In this respect my argument does not foreclose on the possibility of radicalism in the *theatre* of the future. But four main characteristics of the radical in performance that emerge from my search are currently found much more commonly together in performance beyond theatre. For the moment I shall name them, somewhat gnomically, as: dialogic exchange, participatory engagement, performative absence, and aesthetic reflexivity.

These cryptic phrases signpost the ideological direction of my overall argument, which aims to identify some of the features of what I call *democratised performance*. For it is clear that speaking about the sources of radicalism in performance tells us nothing of its content. As Jan Cohen-Cruz notes of Nazi rallies in a recent collection on radical street performance:

> radical performance encompasses left- and right-wing politics. Broadcasting the Aryan ideal to the masses…the 1934 Nuremberg Party rally is a paradigm of street theatre as media opportunity.
>
> (1998: 169)

In general terms, then, radical performance is made problematic by cultural praxis, in that it invites an ideological investment that it cannot of itself determine. In that sense, it is always a creative opportunity to change the world for better or worse, a performative process in need of direction. And ultimately this is why, for me, hovering about the cusp of a paradigm shift, straddling the fences between theoretical camps, is currently the only viable ideological option. Disgusted by the murderously oppressive histories of modernity, suspicious of the absolute relativism offered by post-modernity, to me the tenuous promise of a continually revised and renewed democracy seems like the only hope of balancing the best in both Baudrillard and Brecht. For in order to strengthen a Brechtian belief in the possibility of an expanding realm of justice, equality and freedom in the real world of the next millennium, we may need Baudrillard's insights into the delirious promise of late twentieth-century post-modernity.

'On the cusp of the paradigm shift'

But…in post-modernism, incredulity and scepticism are the order of the day; take them away and the whole theoretical gamut tends to evaporate. In its most extreme forms, in the hyper-real world imagined by Baudrillard, where the real is totally engulfed by the contemporary maelstrom of signs, scepticism turns against itself and generates nihilism. How, then, might we at least partly square the vicious circle produced by a desire to embrace the post-modern paradigm along with the others? Paradoxically, the answer lies in post-modernism itself.

The witty title of John Frow's essay 'What was postmodernism?' signals a humorous doubt that leads him to demonstrate convincingly that 'the concept of postmodernism is logically incoherent' (1997: 26). Despite this scepticism, though, in his conclusion Frow quotes with approval Gerald Graff's view of the post-modern:

> ...it is difficult to take the concept seriously yet not easy to dismiss it [because] once a certain number of people believe that the concept of the Post-Modern marks a real change in the cultural climate, the change becomes a reality to be reckoned with, even if the reality is not exactly what most users of the term think it is.
>
> (1997: 63)

One of the uses of the term that Frow attacks with particular virulence is when it is taken to indicate an historical epoch:

> Pseudo-totalities generate pseudo-histories; the epochal sense of the concept of the post-modern depends for its existence on such historico-pseudo fictions.
>
> (1997: 53)

In other words, some of the cultural changes that 'post-modernism' signifies are certainly real, but the idea that it marks a new phase in the history of the world should currently be treated with vigorous caution, as it may best be thought of as a seductive fiction.

This line of thought provides definitions for three key terms in my overall argument, as follows: 'post-modernism' will refer to the theoretical perspectives on the post-modern developed by writers such as Jean-François Lyotard, David Harvey, Fredric Jameson and, of course, Baudrillard; 'post-modernity' will indicate the post-modern understood as an *as yet fictional* historical phase posited by post-modernism; and 'post-modern' itself will designate the zones of ideological contention and the areas of cultural tension that the term produces through its implicit opposition to the modern. Hence, when I refer to a 'post-modern performance' I am not talking about a genre with specific aesthetic characteristics, but a practice that significantly participates in the tense and contentious climate created by post-modernism (theory) in respect of post-modernity (as yet fictional historical phase). These usages aim to recognise the weight of the debates about post-modernity, while reinforcing my reservations about some of the mystifying effects of the post-modern (zones of contention) and the limitations placed on radicalism by post-modernism (theory). The world may indeed be entering a new epoch as envisaged by post-modernists, but because we are by definition a wholly integral part to it we cannot be sure that a paradigm shift is actually happening.

These formulations still recognise that major historical shifts as conceived by Thomas Kuhn or Michel Foucault may fundamentally change the realities of the world as it is experienced: the Copernican revolution that stopped the Sun going round the Earth in 1543 eventually altered people's view of everything else (Kuhn 1970; Foucault 1970). The explanatory power of Kuhn's notion of the scientific paradigm and Foucault's concept of the epistemes of knowledge provide insight into the major changes in Western history generally, and can be usefully applied to theatre and performance histories, as Joseph Roach, for example, shows in his acute study of the player's passion (1993). But both Kuhn and Foucault warn that an ability to spot a paradigm shift in the past is no guarantee that we might accurately identify one in the present, as it is happening. So while there is no doubt that we are experiencing enormous changes in human cultures, it is appropriate to be cautious about granting full paradigmatic status in the contemporary to post-modernity.

'Aha!,' responds the lively reader, 'this Introduction has already used the idea of a *paradigm shift* between modernity and post-modernity as a key concept, and you have talked about hovering or balancing *on the cusp* of such a shift, and you have said that you intend to investigate radical performance in the culture around the cusp of the paradigm shift.' But if we understand the paradigm of post-modernity as a fiction, then these phrases become *metaphors* in the discourse between paradigms, and the word 'cusp' can be the obvious trigger to remind us that in this book post-modernity is a fiction. For how can something as complexly multifaceted as a historical paradigm shift have such a thing as a cusp?

This methodological move underlines the vital importance of reflexivity as a process in the analysis of contemporary cultural change, because when we are dealing with material that is so close in time and so complex, it is essential to expose and interrogate the assumptions of the analytical perspectives in play. The idea of reflexivity, as Scott Lash and John Urry demonstrate, has become central to many accounts of social process in the contemporary world (1994). They argue that 'reflexivity' generally signifies the ability of people (and sometimes systems) to question and/or interpret the assumptions informing the social worlds through which they live. They also discuss how:

> ...social agents are able increasingly to monitor and organise their own individual life-narratives and how society itself...is even more able to be self-constituting.
>
> (1994: 5)

Hence, the critical strategy of pointing to the fictional 'cusp of the paradigm shift' aims to bring reflexivity into the argument and structure of this book. So when I talk about 'hovering' around the cusp and its culture, I am also signalling the necessarily provisional nature of analyses of contemporary cultures as the millennium turns. Paradoxically, this means that it is especially fitting to investigate radicalism in those cultures through the fleeting and fickle example of performance. For to frame generalisations that might stick to the current processes of enormous political, ethical, genetic and ecological change, we probably have little choice but to catch them on the wing.

The structure of the book and ways to read it

The book is in two parts. Part I explores the contemporary tension between theatre as a disciplinary system and performance beyond theatre as a liberating radical force. Chapter 1 argues that the theatre estate in post-industrial societies is a victim of its own general success in the late-capitalist global market-place of culture. In embracing the disciplines of new consumerism, the theatre and its performances succumb to a commodification that stifles radicalism in the moment of its birth. Because the commodifying process is created by the current protocols of audience membership contemporary theatre is unlikely to crack this dilemma, even as it stages the most radical of post-modern plays. Chapter 2 responds to this problem by proposing that an effective politics of performance may be found in practices that have reached beyond the theatre in order to re-vision the creative process itself. A post-modern perspective on the potential of radicalism in performance beyond theatre opens up a rich array of ways in which the dominant may be subverted. But to transgress the relativism of post-modernism such performances have to be articulated to existing democratic processes in order to challenge and extend their limits. Key to this is the transformation of the spectator into participant in the making of new kinds of culturally activist aesthetics.

Part II searches for the sources of radicalism in contrasting types of performance beyond theatre, concentrating particularly on practices in places that offer the greatest threat to the radical. Chapter 3 analyses the dramaturgies of protest events and demonstrations as they have evolved during the past forty years. Despite constant incorporation into the society of the spectacle created by the expanding globalisation of the media, protest as performance has forged new ways of figuring widespread civil desire as a radical force in the struggle for democratic rights. The emergent aesthetics of protest spectacularly participate in the cultures of the cusp to extend the bounds of the politics of performance. Chapter 4 shifts focus from the mass movements of public protest to the radical possibilities of individual creativity stemming from conditions of extreme oppression, by investigating playwriting in prisons and the performer in blackface minstrelsy. The argument searches for sources of personal autonomy and empowerment through performance in the virulent panoptic systems created by contemporary criminal justice and the historic formations of colonialism. A review of the critical moral dilemmas thrown up by such volatile material suggests an ethics of performance that offers a principled embrace of cultural pluralism. Chapter 5 continues the concern with history through an analysis of heritage performance and reminiscence theatre. The chapter argues that the collapse of history into fiction in post-modernism challenges the radical potential of collective cultural memory and individual recall, but history can be rescued from the reign of nostalgia by the performance of the past as a reclamation of its radical instability in the present. The ubiquity of memory makes such performance available virtually to everyone and so invites speculation about the possibility of a genetics of performance that could carry an endemic radicalism. Chapter 6 again shifts focus from the broad reaches of performed history to the narrow confines of performative mazes, through an investigation of the aesthetics of immersive participation created by the post-war, international avant-garde. The analysis anatomises the issue of how submission to sensory deprivation in performance can produce a grasp of virtual community that radically engages with the growth of global risk in the contemporary world. The spasmodic popularity of such apparently tyrannical forms suggests that they touch on crucial components of radicalism in the culture of the cusp, which may be best approached through a new ecology of performance.

My search for sources of the radical in performance ends with an Epilogue that encapsulates some of the major stages of the journey, but also suggests, I hope, a new beginning through the ways it briefly revisits the diverse registers found in the body of the book. The range of styles includes several that can be found in many an academic text on performance and theatre, from close analysis of particular shows to difficult discussions of theory, from explanations of critical methodologies to explorations of socio-political contexts, from impressionistic pen-sketches of particular performative moments to speculative musings on the implications of an argument, or a factual oddity, or an unusual or typical experience. However, as you will already know if you have read the Prologue, I also include short passages of autobiography – or *possible* autobiographies – that begin each chapter. Why? I hope answers can be found in any resonances that readers may detect between the moments of a personal past – often deliberately couched in the argot of the times – and the histories traced of the politics of performance in the wider cultural scene.

. . . because this is a story that hopes to be at least partly true to its historical moment by subverting, as they say, closure. Hence, besides the yawning stylistic chasm between autobiography and academic treatise, there are certainly many gaps, lacunae and discontinuities, and of course an abundance of unintended deferrals and differences in this text. In a book that purports to play with post-modernism one could hardly expect less. Moreover, in hovering around the cusp of the paradigm shift, looking for sources for the radical in performance in unlikely places, I am by definition dealing in incommensurable materials, contradictory positions and inimical concerns. The main tactic I employ in trying to push past the inevitable logical discomforts of such a project is to transform contradictions, wherever they seem to be significantly produced, into paradoxes. For perhaps it is only in paradoxical formulations that the true measure of the reflexivity needed to engage fully in the culture of the cusp, hoping Baudrillard and Brecht might dance gracefully together, can be found. Just because everything is different doesn't mean anything has changed.

Accordingly, I invite the reader, should you wish, to encounter this text in a number of ways: from start to finish – another detective story; through strands of similar sections – the autobiographical parts *might* make chronological sense; by comparing similarly headed sub-sections across chapters – there are signs of a semi-submerged system there; by taking the chapters of Part II in a different order – the arguments may be cumulative in a number of directions. Any of these approaches to reading will traverse a range of stylistic shifts and hopefully enact the kinds of reflexivity that are crucial to the performative nature of the radical around the cusp of the paradigm shift. And if that creates contradictions, as it almost surely will, then at least you may amuse yourself by turning them into paradoxes, remembering all along Foucault's fabulous joke: all modern thought is permeated by the idea of thinking the unthinkable.

Radicalism in theory and practice

The impact of the post-modern and the onset of post-modernity demand that we sometimes develop quite knotty theoretical explanations for effective radicalism in performance. So I end this Introduction with an example to illustrate that in practice the production of radicalism can be relatively straightforward, though probably never easy.

The Chilean director and actor Hugo Medina has described how during Pinochet's reign of terror the people would show they knew the houses of torture by silently pointing at them as they walked past; everyone knew the significance of the pointed finger, yet the dictatorship was powerless to prevent it because virtually everyone did it. Hence, the everyday act of pointing was transformed into a collective gesture that was beyond the power of control of one of the most violently oppressive post-war regimes, because to eliminate it the regime would have had to destroy the people upon whom its power ultimately rested.

In other words, there are forms of resistance that, decisively, are not articulated to the dominant structures of authority and power in ways that make them automatically recoupable by those structures, and those forms may produce a radical freedom that is not just negatively against a regime but positively for some value or ideal that lies well beyond its ideological territory. Even in the most unlikely corners of the culture of a paradigm shift, say, in the most abstruse interstices of modernity and post-modernity, radical performance can insinuate pathologies of hope.

Part I

Theatre and performance

On the cusp of a paradigm shift

Chapter 1

The limits of theatre

Describe a circle, stroke its back and it turns vicious.

Ionesco

An afternoon at the theatre

I was nineteen and a budding internal exile when I first went to a proper theatre. Four years of working in a Manchester factory as an engineering apprentice had become intolerable, so I'd followed my friend Alex the civil servant to the south coast where he'd got a new post and rented a caravan on a cliff-top overlooking the wide blue stretch of the English Channel. Once there, I attached myself to a bit of genteel glamour, I thought, by getting a job as a waiter in the poshest hotel, reading the 'quality' Sunday newspapers, and finding myself a German girlfriend. Going to a *real* theatre seemed like another logical step in putting a distance between myself and the drab worthiness of Northern engineering.

As I was working evenings I had to go to a matinée performance, and alone because my chambermaid partner Ingrid was on the afternoon shift. I think it was a mid-week afternoon, but certainly it was bright sunshine and hot as hell on the promenade, which was probably why the theatre was packed. I remember lots of bright floral dresses and brass-buttoned blazers with white open-necked shirts, and the grey and silver hair of age, a whole sea of it surrounding me as I sat in the middle of the dimly-lit stalls – I'd been determined to get a 'good' seat – feeling brazenly under-dressed and embarrassingly under-age. The accents around matched those of the people who, usually with hardly a glance at me, ordered wines I'd never heard of from the posh hotel's dreary cellars. I literally crossed my fingers in the hope that if any of them were waiting in this audience they wouldn't recognise me out of my waiter's uniform. Such disjunctions of region, generation and class confirmed me uncomfortably as an exile in the making, an impostor bluffing his way into an alien scene. So the show, which I knew nothing about except the title, came as a revelation and a devastating spur. It was Keith Waterhouse and Willis Hall's *Billy Liar*.

Only two things about the production itself stick like fresh burrs in my memory now. I have a vague sense of the setting as Northern working class that focuses indistinctly around a dark-wood, double-fronted sideboard against flowery wallpaper. That sideboard and wallpaper merge with those in my paternal grandmother's front parlour, which became her dying-room when I was four. I would stand by her high bed, chin lightly brushing the candlewick counterpane, her barky hand tendrilled gently round mine, amazed at the map of her old, old face. A silent falling away of working-class history in the proud but mean two-up two-down terraced house, repeated millions of times in the industrial towns and cities of Northern England. Her kind of dying was the beginning of the end for the class that forged the industrial revolution, whose labour built the British Empire, and into which I was born.

The irony that a flimsy wood and canvas theatrical set could carry such a charge emerges only in retrospect from that summer seaside show at the beginning of the 1960s – at the time I was too busy empathising with Billy the liar. But now the personal and political loss it signals hovers in bleak contrast to the hopes that sustained my class and generation then. Was it some lie we were beginning to live? Was Prime Minister Harold Macmillan's famous claim that 'you've never had it so good' just one of the early signs ushering in the age of consumerism and the commodity, the hyper-real, and the loss of history: the whole glitzy cultural gamut of post-modernity itself? Or was the kernel of hope anyway buried deep in the ephemeral?

Billy Liar stands excited in front of the sideboard, carried by a full flight of words into a vision of his own making. He was a mad dreamer in a chequered sleeveless pullover, failing completely to put one over on his real auditors, those of the white and silver hair, and so becoming a figure of pity and fun. I remember deeply resenting the audience's patronising sniggers, because I was enthralled by the dancing pyrotechnics of the language and the choreography of energy and the sheer love of fantasy that tumbled out of that actor's ecstatic delivery. Here was a glimpse into a world of the imaginary unfettered, a creative hands-on promise of Oz, and the best response my elderly neighbours could manage was a cynical snobbery. Well, they were not going to stop me from crossing into the kingdom of youthful imagination. It would be my generation that flew past the old constraints to make a new kind of world and a new kind of art, and, unlike Billy, we would do it without lying. In the sticky heat of a middle-class and ageing theatre, in a country of impossible contrasts, there seemed everything to play for.

Theatre, power and authority

My lonely initiation into theatre on that sweltering afternoon confirmed me as an imagination addict, but also marked my psychic card, possibly forever, against the pretensions of Western theatre culture. Since then I have never felt entirely at home in theatre buildings, even when I had every 'right', as a bona fide professional theatre worker or a tenured academic researcher, to be there. One explanation for this can be found in Henri Lefebvre's idea of *abstract* space, which frames theatre largely as a 'space of domination', shaped by the ruling ideologies of society, made for purposes of power and control that too often work against the interests of the majority (Lefebvre 1991: 49–52; Nield 1996: 208). In a similar vein, Pierre Bourdieu sees theatre as producing 'a miracle of predestination', through which different groups – playwrights, actors, critics, audiences – are constructed according to hierarchical principles (1984: 234). From these perspectives a theatre building is not so much the empty space of the creative artist, nor a democratic institution of free speech, but rather a kind of social engine that helps to drive an unfair system of privilege. The theatre achieves this through ensnaring every kind of audience in a web of mostly unacknowledged values, tacit commitments to forces that are beyond their control, and mechanisms of exclusion that ensure that most people stay away. Hence, performances in theatre buildings are deeply embedded in theatre as a *disciplinary system*. This chapter explores that idea through an investigation of the new disciplines of theatre that have developed in the late twentieth century.

My analysis will concentrate on three main aspects of contemporary theatre as a disciplinary system. Firstly, I will consider theatre as a process of audience training that strives to echo and reinforce shifts in modes of perception and reception happening in the wider cultural economy: my focus here will be on the ways that increasingly theatre has participated in consumerism and commodification. Secondly, I will analyse theatre as a system of cultural production that aims to shape the formations of society, such as class, gender, generation, race and so on: here I will investigate how British cultural policy has influenced the construction and constitution of theatre audiences. And thirdly, I will explore theatre as a method of spatial indoctrination that aims to embed normative social values in the behaviour of its participants: for this I will draw on performance theory to anatomise the pleasurable submission produced by theatre buildings. These aspects of theatre, of course, always tend to be mutually reinforcing, holistically modelling changes in the distribution and circulation of power in the wider socio-political order.

I shall argue that, during the past forty years or so, the networks of theatre buildings in post-industrial societies have participated in the generation of a powerfully seductive nightmare that conforms to Michel Foucault's idea of the social disciplines:

> ...the disciplines characterise, classify, specialise; they distribute along a scale, around a norm, hierarchise individuals in relation to one another and, if necessary, disqualify and invalidate.
>
> (1977: 223)

This claim may seem paradoxical, given that the global 'success' of late capitalism has created a much wider variety of theatres, arts emporia and entertainment centres. The public can now choose from a greater range of types of theatre than ever before. But this new pluralism, as we shall see, masks a deadening cultural conformity. So while the onset of the post-modern seems to have enhanced the available pleasures of performance, it has also blurred the disciplinary functions of theatre, submerging its similarities to other systems of control in society. And the disciplinary nature of these wider systems itself remains relatively invisible, even though they spectacularly promote new normative values through the way they shape the ideological modalities of the social. Hence, the developing theatre estate is integral to the disciplines of late capitalist consumerism, paralleling the spread of shopping malls, heritage sites and other tourist venues. All this and much more in contemporary society is geared to the production of what Foucault resonantly calls 'insuperable asymmetries and excluding reciprocities', great chasms of economic or cultural or social inequality, which prevent people from recognising the full extent of their common ground.

In line with this, I will argue that increasingly theatre has become a social institution from which equality and mutual exchange – the practice of citizenship through common critique, say – is all but banished. Far from showing us the shape of new freedoms, the theatre estate in Britain and elsewhere has transformed itself into a disciplinary marketplace devoted to the systematic evacuation or diffusion of disruptive agencies, oppositional voices and radical programmes for progressive social change. This has been part of a paradoxical global trend in which the appearance of new freedoms in the expression of difference is fostered under a cross-cultural flag of encroaching conformism. To illustrate this paradox I will briefly analyse one of the prime aesthetic movers in this historical shift: the international musical.

An 'innocent conspiracy'

The olive skin undulates seductively under the pulsing multicoloured lighting as the girls gyrate in Dreamland. The costumes are simply maximum-exposure bikini, high-cut over the hips and low-cut between the breasts, but the hair-dos are exotic-elaborate and the strappy shoes have stacked heels that throw the body into a provocative pose. The music pounds to a Western beat that quickly has the audience in the plush auditorium tapping their feet and clapping their hands in happy syncopation. But the girls mostly dance with their backs to them, because there is another audience upstage which is freer in its reaction, leering and whooping and urging the dancers into ever more erotic shimmies and shakes. This second audience is fully clad, for the most part in heavy boots, battle fatigues, dog-tags and holstered guns, clutching tubes of beer and grooving with the action. The soldiers are high on the women. The Western men are consuming the 'Oriental' chicks.

Figure 2 **The bar-girls dance in Dreamland,** *Miss Saigon,* 1989

Note: The GI audience faces the real audience and the dancing women are surrounded by an ambivalent gaze

Source: Photograph by Michael Le Poer Trench. Reproduced by kind permission of Cameron Mackintosh and Michael Le Poer Trench

This is the scene in the Vietnamese night-club that opens one of the most successful musicals of the twentieth century: Alain Boublil and Claude-Michel Schönberg's *Miss Saigon*. The show was premièred at the Drury Lane Theatre in London in September 1989, but advance sales ensured that it had already grossed £5 million before the first audience witnessed the Dreamland dance. The London production celebrated its tenth anniversary in 1999 and the new millennium will probably see it enjoying many more. There are no statistics available for the show alone, but it certainly played a significant part in the phenomenal economic success of the musical on the metropolitan stage in the early 1990s. For example, between 1989 and 1993 the modern musical's percentage share of total box office takings for London theatre rose from 35 per cent to 50 per cent (£53.9 million to £107.3 million in cash terms). In 1993 this represented a 42 per cent share of total attendance at the city's theatres, or about 5.5 million people. One in three of these, or 1.8 million people, were tourists from overseas (Dunlop and Eckstein 1994). Given this, plus productions of the show staged in many capital cities of the world, and *Miss Saigon* – together with other so-called mega-musicals such as *Les Miserables*, *Cats* and *Phantom of the Opera* – can justifiably be called a global phenomenon, a crucial cosmopolitan part of the international cultural industries in a late capitalist, post-modern world.

The show is global in a number of other senses, too. First, it is set during the first war that figured on the international tourist map. In 1967 Mary McCarthy described the spectacle as starting even before her plane landed at Saigon airport: 'the tourists, bound for Tokyo or Manila, were able to watch a South Vietnamese hillside burning while consuming a "cool drink" served by the hostess' (1968: 12). Second, its story deals with the cross-cultural fate of a *bui doi*, or 'dust of life' as they are called in Vietnam, one of the many thousands of Vietnamese children fathered by American GIs: will he be left to the chances of war or flown out to a safe and opulent future in the United States? Third, successful casting of the show depends on the recruitment of an international troupe: for the first production performers were drawn from the USA, England, the Philippines, France, Hong Kong, Italy, Japan and Holland (Behr and Steyn 1991: 141). From the outset *Miss Saigon* was designed by its producer for global distribution: '...Cameron Mackintosh is *internationalising* the musical, looking for collaborators beyond the West End to Europe, North America, the Philippines even...' (Behr and Steyn 1991: 132 – their emphasis).

The global positioning of *Miss Saigon*, like other international musicals, is crucial to how it operates as a commodity and as a key indicator of the relentless drive to commodification in Western theatre. But comm-odification, as we shall see in more detail shortly, always aims to disguise its central purpose, to produce a product with invisible ideological seams. It follows that one of the best ways to discover how commodification works in theatre is to identify faults in the way the fabric of a show has been put together. In the case of *Miss Saigon* this means an investigation of the cross-cultural controversies raised by Cameron Mackintosh's prod-uction. This in turn will shed a little initial light on the show's participation in the paradigms of both modernism and post-modernism.

Significantly, it was not its treatment of the Vietnam War as fit setting for a musical that caused a furore when *Miss Saigon* was planned to open on Broadway in 1991, but the casting of the character of the Engineer, the part-French, part-Vietnamese owner of the Dreamland night-club that supplies prostitutes for the GIs. In London the Engineer was played with great success by Jonathan Pryce, who to achieve the requisite Eurasian appearance initially used prosthetic eyepieces and bronzing lotion. When Cameron Mackintosh proposed that Pryce play the part in New York, Asian and other members of the actors' union AEA (American Equity Association) protested against the granting of a visa to Pryce, arguing that it raised an 'issue of racism' and that 'It is time for...the Asian American community to stand in the way of yellowface...and...such an abomination of casting naively' (Behr and Steyn 1991: 182). Here was a dispute about the rights of the minority to protect the interests of their difference – a central theme of post-modernism – apparently based on an appeal to a racial authenticity that was essentialist – a central aspect of modernism. But what *triggered* the dispute was the way in which racial thresholds, in the AEA's view, had been unacceptably transgressed by the commodification of the actor. For Cameron Mackintosh it was essential that Jonathan Pryce should play the part in New York because he had been a major factor in the highly profitable commercial success of the show in London. Again, key aspects of post-modernism – that appearance has taken the place of the real, that many subject positions are available to the individual – were placed in acute tension with modernist principles – such as the integrity of the artist and the inviolability of art.

It is not surprising that a commercial show that was so crucially dependent on cross-cultural exchange between East and West, 'First' and 'Third' worlds, should run into these types of problem at the end of the twentieth century. By inevitably engaging with issues of colonialism in a context so dependent on commodification it risked producing ironic ethical turbulence at every turn. Hence, the video of the making of the first production, available for sale in theatres and some audio stores, shows auditions for the bar-girls in New York, Los Angeles, Hawaii and Manila, in which a row of white men gaze on a series of conventionally beautiful young Oriental women. Ironically, the film dwells on an image of the patriarchal colonial power that had created the setting of the show, the war in Vietnam, in the first place. But when it emerges that one of these young women had been a Vietnamese 'boat person', the editing tactfully cuts to another topic, as if the film-maker cannot bear too much reality.

When the Filipino women who were to play the bar-girls were brought to London for the original production, the collusion of commodi-fication and oppression was thrown into exceptionally high relief by the way in which they were inveigled into semi-nudity on stage. In the authorised account of the show, its director, Nicholas Hytner, is reported as follows:

> 'Here were young people from a chaste and pious Roman Catholic culture coming to late twentieth-century London for the first time where the idea of living through a sensual relationship on stage is no problem,' says Hytner. An *innocent conspiracy* took place, with the co-operation of all the production team concerned. The costumes for the opening bar scene...were 'not ready' until the very last minute, just before the dress rehearsal. Even so, 'they came as a real shock to them,' said Hytner, and it took a good deal of eloquence on his part to persuade them to wear them. In the process, he lectured them on the art of the theatre. 'I tried to explain that you don't necessarily have to have three daughters in order to play King Lear.'
>
> (Behr and Steyn 1991: 156–7 – my emphasis)

The recourse to Shakespeare to justify a deception alerts us to a monu-mental conflict. The women are considered so constrained by their culture that, apparently, they must be tricked into freedom. The resulting cross-cultural transition can be seen as a post-modern liberation, the dead hand of history and tradition lifted to release them into sensual pleasure and joy in appearance. 'Once they realised they looked good, and moved well,' say Behr and Steyn, 'their reservations disappeared' (p.157). But of course the transformation is also into becoming an Orient-alised sexual commodity to be gazed at on the international Westernised stage, and from this perspective we can see bearing down on the women all the weight of modernism in its most troubling racist, sexist and colonialist guise. So the 'conspiracy' frees the women to more fully express their sexuality, but at the price of conformity to the ideology of consumerism and the international market-place. These tensions are endemic to the whole of *Miss Saigon* because it combines an ideologically explosive subject – the war in Vietnam – with an extremely fraught current issue – the exploitation of the 'Third World' by the liberal capitalist democracies – and aims to transmute them into a global commodity. The performative structure of the opening Dreamland scene encapsulates this ambivalence: the real theatre audience may choose to be appalled at the gross enjoyment of the onstage audience of GIs, or it may gain an oppressive pleasure from authorised sharing in the lascivious gaze of the guys. Hence, *Miss Saigon* is riddled with the kinds of ideological contradiction that are common around the cusp between paradigms, a fate audaciously signalled by Behr and Steyn's claim that such a carefully orchestrated deception can indeed be thought 'innocent'.

The commodification of culture

The contradictions of *Miss Saigon* result from its position in the global cultural market-place, but whether or not an audience perceives those contradictions is determined by the specific conditions of its reception. The theatres in which the show is staged operate to disguise such contradictions, in order that audiences may consume the spectacle in untroubled enjoyment. To enter into such enjoyment, audiences must therefore submit to the disciplines of a theatre that transforms live performers into commodities. For the rest of this chapter, therefore, I shall be concerned with the disciplines that produce the commodification of cultural *consumption*, using theatre and live performance as a kind of test case for consumerism's effects in the wider sphere of general socio-political exchange. From this perspective the last twenty years of British theatre and live performance is an especially rich field for analysis, because monetarist Thatcherism was its main political context and because free-marketeering, as Will Hutton has trenchantly shown, provided the 'ideas around which the British (and much of the world's) economy and society have been organised' (Hutton 1996: 236).

The invasion of a new cultural economy into British theatre in the 1980s and 1990s can be clearly traced because much of the sector traditionally had been subsidised in order to *protect* it from the reign of the consumer. But under Thatcherism this protection was reduced and theatre became subject to increasing market pressures. The effects of this major reorientation turned the whole theatre estate into a kind of post-modern playground, in which a widening variety of styles and venues masked an underlying tendency to ideological conformity. To explain this paradox I will focus more closely on the processes of consumerism, and ask what it might mean to 'consume' a theatrical performance and how such 'consumption' might affect the social power and authority of the theatre's 'consumers'. This analytical angle on the perception and reception processes of audiences raises more general issues about the commodification of theatre and performance, and about the relationships between commodities, consumption and the (re)production of culture. The rest of this section offers a brief discussion of theories of commodification, before we return to their bearing on British cultural policy and the practical operations of theatre.

In wrestling with the idea of the commodity, critical theory often takes Marx's explication of commodity fetishism as its starting point. The production, exchange and circulation of commodities are seen by Marx as phantasmagoria, through which we are entranced into forgetting about the exploitation of labour by capital, and that denies access to knowledge of what is 'really' going on in capitalist society (Marx 1970: 71–83). So production of the commodity disempowers the consumer; any authority or power that it produces is little more than an alienating fantasy (Eagleton 1990: 84–8). Theorists who follow Marx have inflected this approach to the commodity in ways which are of particular relevance to theatre's contribution to culture in the late twentieth century. Horkheimer and Adorno, for example, argue that the arts, including theatre, have succumbed to commodification and the market as a result of the spread of mass media, especially during the second half of the twentieth century: the reproduction of the 'original' aesthetic event transforms it into a commodity like any other (Horkheimer and Adorno 1972). A related argument can be found in Lukács (1971), who in turn influenced the early writings of Baudrillard, where the commodity begins also to take on a dematerialised quality as a consequence of the over-production of signs in highly mediatised societies (Baudrillard 1988).

There are, of course, more strands than this in the historical development of concepts of commodification (Frow 1997), but a significant recent one has been developed by feminist cultural critics, in a shift of interest towards an area that Baudrillard pioneered: namely, the commodification of consumption, rather than production. Shopping has been a key cultural trope in this shift and the spread of shopping centres and superstore malls has provided its main institutional target. In these cathedrals of consumerism the processes of commodification begin even before anything is bought, because the exchange between shopper and environment has in one way or another already been paid for: the shopping 'experience' as a process of consumption is commodified (Morris 1993; Willis 1991). This approach to the commodification of consumption can, of course, be applied to other cultural realms, including heritage sites, arts centres and theatres; but whether the focus is on production or consumption, the abiding tendency in this long history of thinking about the commodity form is to see the process of commodification as signifying *loss*: of autonomy, of power, even of meaning itself.

The various inflections of this line of thought in post-modernism have led to some startling conclusions, such as Fredric Jameson's famous contention that the commodifying 'logic of late capitalism' is producing:

> the disappearance of a sense of history...in which our entire contemporary social system has little by little begun to lose its capacity to retain its own past, has begun to live in a perpetual present and in a perpetual change that obliterates traditions.
>
> (Jameson in Foster 1985: 125)

In the 1990s, a Britain in the grip of the heritage industry seemed to be bearing this out, as Robert Hewison has forcefully argued: the cheerful tourist visiting a past that he or she knows has been recently manufactured in high-tech factories is a paragon of post-modernity (Hewison 1988). From this angle, disempowerment is written into the texture of everyday life because everything – including our consumption of the past – may be turned into a commodity, with the result that there may appear to be no value system apart from commodification. Hence, heritage may be taken to exemplify the reign of Baudrillard's vision of the hyper-real throughout culture, in which all referents to the real disappear, to be replaced, in a kind of total ironic miming of Marx's commodity fetishism, by an endless precession of simulacra (Baudrillard 1994). Considered as purpose-built houses for simulation, theatre buildings and their products obviously can fit easily into this pessimistic vision of the contemporary cultural emporia.

Another strand of recent cultural theorising offers a more hopeful perspective. The thinking of de Certeau, Bachelard and Lefebvre investigates the ideological permeability of everyday life and its potential for providing 'gaps' for resistance in the consummate empire of the commodity (de Certeau 1988; Bachelard 1994; Lefebvre 1991). Michel de Certeau, for example, spots the potential for resistance in the art of 'making do' as practised by the subordinate:

Innumerable ways of playing and foiling the other's game, that is, the space instituted by others, characterise the subtle, stubborn, resistant activity of groups which, since they lack their own space, have to get along in a network of already established forces and representations. People have to make do with what they have. In these combatants' stratagems there is...a pleasure in getting round the rules...

(1988: 17)

In a related vein, Susan Willis offers interesting reflections on historical theme parks and heritage sites, when she claims that the *active participation* of the visitor in re-imagining a past culture *through* commodification has the potential to 'produce a critical rupture with the present' (Willis 1991: 15). The sources of such ruptures and resistances in performance are the subject of this book, so it is of some significance to my overall argument that various versions of the debate about the disempowerments of the commodity form and the empowering potential of performative participation animate the thinking of many cultural analysts and theatre theorists (Fiske 1989; Frith 1983; Hebdige 1979; Auslander 1992; Phelan 1993; Read 1993).

The origin of this debate in the writings of the Frankfurt School – Lukács, Adorno, Habermas and others (Thompson 1990; Bottomore 1984) – is testified by the enormous influence of Brecht's friend, Walter Benjamin, who framed one of its most potent formulations for the practice of performance. In a now famous essay Benjamin prefigured Baudrillard and Jameson in arguing that:

The technique of [mechanical] reproduction detaches the reproduced object from the domain of tradition. By making reproductions it substitutes a plurality of copies for a unique existence...[and it leads to] the liquidation of the traditional value of the cultural heritage....

(1992: 223)

Such 'unique existence' Benjamin characterises through the concepts of 'aura', 'authenticity', 'cult value' and 'ritual'; moreover, he identifies its last (?) glimmerings in a contrast between film and stage acting:

The aura which, on the stage, emanates from Macbeth, cannot be separated for the spectators from that of the actor. However, the singularity of the shot in the studio is that the camera is substituted

for the public…the aura that envelops the actor vanishes, and with
it the aura of the figure he portrays.

(1992: 231)

What is important to the overall argument of this book is not the problematic concept of 'aura', but Benjamin's attempt to grapple with the
general meaning of the unique performance. For when consumerism
seems designed to commodify every aspect of culture, including the
face-to-face encounters of live performance, the issue of the possibility
of radical resistance becomes ever more urgent. I will return to this
question in the next chapter, but my main concern now is to show how
in the past twenty years British theatre, in line with theatre in the rest of
the so-called developed world, has undermined that urgency by
succumbing to new pressures of commodification in the market-place
of culture.

Commodification *via* State subsidy

During the 1980s and into the 1990s, British subsidised theatre, in
common with other cultural institutions, was subject to massive political
pressures that aimed to make it more market and consumer oriented.
Under Thatcherism, there was a fundamental shift in the ideology of
the funding agencies, particularly the Arts Council, and in the ways that
their 'clients' – in this case the national, repertory and alternative (or
fringe) theatre companies – related to the public. These developments
can be described variously as: a new *rapprochement* between State subsidy
and market economics; a move from essentialist to instrumentalist views
of the functions of the arts in society; an undermining of élitism by
populism; and as a struggle between modernist and post-modernist
cultural dynamics. As these alternative descriptions suggest, the changes
were fairly complicated and their implications for the practice of
theatre are hard to determine precisely, but they can be summarised
generally as an attempted transfer of authority, if not power, from
producers to consumers. The main means used to achieve this transfer
was an increasing commodification of theatre and performance, their
transformation from traditionally defined 'art' into contemporary
cultural 'product'.

Traditionally the Arts Council of Great Britain (ACGB) had
subsidised producers, mainly through grants to theatre companies. Its
policies were based on the modernist/liberal-humanist view that the
artist has something special to offer to society that transcends any

particular political or economic regime. Art puts people in touch with 'universal' values, so it deserves protection both from market forces and State interference since, like education, health and social security, it is an essential ingredient in the satisfied citizen's life. Hence, Roy Shaw, Secretary-General of the Council from 1975 to 1982, approvingly quotes Iris Murdoch's dictum that art is 'a training in the love of virtue' (Shaw 1987: 23). This notion derives from a very long tradition of essentialist cultural critics and art theorists which includes, for example, Ruskin, Wordsworth, Arnold, Tolstoy. Fundamentally, this modernist tradition holds that art has *inherent* redemptive, rejuvenative or recuperative qualities, and that its transformative power is somehow placed *in* the artwork by the superior productive abilities of the artist. The tradition sees art, in essence, as closer to the Church than the market-place.

In the 1970s, Arts Council policy generally had stuck to this line, though it was tempered by a growing commitment to arts education as a way of broadening access to the 'high arts'. Such attempts to democratise an existing cultural agenda, however, attracted rising accusations of élitism from anti-authoritarian formations, such as the Council of Europe and the British community arts movement (Simpson 1976; Kelly 1984). Ironically, in the 1980s the Council's policies met a similar challenge from a totally different ideological direction, as the 'reforms' of the Thatcher government demanded greater 'accountability' and 'value for money' in public institutions. The pressure shifted the Council towards a more populist stance, and simultaneously eroded the so-called 'arm's length principle', which was supposed to stop State interference in the 'freedom' of the arts (Hutchison 1982: 27–40). Thus neo-conservatism sanctioned a more interventionist role for the Council so that it could open up the subsidy system to market forces.

The rhetoric of this process is interesting for the ways in which it echoed Thatcherite doctrine. So we find William Rees-Mogg, the high-Tory former editor of the *Times*, who in 1981 had been appointed as Chairman of the Council, by mid-decade arguing in a lecture entitled 'The political economy of art' that:

> The qualities required for survival in this age will be the qualities of the age itself. They include self-reliance, imagination, a sense of opportunity, range of choice, and the entrepreneurial action of small professional groups. The State should continue to help the arts but the arts should look first to themselves, and to their audiences, for their future and their growth.
>
> (1985: 8)

Such developments, Rees-Mogg urges, are a necessary consequence of an all-pervasive historical abandonment of 'the great twentieth century thesis...[of] collectivism and mass forms of production and power' (1985: 1). The end of communism/socialism is signalled by the emergence of a new class – the 'affluent and technically qualified...electronic middle class' (1985: 5) – that will dominate the social structure. Through them the Arts Council was to become a singular force in the widespread trend to establish a new economic base for Britain in the service industries. Moreover, the yuppies and the meritocratic service class, identified in due course by sociologists and cultural critics as the social formation most in tune with post-modernism, were to be the vanguard consumers of a new arts renaissance (Featherstone 1991: 35).

Rees-Mogg, somewhat cheekily, had borrowed the title of his lecture from Ruskin, but the name of the Arts Council pamphlet that translated his arguments into practical objectives was straight out of the Book of Thatcher. 'A Great British Success Story' was offered as a twenty-page 'Prospectus' spelling out the advantages of accepting 'An invitation to the nation to invest in the arts' (ACGB 1986). This glossy panegyric employs the language of big business and the stock exchange to outline the 'Dividends' that would result from a new combination of State grant aid and private sponsorship, including: (i) low-cost job provision (at £2,070 per head per annum: 'a bargain price'); (ii) regeneration of depressed inner-city areas; (iii) vital creative stimulus to the wider (commercial) entertainment industry; (iv) substantial tourist income; and so on. Significantly, 'pleasure' for 'millions of people' comes at the end of the list. The arts are framed generically as 'the arts industry', and their operations are transformed metaphorically into a business company: 'The arts have an excellent sales record, and excellent prospects. *Customers* are growing in number, and with increased leisure one of the certainties of the future, *use* of the arts will intensify' (my emphasis). The pamphlet claims that the arts may provide a society with 'vision', but its main argument carries the clear implication that they are essentially akin to other types of consumer product.

This rhetorical trend in cultural policy-making framed the relationship between art and its audience in a relatively new way, and fostered new types of ideological role for both in late capitalist society. In Europe the new orthodoxy was given vigorous impetus in 1987 through the publication of an impressive report by John Myerscough, *The Economic Importance of the Arts in Britain*, which drew on extensive empirical evidence to provide ammunition for an:

...argument [that has] moved on to a higher ground, by relating the role of the arts to the fact that we live in an era of industrial restructuring characterised by the growing importance of the service industries...and of industries based on new technologies exploiting information and the media. The success of cities in the post-industrial era will depend on their ability to build on the provision of services for regional, national and inter-national markets....The arts fit *naturally* into this frame....

(Myerscough 1987: 2 – my emphasis)

Hence, art can be used as a cultural magnet to attract 'footloose senior executives' in search of lucrative locations for the new information industries, and it can be used to tool-up civic systems by becoming a 'catalyst for urban renewal'. Again theatre and concert audiences, museum buffs and gallery-goers are transmuted into 'arts customers', but the pressure to so conceive them is now increased by the stamp of empirical authority. Mighty statistics promote the notion of art as a service commodity, and an especially superior one; not because its inherent qualities put us in touch with supposed universal human values, rather because it can trigger off huge transformative forces in the process of social restructuring for the post-industrial/post-modern age.

From this position it is but a short logical step to conceive the arts customer as the fulcrum of 'success', for the instrumental vision of this emergent policy orthodoxy shifts the location of cultural authority in the creative processes of art from the producer to the consumer. This is justified because, after all, in a *service* relationship it is the consumer who, at least in theory, always calls the tune. This narrow view of audience creativity gradually became official policy, as can been seen from the 1987/8 Arts Council annual report, in which the Council's Secretary General, Luke Rittner, drew attention to 'the unique and precious commodity that the arts represent'; while Chairman Rees-Mogg suggested that:

We are coming to value the consumer's judgement as highly as that of the official or expert....The voice of the public must...be given due weight...[and] the way in which the public discriminates is through its willingness to pay for its pleasures.

(ACGB 1988: 2–3)

By the start of the nineties, then, British cultural policy (as represented by the ACGB) had been refashioned by monetarist ideologies that favoured the commodification and marketisation of art. At least at the level of rhetoric, this discursive realm relocates authority in the image of the consumer as sovereign queen or king.

Before we consider the impact of the Arts Council's policy revisions on theatre itself, it is worth noting that the new policies were implicitly contradictory, for they signalled a significant erosion of cultural boundaries that the ACGB had been set up to patrol. For example, talking about the arts as an industry or business comparable to others in terms of productivity and efficiency suggests that there is no fundamental difference between art and other 'commodities', and therefore ultimately no need for a State system of subsidy for the arts. The arguments that locate art as part of the wider cultural industries problematises its definition (Mulgan and Worpole 1986). The notion that production should follow demand implies, in post-industrial society, a pluralism that challenges the hegemony of essentialist 'high-art' traditions.

Hence, the new policies were part of the wider cultural swing towards de-traditionalisation and the abolition of hierarchies of value promoted by post-modernism. To work in this system of cultural production, even if you were staging the most modernist of shows, implied a vote for post-modernity. Consequently, the Arts Council's position, with roots still firmly entwined in the high-art traditions, became increasingly paradoxical. For example, its frequent insistence that subsidy should only support artistic 'excellence' highlighted the growing problem of how to identify exactly what that might mean, and ironically it evoked traces of the Council's élitist past at the very moment that it engaged in the populist present of the post-modern. Some politicians were not slow to spot the core institutional issue raised by these developments: both Labour and Liberal Democrat policies for the 1992 General Election recommended that the Council should be abolished. The Tories, apparently happy with the rhetoric, wanted it kept.

The impact on theatrical practice

The transformation of the arts patron into a customer of culture involved the redesign of many of the theatre's disciplinary mechanisms. Throughout the 1980s and into the 1990s, theatres in the subsidised sector were encouraged by a variety of ACGB schemes to follow London's West End in working to improve the ways they 'treated' their audiences, especially through advertising, at the point of sale, and in front-of-house (foyer) services. Increased spending on marketing produced promotional material that generally was better designed, slickly printed and eye-catching, while copy-writing tended towards extravagant hype (for example, the English Stage Company makes Shakespeare 'the hottest ticket in world theatre'). Many theatres adopted quasi-corporate identities, complete with obligatory logos. Ticket buying was made easier by box office computerisation and credit card payment, and pricing policies reflected a greater awareness of untapped markets through subscription and discounting schemes. A telling example of this general refocusing is provided by the Arts Council-led, 1991/2 National Strategy for the Arts, which notes:

> the inspired use of the phrase 'Theatre Receptionist' for 'Box Office Assistant' at the Theatre Royal Stratford East, [which] has been shown to encourage wider staff recruitment from communities alienated by the more technical term. It has also led to more positive attitudes to *customer* care....
>
> (Barnard 1991: 2 – my emphasis)

The general aim of these developments was to increase 'access' (a 1980s arts catchword) through what the National Strategy somewhat euphemistically calls 'audience development' (NAMSU 1992). So the notion of theatre as a cultural drop-in centre spread, as foyer areas were redesigned to make them more 'welcoming', and bar and restaurant services were developed, both to increase income and to encourage casual use by non-theatre-goers. Big, European-funded refurbishment schemes, such as the £6 million project at Newcastle-upon-Tyne's Theatre Royal (1987/88), and brand new theatres, such as the West Yorkshire Playhouse in Leeds (1990), invariably included facilities for corporate entertainment as essential aids in attempts to woo major sponsors. Bolt-on entertainment such as foyer-cabaret, film screenings and music events became commonplace. Through all these processes the pleasures of *theatre-going* gained as much – arguably more – emphasis in the consumption of theatre as any enjoyment of the production and performance itself.

A cognate commodifying trend occurred in patterns of subsidised theatre programming: on the one hand, there was a drift towards populism, signalled by 'a decline in the presentation of classical drama... and a rise in musicals...and plays by Alan Ayckbourn...' (Cork 1986: 8); on the other hand, less original work was available as fewer new plays were staged and as adaptations grew from 5 per cent of the national repertoire in 1981–5 to an astonishing 20 per cent in 1985–9 (Barnard 1991: Tables 1 and 2). Moreover, the distinctions between the different theatrical sectors were crumbling, as regional repertory theatres mounted co-productions with leading alternative theatre groups (the Leicester Haymarket Theatre led the way) as these groups (such as Theatre de Complicite and Tara Arts) staged shows at the National Theatre, and as National Theatre productions, such as David Edgar's fringe-inspired *Nicholas Nickleby* followed by *Guys and Dolls* and *Les Miserables*, transferred to the West End and Broadway. The increasing predictability of theatre programming was masked by promotional hyperbole that claimed every production to be exceptional, while the individual customer's uses of the theatre estate was pushed towards a uniformity set by mostly invisible economic imperatives. Just like the new shopping centres, theatres everywhere aimed to provide customers with the same types of facility, but at the cost of producing a narrower range of products.

As a 'customer' of the theatre, the audience member ironically had a growing number of performance-related commodities to attend to, as the 1980s witnessed a remarkable proliferation of theatre sales lines: T-shirts, badges, hats, posters, pennants, playscripts, cassettes of show music, videos of the making of the show – if it could carry an image and/or title of the production it was pressed into service. The performance itself might become a fading memory, but its traces could be registered in countless objects, the consumption of which might magically recapture the moment of gazing at the stars onstage. Hence, some especially successful shows acquired their own logo – one thinks of the half-mask of the *Phantom of the Opera*, or the waif-face of *Les Miserables*, or of course the helicopter visage of *Miss Saigon* – which by a process of semiotic condensing 'becomes' the show. Susan Willis succinctly notes that, partly because of their proliferation in contexts separate from what they signify, 'the logos become essentialised in relation to the de-essentialisation of the commodity itself' (Willis 1991: 60). In other words, the power of performance is sucked dry by the peripherals of theatre as it is transformed into a service industry with subsidiary retail outlets. The commodification of the theatre is achieved by reshaping the patron in the image of the consuming shopper.

In post-industrial, post-modern societies such transformations of cultural behaviour have multiple sources, but in this respect three developments in the whole estate of British theatre are worthy of particular note. First, the marketisation and commodification of theatre offers growing opportunities for 'secondary consumption' of performance, in which the possession and use of spin-off artefacts may become a potent substitute for the experience itself. Hence wearing the *Miss Saigon* T-shirt and/or a Royal National Theatre peaked cap may be even more culturally charged than an evening in the stalls watching a show. Performance is transformed into an associated commodity that may totally substitute for the live event. Second, the middle-class domination of theatre, and especially subsidised theatre, may be challenged by a growing heterogeneity of actual audiences. This is most marked for London, where there was sustained growth in the proportion of tourists and day visitors using the National and West End theatres, until they constituted over half of the total attendances (Dunlop and Eckstein 1994). Figures for the regions show a much smaller proportion of tickets bought by non-residents, but a much higher proportion of C2DEs – blue collar and manual workers – than is commonly supposed by critics who claim a middle-class hegemony for theatre (Feist and Hutchison 1990: 37; Myerscough 1987: 25). Third, the trend towards heterogeneity in audiences may be accelerated both by the collapse of the traditional aesthetic hierarchies under the pressure of populism and by the erosion of boundaries between theatre and the other 'cultural industries'. The increased crossover of productions and, crucially, performers between theatre and film, TV, video and radio breeds a familiarity (especially through well-known names and faces) that undermines exclusiveness. Similarly, the growth of the theatre 'package tour' – a coach trip, a meal, a show and a hotel room at an all-inclusive bargain price – turns mainstream metropolitan theatre-going into an accessible outing. So as the cultural barriers diminish theatre becomes the subject of a widening plurality of uses. Its place in the big business entertainment account is matched by its contributions to the heritage industry, while the once heterogeneous local audience is infiltrated by the domestic version of what Urry, following Feifer, calls 'post-tourists' (1990: 100–2): people for whom there is no correlation between *particular* cultural zones and self- or group identity, who collect theatre experiences in order to construct the deep surfaces of the post-modern personality.

The net results of these trends for theatre and performance, *vis-à-vis* the distribution of power and authority in the social, are paradoxical. On the one hand, the location of theatre in the whole cultural realm is enhanced. We can identify this empirically, perhaps, in ticket sales and yield, where the total number of attendances held steady in the second half of the 1980s even though the rise in ticket prices outstripped the rate of increase of average earnings (Feist and Hutchison 1990: 4). The most likely explanation for this is that the theatre came to rely less on the established audience, and so was used by a growing number of people (who would, on average, pay less each). This suggests a rising social *status* for theatre as a symbolic commodity, an improvement reinforced by the more widespread growth of secondary consumption through artefacts and media reproductions. Consumers of theatre – both primary and secondary – stand to gain more authority from this enhanced general status. On the other hand, the lack of cohesion brought by the expanding heterogeneity of actual audiences, the separation of theatre from any particular social formation, suggests a dispersal of power. It becomes increasingly difficult to employ Bourdieu's concept of 'distinction' (1984), or to talk, say, about the middle classes using theatre to consolidate their position in the social pecking-order. Instead, we have the post-modern spectacle of a fragmenting democratisation of consumption, a growth in access that increasingly turns theatre as a cultural resource into a commodity of capital.

The implications of these developments for an assessment of the shifting patterns of cultural power and authority around the paradigm cusp are very complex. But we can begin to address the issues by considering the ways in which power and authority may be negotiated through live performance; and this returns us to our core concern, namely, what might it mean to 'consume' theatre and how might this affect performance as a discourse of power? I shall use the final sections of this chapter to briefly explore the main theoretical issues this question raises. These depend centrally on the pivotal distinction that shapes my argument in this part of the book, between theatre as a disciplinary system and performance as a source of radicalism.

Theatre as a service industry

The significant changes in the patterns of use of the theatre estate in Britain towards the end of the twentieth century demand a re-evaluation of the currently dominant explanations of the social functions of theatre generally. The most influential of these derive from the cultural theories of Gramsci and Althusser in arguing that theatres are mainly used by the middle classes – or electronic or service classes – to confirm and strengthen their power base within the social hierarchy (Althusser 1971; Gramsci 1971). The acquisition of cultural capital, especially in the form of the high-art tradition, endows authority on the middle classes; but at the same time it subjugates them to the powers of the dominant order. (McGrath 1981, 1990; Bourdieu 1984). The paradoxical empowerment/disempowerment brought about by middle-class colonisation of the theatre estate has been explained most commonly in terms of a simple duality: empowerment is achieved through the *active* occupation of the institution of theatre, while disempowerment is the result of a *passive* consumption of that theatre's repertoire of performances (Craig 1980: 13–14; Gooch 1984: 34–5). Now this account both over-simplifies and inverts the ways in which such theatre (and perhaps any theatre) aims to function. That is to say, we may arrive at a more accurate picture if we think of the active use of the theatre institution as usually accompanied by a *passive* – or, more precisely, *implicit* – acceptance of its meanings and values; while the apparently passive consumption of its productions may mask an *active use* of their codes.

Most Western theatre is a curious cultural institution in that it requires us to pay for an acute deprivation of our freedom of movement. As with cinema, to gain access to the performance we agree to be channelled through an ever more limiting physical regime, until we are seated to focus within a narrow angle of vision, normally to remain there for a period we do not determine. Moreover, once the actors begin their work the audience is under a much greater injunction than can ever occur in cinema. Anyone who has felt like leaving a performance in theatre during its course will know what constraining forces are built into the conventions created for its consumption: the live actor is like a visceral magnet pulling on the human fillings of the audience. Viewed from this angle, the theatre consumer certainly does not call the tune; considered as a service industry, theatre offers what must be one of the most exacting producer–consumer contracts of all. But what might such an extreme contractual arrangement signify?

One way to begin answering this question is to analyse the architecture of theatre in relation to its social context, in order to understand what the performance theorist Richard Schechner calls its 'sociometric design' (1988: 161). For example, Schechner draws attention to the salient features of nineteenth-century proscenium theatre, which include: a hierarchy of seating/prices, with the most expensive boxes having a poor view of the stage but being splendidly placed for the display of their patrons' privilege to the rest of the audience; an auditorium decorated to suggest opulence, wealth and comfort (though this diminishes with seat price); the effacement of the machinery of production by the proscenium arch and curtain; and the correspondence between the open arch and a shop window. In these and other ways:

> …the proscenium theatre is a model for capitalism. Today, as capitalism evolves into corporatism, new kinds of theatre arise. Cultural centres and regional theatres – art fortresses run by impresarios overseen by boards of directors – are examples of corporatism.
>
> (Schechner 1988: 164)

One might take issue with the detail of this account, but the substantive point is surely sound: in consuming theatre as a service we are more or less implicitly consuming the ideologies of the society that built it. It does not matter much that we might have a critical attitude to those ideologies, that we might, for example, find the London reconstruction of Shakespeare's Globe Theatre quaint and uncomfortable; the fact of their use is in part an animation of the values inscribed in the architecture. So the ideology of theatre architecture as abstract space (Lefebvre) is embodied in the behaviour of the audience. It insinuates theatre as social memory, a history that is assumed to be shared, in the flesh and blood of its users, doing for them what Bachelard claimed for personal memory itself: 'In the theatre of the past that is constituted by memory, the stage setting maintains the characters in their dominant rôles' (1994: 8).

Now in the post-industrial and post-modern world, as Schechner points out, we are confronted by a variety of theatre architectures that model a range of ideologies. Where formerly there was a dominant form – the proscenium arch – which could be considered the 'natural' shape for theatre to take, now the logic of late capitalism has led to a plurality of sociometric models. This then produces a potential for the uncovering of any hegemony, any mechanism of dominance, written into theatre viewed as a disciplinary machine for the production of cultural commodities. As for other commodities, this gives the illusion of choice, of a radical escape from ideology. But the proliferation of theatre forms is simply another version of what Ivan Illich calls 'radical monopolies': 'the dominance of one type of product rather than one brand...when one industrial production process exercises an exclusive control over the satisfaction of a pressing need' (1985: 52). Of course, there may still be alternatives offering a radical criticism of the radical monopoly, but for most people these are relegated to subordinate status in the cultural system. The mechanism for achieving such subordination has been the marketisation and commodification of the whole system, further reinforced by the media's recycling of its products; for the components of the contemporary pluralism of theatre are now made to signify, more or less obliquely, consumerism as a cultural practice.

Hence, Western theatre in the late twentieth century *may* be the site of increased access to, and a variety of uses of, what was previously a protected domain for the construction of middle-class power, but the newly heterogeneous audience is still the object of consumerism. That is to say, the contract created by the modified conventions of the theatre experience implicitly underwrites commodification. In a sense, the audience's bodies embody the ideology of theatre as a commodity form because by their compliance they consume its meanings and values. As we have already noted, this is the case even if, as is often argued for post-modernist cultural practice, the audience entertain the theatre ironically, with a self-reflexive awareness of themselves as the consuming commodity. Such irony may produce a sense of power, but the irony, as it were, rides on a submission enforced by the growing separation of producer and consumer, actors and audiences. Within the theatre's walls, consumption of theatre is increasingly an abdication of authority and a relinquishing of power, especially when performance itself succumbs to commodification.

Performance as a commodity

The idea of the passive audience for performance usually has been associated with mainstream theatre. In the Marxist tradition the notion derives directly from Brecht's idea of *culinary* theatre, in which a gullible audience is seduced into a glazed ecstasy of sensory indulgence that is deeply conservative (1964: 89). The image of the dispossessed audience has also been potent for other critical traditions including, perhaps surprisingly, theatre semiotics. Thus Marco de Marinis, in an important essay on 'The dramaturgy of the spectator', directly links what he calls 'closed' performance texts to 'the passive and standardised means of consumption found in mainstream theatre' (1987: 104). This interpretation arises because theatre semiotics are often more concerned with describing the structures of theatrical sign systems, rather than to determine the meanings that the audience may construct through its use of the signs. Hence, the dominant image of the audience informing these critical traditions is clearly one of disempowerment: consumption conceived primarily in terms of exchange (rather than use) value, the audience excluded from the means of production.

In a broader framework of analysis the idea of the disempowered audience may also be related to the theoretical tradition initiated by Bakhtin, which has grappled with the functions of the carnivalesque in society (1968). The carnivalesque is a cultural practice characterised by excess, immersion and the elimination of distance between subject and object. This in turn has been linked by contemporary cultural critics to the development of post-industrial consumerism, so that, for example, shopping malls, department stores, theme parks and heritage displays are identified as sites of carnivalesque indulgence. Susan Willis, for example, suggests that 'the amusement park is not conceived of as a site of production, but is felt instead to be a commodity itself' (1991: 16);

while Mike Featherstone draws on Baudrillard and others, in arguing that consumers of such sites are aware that they are simply simulations and therefore have the 'capacity to open up to surface sensations, spectacular imagery, liminoid experiences and intensities without...nostalgia for the real' (Featherstone 1991: 60). I have already noted how theatre can take its place in this phantasmagoria of commodity fetishism, but what are the processes whereby the *live performer* is, as it were, de-natured through commodification?

A common explanation in theatrical theory points to the performer's display of skill or technique. So Grotowski represents a long line of analysis when he claims that the 'courtesan actor' presents the audience with little more than 'an accumulation of methods, artifices and tricks...a collection of clichés' (1968: 34). This is an analytical seam that feminist theatre critics, directors and actors subsequently have extended out into the audience, as it were, arguing for example that in a patriarchal society 'the very fact of my biology on stage commodifies my presence' (Love 1995: 275). Such a theatre of prostitution is seen as producing a pathology of performance that the performer cannot control, or which is totally lacking in any sense of authenticity. Performance becomes an 'unreal' exchange, merely a simulation, and of course it is particularly prone to being perceived in this way as it is so obviously founded on artifice. Parallel lines of thought led the remarkable theoretician of theatre, Herbert Blau, to write:

> As we think of a new audience for a new theatre in what remains of a class society, this [the current situation] is likely to give us a sense that we come together *(de)classified*, as if the power to be an audience, for those who are one, is not the spontaneously live ideology but the fringe benefit of collective dispossession.
>
> (1990: 357)

Here, then, is the domain of the completely disempowered, where the audience is located at what should be the cutting edge of culture, the perfect place for self-reflexive critique (as Brecht saw it), only to be robbed of such power by their internalisation of consumerism's capacity for commodifying the living body.

This was the paradoxical cultural pathology that was at play in *Miss Saigon*, where the Filipino women performers ostensibly gained a freedom of expression that their original culture denied, only to be (potentially) *doubly* transformed into a sexual commodity by the onstage and offstage audiences, in a kind of feedback loop of reception that secures the ideological trick of disempowerment. The paradox arises because the creative freedoms of performance reinforce the chains of theatre as a disciplinary system. Hence, the processes of commodification in late twentieth-century Western performance in the theatre are created through the protocols of audience membership, which massage the consciousness of spectators into a tacitly willing collusion in their own dispossession. Whilst I have used the example of the commercial musical to highlight the pathology, my argument suggests that the paradox is endemic to the whole theatre estate in post-industrial, post-modern societies. A couple of examples from recent British productions of 'political' plays on the mainstream stage will illustrate the point. These plays *appear* to be attacking the injustices produced by late capitalist hierarchy and exploitation in modern democracies, but in the process of being staged in theatre buildings, in submitting to contemporary theatre as a disciplinary machine, they succumb to what they attack.

The commodities of theatre

When Ian McKellen played Richard III at the National Theatre in London in 1990 the director Richard Eyre created a cinematic style of fades and jump cuts, orchestrated with a specially written sound-track. The critical reception was unanimous in its admiration of McKellen's acting, celebrating it as a virtuoso performance. Hence, the theatre mimics the cinema to create a star vehicle that delivers privilege to the necessarily select audiences for the show *and* simultaneously subjugates them to the dominant processes of cultural production. This ideological nexus is ironically enhanced by the setting of the play in 1930s Britain, with McKellen playing Richard III as a close cousin of the fascist Sir Oswald Mosley, because through the fictional world of the play the production then mounts a bitter attack on a fascistic attempt to debase the dominant order. Paradoxically, the better McKellen's performance, the more the audience is likely to be seduced into acquiescence to a hierarchical system that commodifies *them* as figures of subjugation. But even if the production engineers a critique of inherited privilege, the excesses of McKellen's brilliant portrayal reinforce its status as a high-value commodity in the cultural market-place, inviting the audience to position themselves as its consumers. They may enjoy a live performance, and that performance may even have radical elements, but in the sociometric spaces of a National Theatre interpolated by late capitalism into a system of global commodification, they are also actively engaged, through the protocols of audience membership, in the transmutation of that performance into a commodity. In a further ironic sequence, this *Richard III* became part of the process that conferred knighthoods on McKellen and Eyre, and had the concrete edifice on the South Bank of the Thames renamed as the *Royal* National Theatre. Theatre and performance as commodities gain the monarchic stamp of approval and audiences become commodities in a right royal system of consumption.

A similar process stimulated the success in 1998 of Mark Ravenhill's *Shopping and Fucking*, which graphically and wittily explores how the metropolitan sex industry sucks especially vulnerable young people into its degrading rituals of exploitative ecstasy. Directed by Max Stafford-Clark for the touring Out of Joint Theatre Company, the production transferred to London's West End, where it succeeded in attracting youthful audiences to witness its bizarre combination of neo-Brechtian design – an upstage free-standing wall flashes out one-word themes for each scene in designer neon – with farcical action that extravagantly out-Ortons Joe Orton at his brutal best. The show – which has already been produced in New York, Johannesburg and other global cities – dramatises the commodification of desire through a knowing post-modern take on the constructedness of sexual identity. The plot ensures that the characters are tested continually to reconstruct themselves as each others' sexual objects, with money circulating at the cold heart of every desperately lustful exchange. The bleakness of this scenario would seem to offer sufficient resistance to the seductions of West End privi-lege, by implication staging a critique of the sociometric architectonics of the theatre as market-place for the human. But the contrast between, on the one hand, the story of degrading sexual commercialism on-stage, and, on the other hand, the commercialisation of degradation by the theatre in staging the show, produces a irony that paradoxically evaporates in the pleasures of performance. In their enjoyment of the display that turns the sexual subject into a commodity, the audience participates through the machinery of theatre as a disciplinary system in a process of consumption that does exactly the same to them.

So whether positioned more closely to the modernist classical canon (a 'political' *Richard III*) or the post-modernist parodic contemporary (in the 'politics' of *Shopping and Fucking*), productions that occupy the estab-lished edifices of the theatrical estate today trade under the unavoidable sign of global commodification. What is exchanged in that trade *may* become a radical critique of its own assumptions – an attack on the values of consumerism, commodification and the market-place, say – but the disciplines of the estate have been developed so as to threaten commodification of even the subtlest and supplest radical impulse. Hence, as the new millennium extends, the radical in theatre is likely to become an increasingly rare phenomenon, which is why I turn next to consider how the radical may survive and flourish through the excesses of performance.

Chapter 2

The excesses of performance

The superfluous, a very necessary thing.
Voltaire

London Arts Lab to Diamond Head Crater

The mime play delivered itself to my imagination almost ready-made in a moment of somnolence on a sunny summer beach on the south coast of England in the late 1960s. All I had to do was find a way to describe the string of crisp images showing the falling spiral from birth to death to birth/death of a bowler-hatted man with no eyes. The only other characters were bowler hat's *doppelgänger* and a working-class stage-hand who crazily tries to break through the fourth wall from the auditorium to the stage, using an escalating succession of tools and weapons, in a vain attempt to stop bowler hat from hanging himself. The movements of these figures were etched with acutely impossible precision in my imagination; otherwise the main demands of the play were technical. A stage full of huge transparent eggs that gently swayed as if on the seabed, *doppelgänger* slowly easing himself through a long birthing tube, candles that lit themselves, a face with a forehead that fell in utter smoothness to the cheeks, and a suicide high up on a totally blank wall through which a spotlight has to shine.

Back in Manchester I took the mime play to the University Drama Department. Claire Venables and Peter Thomson kindly had a look at it, professed themselves impressed, but couldn't see any way that it could be staged in the North. Its physical and technical demands were well beyond current known competencies, though its style and themes might well strike a chord. It was Peter Thomson who had heard that a new arts centre, or something like that, had recently opened in London's Drury Lane. It was called the Arts Lab and already had a reputation for wild experiment that somehow paralleled the growing student revolt of '68. I hitch-hiked down to London and approached the Arts Lab out of the blue. I can't remember walking into the building, but the moment I looked at the pink stencilled sheet that gave details of the programme is as vivid as a sunset in Hawaii. Somebody called Stephen Berkoff was planning to do Kafka's *In the Penal Colony*, a group called the People Show were going to do Show No 19, there was an exhibition coming up by an artist called Yoko Ono, and a Dutch company going by the name of the Will Spoor Mime Troupe was already showing *Art of Fugue*.

I bought a ticket for Will Spoor's production and was amazed at what I'd stumbled into. The Arts Lab theatre was just an oblong space with a fit-up control box at one end and flexible seating for up to a hundred people. I watched the show in delighted disbelief as it unfolded in a combination of high-precision movement and low-cost technical invention. It was brilliant: irreverent, witty, subversive, rude and above all stunningly skilful and imaginative. When it was over I hung about the theatre and introduced myself to Will Spoor and he graciously agreed to read my play. Four days later a letter arrived from Amsterdam saying the company would be on its way back to London as soon as I'd arranged for the availability of the Arts Lab theatre.

My memories of the huge shimmering eggs of the show's opening scene still produce a recalcitrant sense of unbearable fragility. The achingly slow slither of Tony Crerar as the *doppelgänger* through the long birthing tube – or was it an intestine? – that stretched the whole width of the stage, still evokes a choking smother of claustrophobic anticipation. But most of all the sheer exhilaration of knowing that anything goes still lingers in the memory banks like a bomb waiting to go off; *really* anything, so long as it could be done unreasonably cheaply and cheerfully as a fillip to the cultural iconoclasm of the Arts Lab. Back then, there seemed to be no significant limits to what we might allow the imagination to do if we were ingenious enough, and the audiences seemed ready even for the untrammelled assaults on their senses that we dished up in the scene that attacked the fourth wall (reminding the *Guardian* critic, to my delight, of the Crazy Gang). It seemed only right that the show was a sell-out, because we were just luckily riding the wave of a great generational upsurge of creative energy. We were part, after all, of the first counter-culture.

Less than two years later and I was in Honolulu's Diamond Head Crater choreographing a spectacular happening for an audience of two or three thousand people. My mime play eggs had metamorphosed into a massive transparent box inside which twenty near naked bodies writhed and squirmed and slithered till they brashly broke out into the bright Pacific sun, trailing long entrails of thin translucent tube filled with coloured smoke that slowly seeped out to shroud the crowd, who became dancing spectres in a swirling dream. As Honolulu then was San Francisco's closest counter-cultural cousin, *and* the main rest and recuperation centre for Vietnam GIs between tours of duty, the sight was redolent of horrific ecstasy, the Aquarian dream turning sourly towards nightmare. As the US army helicopters hovered in surveillance over the smoke-strewn festival, I remember thinking how easy and how impossible it would be for them to wipe us all out with a quick falling splurge of napalm. I recall as well reflecting wryly about how my polythene passions, my fixation on the cheaply transparent, had become the vehicle delivering me up to a new internationalism in popular experimental performance. Such oddities seemed to speak as part of a growing chorus of ironic subversion that was only the beginning of a much greater ground swell of dancing reaction against a world we were certain was in need of radical change.

An explosion of performance

In the past forty years there has been an explosion of performance beyond theatre as the generations born since the Second World War have experimented in unprecedented ways to push back the boundaries of creative freedom. Named variously as underground theatre, fringe theatre and alternative theatre in the West, and as theatre for development, theatre for liberation, popular and people's theatre in the rest of the world, what began in the 1950s and 1960s as a few scattered efforts to reinvent the socio-political role of performance quickly mushroomed into a global phenomenon (Epskamp 1989; van Erven 1988, 1992; Fotheringham 1987; Itzen 1980; Kerr 1995; Kershaw 1992; Shank 1982). By the end of the twentieth century a plethora of innovative practices could be grouped around these broad headings, including community theatre, grass roots theatre, feminist theatre, women's theatre, lesbian theatre, gay theatre, queer theatre, black theatre, ethnic theatre, guerrilla theatre, theatre in education, theatre in prisons, disability theatre, reminiscence theatre, environmental theatre, celebratory theatre, performance art, physical theatre, visual theatre and so on. Virtually all of these genres established themselves, at least initially, beyond the cultural mainstream, often against intense opposition from traditionally-minded theatre critics and historians. One major tactic of marginalisation has been the usual slapping on of negative labels: 'fringe', 'small scale', 'off-off-Broadway' and also, with a supreme pejorative sneer, 'political' being among the most common. But even sympathetic commentators have often fallen short of doing full justice to either the scale or the aesthetic and ideological radicalism of wave after wave of experimentation. Paradoxically, a common mistake has been to link some or all of the new theatre movements too forcefully to the historical avant-garde of the early twentieth century.

Examples of this historiographic sleight-of-hand are easy to find, but James Roose-Evans and Margaret Croyden were especially influential through the early 1970s publication of full-length studies that traced a genealogy of experiment from and through the naturalists, symbolists, constructivists and surrealists to such later luminaries as Grotowski, Brook, Barba and Robert Wilson, Ariane Mnouchkine, Jerome Savary, together with groups like the Living Theatre, Open Theatre, the Performance Group and the Bread and Puppet Theatre (Croyden 1974; Roose-Evans 1984). The problem is not that the genealogy is wholly inaccurate: established experimentalists such as Grotowski, Brook and Barba, for example, overtly locate themselves as an extension of the earlier modernist avant-garde tradition. But the inclusion of groups such as the Living Theatre, which professed a revolutionary rejection of the past itself (Beck 1972), surely signals that too many aesthetic eggs are being placed in the same historical basket. Later historians of the even more wayward practices of performance art and live art, such as RoseLee Goldberg and Henry M. Sayre, have compounded the issue by extending the line to include, respectively, the 'media generation' of 1968 to 1986 (Laurie Anderson, Richard Foreman, Karen Finley, Squat Theatre, etc.) and the whole of the 'American avant-garde since 1970' (Goldberg 1988; Sayre 1989). The chief historiographic problem of such genealogies is that they might erase some of the provocative richness of the new aesthetics, and so promote a failure to recognise the full range and power of the radical new relationships that have been forged between art and the social, performance and culture. Marvin Carlson wisely warns us that:

> ...to concentrate largely and exclusively upon the avant garde aspect of modern performance art, as most writers on the subject have done, can limit understanding both of the social functioning of such art today and how it relates to other performative activity of the past.
>
> (1996: 81)

This question of the 'social functioning' – or the political or ideological significance – of contemporary performance is what makes the issue of avant-gardism so crucial to an assessment of performance's potential to undermine the disciplinary forces of theatre, to circumvent commodification or to further new forms of radicalism.

The post-modernist critique of the modernist avant-garde of the early twentieth century has helped to clarify this problem, whilst also often slipping into another kind of categorical trap. The starting point here is that the aesthetic objects that were once considered supremely radical now grace the boardrooms of international corporations or hang in the reverent spaces of the national galleries of the world. In Nick Kaye's terms, they suffer this fate because they were from the outset projected 'towards an autonomous aesthetic sphere' (Kaye 1994: 21). In their quest for the essence of aesthetic originality, say, such artworks were already incorporated into the teleological master-narratives of modernism, the dream of steady progress to Utopia. The parallel trend in theatre can perhaps be identified most tellingly in the aestheticisation of Brecht in post-war European theatre, where a celebration of the formal character-istics of Epic theatre ironically replaces the political relevance of his plays (McCullough 1992; Eddershaw 1996). In other words, mainstream culture will always catch up with particular avant-gardes and incorpo-rate them into dominant ideologies because that is their socio-political destiny at their inception, that is what it *means* to be avant-garde (Featherstone 1991: 36–43).

It follows that performance in post-modernity, to avoid this kind of fate, must reposition itself in relation both to past avant-garde traditions and to present cultural conditions. But with regards to the past it cannot propose a complete rejection or break, since that would repeat the foun-dational gesture of modernist art, so its response must take the form of a refusal to treat the past in any way that is not at least tinged with scep-ticism or irony. And with regards to the present, the most common claim has been that post-modern art exists on the margins – or in the cracks or crannies or creases – of mainstream society, the better from which to attack the dominant. But this then colludes with the view of a mainstream critical tradition that would reduce post-modern perform-ance to the frippery of a 'fringe', or the backwaters of an 'off-off-Broadway' (Connor 1989: 240–4).

These are some of the complexities and conundrums for perfor-mance that flow in the wake of post-modern theory. But we may see a way past such dilemmas if we think of the new performance practices of the past few decades as articulated to their local and global socio-cultural contexts in ways that are different *in kind* to those that were created by the modernist avant-garde theatrical movements or figured by most post-modern cultural critics. This difference may be discerned pragmatically by noting how possibly most of those practices have been pursued in *self-created* circumstances, in *fresh* types of venue, *beyond* existing theatres. And while it is true that the success of the successive waves of performance experiment has led to some institutionalisation – as in the British system of studio touring, for example (Kershaw 1993) – that should simply make us more alert to the significance of the continuing effort to side-step the disciplinary structures represented by the physical and social architecture of theatre buildings and other kinds of arts emporia. This widespread aversion signals, I think, much more than a desire for creative autonomy: we might usefully talk in terms of a radical revisioning of the creative impulse itself, a wholesale dismantling of the dominant modes of creativity in order to totally destabilise traditional notions of, say, political theatre, and to open up, through performance, unexpected sources of democratised power. To take just one example, the search in some feminist theatre for the performative equivalent of Cixous's *écriture féminine* can surely be interpreted as carrying such a radical charge (Aston 1995: 45–9; Dolan 1993: 85–97). Viewed from such a perspective, many of the practitioners of contemporary performance are neither avant-gardist, nor marginal, nor peripheral; rather, we may see them as articulated to major socio-cultural formations – counter-cultures, new social movements – in ways that sometimes bestows on their work both a culturally representative and a socially formative significance.

Hence, I think it not unreasonable to claim that contemporary performance has become the ideological 'other' of the institutional spectacle of disciplinary theatre, its excesses mocking the still comparatively straight-laced protocols of established theatrical culture. So the politics of contemporary performance might be construed as founded partly in a global counter-action to the burgeoning reifications of the cultural logic of late-capitalism, the downside of post-modernism, as well as a sometimes anarchical feverish embrace of it blandishments. This chapter, therefore, is devoted to an exploration of new approaches to the politics of performance in the post-modern, acknowledging its often contradictory nature, but focusing especially on its positive potential for reinforcing the processes of democracy.

The promiscuity of the political

Within the post-modern, all art, including theatre and performance, loses its claim to universal significance, to stand, as it were, outside the ideological, and becomes always already implicated in the particular power struggles of the social. As a consequence of radical new ways of thinking – such as in deconstructionist, feminist, post-structuralist, post-colonial and post-modernist theory – the old binary oppositions between, for example, propaganda and art, or politics and aesthetics, or the real and the imaginary, are deeply problematised. In parallel vein the idea of the 'political' has been applied to a widening range of phenomena: now we have the politics of representation, the politics of the body, identity politics, sexual politics, cultural politics…and at an international seminar on performing sexualities a leading English gay critic gave an especially witty and ductile paper on the politics of the limp wrist! (Fowler 1994). In this aftermath of the theoretical explosion it becomes no longer credible to box off 'political theatre' as a separate category, because in one way or another all performance and theatre can be seen to be involved in discourses of power, to be in some sense engaged with the political.

The following argument aims to anatomise the consequences of this diffusion of the 'political' for the analysis of contemporary performance. In particular, I shall be discussing how we might begin to construct a critical approach to contemporary performance that both (a) recognises some of the force of the post-modern paradigm as a liberation from sclerotic traditions of political theatre analysis, and (b) pushes us past the unhelpful idea that 'all theatre is political' by viewing performance in the light of concepts drawn from theories of democracy. My starting point is the inevitable complexity of the political dimensions of perfor-mance when it becomes an excessive dynamic interaction between text and context, performer and society, especially in a world made complex by mediatisation and globalisation. I will consider how the best recent analyses of the political in performance have wrestled productively with the explosion of theory in post-modernism. The second half of the chapter briefly considers the radical implications of performative excess in two highly contrasting but representative cases of post-modern performance: the Wooster Group's *L.S.D. (…Just the High Points…)* and Welfare State International's *Glasgow All Lit Up!* (Coult and Kershaw 1990; Savran 1986).

My overall aim is not to deny that 'all performance is political', but to encourage discrimination between the different ways in which, and degrees to which, particular kinds of performance may become more or less radically efficacious in post-modernity, particularly for the ways in which they may promote democracy. To achieve this we will need to focus on the excesses of performance, to see the ways in which, for example, the richness of signification in performance may subvert the disciplinary forces of its context. My contention is that in the *excesses* of performance beyond theatre we may find new sources of democratising power, new types of cultural democracy, new forms of radicalism. To start us in this direction I will briefly consider the case of a theatrical practitioner who resisted the new orthodoxy that insists that all theatre is political, who was exceptionally keen, in fact, to avoid the political in performance. I choose this as my starting point because such an aversion, like low angled light, might throw the object of our enquiry – the complexity of the politics of performance in post-modernity – into high relief.

The politics of community plays

Consider the paradox of an important woman writer/director who consciously sought to keep politics out of performance, who went out of her way to commission socialist playwrights to write plays that were apolitical, and who stimulated a theatrical movement that aimed to empower not just individuals but whole communities. This was Ann Jellicoe, author of the key 1960s play *The Knack*, one-time literary manager of the Royal Court Theatre in London, who in 1974 decided to distance herself from metropolitan success because the theatre 'seemed totally unimportant in most people's lives' (Jellicoe 1987: 3). Four years later she wrote the first of a series of 'community plays', *The Reckoning*, which she staged as a large-scale production in the secondary school hall of Lyme Regis, Dorset, involving a cast of around eighty non-professional performers augmented by actors from Medium Fair, the community theatre company that I co-directed at the time. Ann Jellicoe has described in some detail how the project was taken up by almost the whole town, and also she has been admirably forthright about her ideological intentions in staging community plays:

> If we set out to challenge the basic political feelings of the communities we serve, we will alienate large sections of them and lose their support....Politics are divisive. We strongly feel that the humanising effect of our work is far more productive than stirring up political confrontation.
>
> (1987: 122)

Some commentators, mainly from the Left, have taken her to task for the apparent *naïveté* of the modernist assumption that art can rise above politics (Woodruff 1989; Reynolds 1992). The issue of the transgressive potential of art hovers close to the main current of my argument, but initially I will approach it obliquely by taking a tightly focused look at the 'politics' of a particular moment in *The Reckoning*.

The play's subject was the 1682 Monmouth Rebellion, which began in Lyme Regis. The staging of the show was in the now familiar promenade style, with the audience standing and the actors working amongst them, especially in crowd scenes. The best of these in *The Reckoning* involved confrontations between local supporters of the rebellion and Royalist Troops. I was in the audience during one of these scenes on the third night of the play's short run, watching the Royalist soldiers hunt out the rebels, when a young woman performer playing a dissenter trying to evade arrest appeared at my shoulder. She jabbed me quite forcefully in the ribs, pointed at one of the Royalists, and in a tone of absolute urgency and passion demanded that I should join her in an attack on his person. So good was her acting that for a moment I felt my body beginning to move aggressively in his direction and my fists starting to clench…before critical caution induced me to smile at her in a sickly attempt to diffuse the power of her subversion. She countered my deflection with a look of withering contempt and moved on to stir up someone else. A couple of days later I discovered that she was a student in the school's sixth form, and that recently she had been publicly humiliated by the teacher playing the Royalist soldier.

Now I remember this scene because of its sense of dangerous *excess*, which I think was generated by the raw conflation or overlapping of several contrasting 'political' dimensions (or frames of reference) that were at play in the moment. In general thematic terms, the scene obviously took a stab at royalism, the willing subservience to the hegemony of inherited power, by urging direct revolt against militarism as a tool of imperial domination. But equally the scene easily exceeded this theme because its potential meanings were produced not just by the text – an anti-royalist gesture in the Monmouth Rebellion – but in its interaction through the spectator with the ideological multiplicity of its current socio-political context, with the pluralism of the post-modern paradigm. So at the same moment that the young performer was representing a dissenter in the Monmouth Rebellion she was also potentially representing: (a) one of her ancestors (as she was born into a Lyme Regis family), (b) her classmates in secondary education, (c) young Western women in the late 1970s, and (d) herself as an individual in that particular time and place – and this list does not exhaust the possibilities. It follows that the *type* of politics animated by the scene, and therefore any particular radical import perceived in the young woman's protest, would vary according to the spectator's positioning in respect of those different realms – a classmate might mostly see institutional politics, a feminist might focus on sexual/gender politics, a party worker might gleefully (Left) or regretfully (Right) note its implications for the politics of State, and so on. It does not follow from this that *individual* interpretations are always primary, as Martin Esslin maintains (Esslin 1987: 21), or that *collective* responses are inevitably oppressive, as Howard Barker argues (Barker 1993: 119–23); rather, it would be more accurate to say that the scene provides opportunities for a collective act of recognition of 'resistance' within which there is scope to inflect 'resistance' with a variety of radical meanings or responses.

The pluralistic significance held in potential by performance derives from its simultaneous occupation of various *realms of representation*, by which I mean frames of reference or, in the stricter terms of semiotics, discursive coding systems (de Marinis 1993). But *also* the power of performance lies in the ways it evades representation by working between or beyond such realms. The moment when my body tensed towards action transcended representation in a phenomenological response. We are talking here, then, only partly about the semiotic excess of performance identified by Anne Ubersfeld, when she writes:

> Theatrical pleasure is, properly speaking, the pleasure of the sign; it is the most semiotic of pleasures....Theatre as sign of a gap being filled....Memory and utopia, desire and remembrance, everything that summons up an absence is, in fact, fertile ground for theatrical pleasure.
>
> (1982: 129)

My argument overall challenges Ubersfeld only in two main respects. Firstly, I doubt that *theatrical* pleasure can now commonly produce such effects without running high risks in the commodification stakes. This is the weakness in Ubersfeld's exclusive emphasis on the theatre as *sign*, because it is through representation that theatre and performance are most effectively commodified. Secondly, much more happens in performance than the production of signs, and it is precisely this experience of performative excess - which *includes* the signifying process – that ushers in the potential of the radical in performance. Hence, identifying the sources of radicalism in performance becomes a question of investigating the excesses of performance.

I have analysed the moment from *The Reckoning* in some detail to show

how it produced an excessive semiotic and phenomenological effect. From this perspective, as Ann Jellicoe insists, the play could not be classed as 'political theatre' in the traditional sense. Nonetheless, we have seen that through its excess in performance the show became rife with potential political meanings, and this throws the somewhat restrictive traditional notion of political theatre into question. We may say that in this analysis the idea of 'political theatre' is challenged by a more pliable approach to the politics of performance.

Current approaches to politics in performance

Traditionally, of course, 'political theatre' has been taken to refer mainly to 'left-wing theatre'. Irwin Piscator was one of the first writers to develop this connection in *The Political Theatre*, which describes his efforts to create a theatre that would champion the cause of the proletariat in its battle with the bourgeoisie (Piscator 1980). His was a Marxist theatre that aimed to promote revolution, to overthrow the institutions of capitalism and to replace exploitation with justice, inequality with equality. Embedded in his practice was a vision of Utopian democracy in which each will 'contribute according to ability and receive according to need'. Many theatre practitioners and writers, from Brecht to Augusto Boal, subsequently have pursued similar convictions and they have established a rich and varied dialogue between theatre and politics. Sometimes this has been simplified by urgency – as in the agitprop plays of the 1930s Workers' Theatre Movement – and sometimes it has been extraordinarily sophisticated – as in the best plays of Brecht or, more controversially and recently, Heiner Muller – but always it has tended to assume that the pictures of the world painted by Marxist and socialist political theorists are fundamentally accurate, revealing truths about 'reality'. Hence, this tradition of 'political theatre' has defined itself in relation to the teleological master-narratives of historical or dialectical materialism.

But the diffusion of the 'political' brought about by globalisation and the explosion of theory has thrown all this into question, so that recent critical texts about the general issue of politics in performance tend to be uncertain and tentative. Sometimes they fall back on relatively well-worn agendas in their choice of analytical perspectives; sometimes they embrace the new fluidity with a febrile excitement. A 1992 British collection of essays on *The Politics of Theatre and Drama*, for example, acknowledges that the current situation offers 'a bewildering and exciting new field', but focuses its discussions on a now familiar list of topics: political (meaning mainly Leftist), alternative, feminist, community and Brechtian theatres being its main categories of concern (Holderness 1992). A 1991 American survey collection, *The Performance of Power*, also reports on 'redefinition and reassessment everywhere we looked' and shifts us closer to the critical ground of post-modernism by invoking semiotics, deconstruction and theories of the gaze as crucial to the 'political' conflicts of subjectivity and identity defined in terms of gender, race, class and sexuality (Case and Reinelt 1991). More recent collections on *Performance and Cultural Politics* (Diamond 1996) and *Crucibles of Crisis: Performing Social Change* (Reinelt 1996) include a yet wider range of socio-political concerns and develop more sophisticated approaches to discussing their manifestations in performance, but both in different ways singularly reinforce the impression that analysis of the politics of performance is still in a state of acute flux.

Theorists who have searched for a fresh start in the general characterisation of the *radically* 'political' in performance – in the sense of a politics of performance that is deeply oppositional to the dominant formations and discourses of its particular society – tend to be interestingly subtle and tentative. For example, Dorrian Lambley develops a Derridean notion of the 'poetic' in theatre, defined as 'a visible gap between signified and signifier', as the source of its potential as a 'credible language of opposition' (Lambley 1992). Philip Auslander is only a little less cautious in an important book on the politics of post-modern performance, which, he argues, consists in the two-fold ambition of 'exposing processes of cultural control' in order to discover 'traces of nonhegemonic discourses within the dominant without claiming to transcend its terms' (1997: 61). These are especially *reflexive* views of the political in performance as they generate a critical awareness of both the protocols of performance – the rules of its particular aesthetics – and the assumptions upon which those protocols are based. Hence, from this meta-analytical perspective a theatrical attack on the oppressions of the State, say, gains in political stature by demonstrating that the nature of its opposition may invoke processes of oppression almost identical to those its sets out to attack: under what circumstances could you justify killing the king for killing others? From such reflexive points of view, all performance becomes politicised.

What is gained through this new reflexivity in critical discourse is a kind of *democratisation* of the idea of the political, resulting from an increasing sensitivity to the ways in which – *pace* Foucault – power relations are embedded in all cultural practices, including those of theatre and performance. What is lost is a stable set of concepts that would enable us to identify once and for all the ideological or political significance of any particular performance text or practice in any context. A performance that could be considered 'radical' or 'revolutionary' or 'progressive' in one place or perspective might be seen as quite the opposite in another. This profound destabilisation of tradition threatens to cast theatre adrift in a constantly shifting sea of 'political' perspectives on performance.

The rest of this chapter explores some of the opportunities opened up by such instabilities in the politics of performance, by addressing the question of political radicalism in post-modern performance. It is useful to focus on the radical because it is the radical that is most thoroughly problematised in the breakdown of binaries and the diffusion of the political in post-modernity. My interest is *in what senses* post-modern shows such as *L.S.D. (…Just the High Points…)* and *Glasgow All Lit Up!* can be considered radical, because that may give us a measure of the kinds of political impact they hoped to achieve in their specific contexts, and perhaps provide some indication of the sources of radical performance in post-modernity. As these two shows may also be taken as representative of a much wider range of practices – *L.S.D.* in relation to presentational performance art and *Glasgow All Lit Up!* in relation to community-based participatory projects – we may consider them in various ways as paradigmatic of much contemporary performance.

So the specific context for the following analysis is Glasgow, Scotland, on a wet and windy weekend in the Autumn of 1990. I went to see the Wooster Group in *L.S.D. (…Just the High Points…)* at the Tramway Theatre on Friday night, and was amused by the 'schizophrenic' audience: avant-garde trendies in expensively tailored leather jackets rubbing shoulders with gangs of thin-frocked, streetwise teenage women, no doubt drawn by the filmic magnetism of Willem Dafoe, one of the group's founder members! Then on Saturday I spent the evening on the streets, following *Glasgow All Lit Up!*, a huge lantern procession with a spectacular finale mounted by the veteran subversive British company, Welfare State International. Over 10,000 people paraded through the puddle-strewn streets of the city centre in an event that blurred genres and juxtaposed disparate codes and obviously appealed to a huge and, for the most part, casual audience. Both shows clearly proved, if any proof is still needed, the post-modern point that traditional distinctions between the experimental and the popular often no longer hold. What is less clear are the political implications, for analysis and in terms of actual effect, of that kind of breakthrough on such

are broken in the name of such deconstructions the precise political purpose of the show is not at all easy to determine.

Auslander addresses the politics of *L.S.D.* in two interconnected ways: in terms of its semiotics and politics of representation, and in terms of its acting styles and the politics of the performer's 'presence'. Semiotically speaking, the show's deconstructive style seems designed to promote reflexive readings – or complex seeings – by overlaying and juxtaposing contrasting and often incompatible cultural codes. Auslander illustrates this point through analysis of the group's use of blackface to present the character of Tituba from *The Crucible*. This may be interpreted as racist (as the use of blackface in an earlier group show, *Route 1 & 9*, had been), but Auslander argues that when:

> ...the actress who plays Tituba goes on, still in blackface, to play Mary Warren, 'the sign becomes separated from its object', leaving the audience to impose its own interpretive schema on the displacement. I would argue that it is precisely at this moment of the emptying of the sign that the gesture becomes political, for it is when the arbitrary character of the sign is asserted that the significance of its imposition by one group on another stands out most clearly.
>
> (1992: 27)

In other words, the use of blackface can be interpreted as opening up a critique of racism. As this aesthetic strategy is a principle in the dramaturgy of *L.S.D.*, the show resolutely refuses to offer a perspective through which audiences might collectively privilege one realm of representation over another. So, theoretically, individual spectators are free to derive contradictory meanings from the piece. In this sense the show develops a deeply radical attitude to the politics of representation, by exposing *all* representations as constructed.

The political issues raised by the performer's 'presence' are even knottier, because, as Auslander rightly argues, presence is associated with the idea of 'charisma', and charisma has often been used by politicians such as Nixon and Hitler to construct systems of domination; hence, 'to invoke the power of presence is to link oneself inextricably to the workings of a repressive status quo' (1997: 63). In arguing this Auslander is following Derrida, who posits that presence is not an essential trait of reality, but a 'reality effect', especially in respect of relations of power (Derrida 1991: 69). It follows that in order to sever any link with existing systems of dominance, performance must find means to deconstruct the performer's presence. Auslander cites two of the key acting strategies of *L.S.D.* as significant steps in this direction. Firstly, he notes the clear refusal of the actors to make a 'greater investment of the self in one procedure [rather] than another', signalled by techniques through which 'signs of emotional commitment in acting were distanced and demystified' (1997: 66). Secondly, he cites the famous Part 3 recreation from videotapes of the group's *Crucible* rehearsal when the actors had all been high on LSD. In staging a meticulously detailed reconstruction of an experience which the actors had had, but which was not directly accessible to them as memory (due to the effects of LSD) the show problematises the nature of identity – how can we decide which is the 'real' actor: the one that was high on LSD, the one shown in the video-tape, or the one exactly recreating a previous experience as seen on the video? In Auslander's view such 'blurring of identity nullifies the possibility of charismatic projection' (1997: 67) by deconstructing the performer's presence, thus questioning oppressive uses of presence in politics.

Such intricacies of analysis of the performance text expose the potential political complexity of post-modern theatre, but the attempt to dispel 'presence' from the performative, even though it is stimulated by no less an authority than Derrida, is almost certainly easier in theory than practice. This is not only because 'presence', or in Walter Benjamin's terms 'aura', possibly has been the most powerful of all the attributes of performance (1992: 215). But also because, as Auslander's analysis reaffirms, the audience plays an unavoidable role in the making of performative effects. So if we turn to the *context* of the Wooster Group's work we may identify other types of construct that crucially affect the reception of the actor. For example, in an acute discussion of the links between the performer's persona and the persona's image as property, Celia Lury adopts Barry King's suggestion that in Western cultures:

> ...there has been a shift from the evaluation of acting as imperson-
> ation, in which the persona of the actor should disappear into the
> part, to evaluation in terms of personification, in which the perfor-
> mance of a part is subsumed by the actor's persona.
>
> (Lury 1993: 72)

Hence, in the very moment of deconstructing texts, Willem Dafoe and Ron Vawter may be perceived by the audience as constructing a persona with all the charisma and presence of a film star. Of course, such interpretive tendencies are likely to be reinforced by the forms of evaluation of acting – the 'reading strategies' of the audience – which predominate in any particular time and place. Ironically, perhaps, the Wooster Group actors' involvement in the media, especially in film (Willem Dafoe has starred in films such as *Platoon* and *Mississippi Burning*, Ron Vawter was in episodes of *Miami Vice*), could encourage the audience to endow them with presence/authority as an integral result of their attempts to evade it. Such may be the ironic outcome of excessive performance in the Wooster Group's show.

This is not to suggest, of course, that the Wooster Group's post-modern aesthetic is apolitical. Their challenge to Arthur Miller's property rights in staging parts of *The Crucible* as a kind of fast-forward replay has profound political ramifications, as David Savran has pointed out (Savran 1986: 191–5). In contrast, though, we may note that there *is* something curiously passive (in the sense of being primarily reactive) in Auslander's idea of *resistance* as the main mode of the post-modern political. His key contention in this respect is that the post-modern political artist offers 'strategies of counterhegemonic resistance by exposing processes of cultural control and emphasising the *traces* of nonhegemonic discourses within the dominant...' (Auslander 1997: 61 – my emphasis). But this seems to me to be a painfully reserved formulation, partly because the dominant discourse may well provide more substantial 'weapons' – such as performative presence – which can be turned back on it in the form of 'attack'. Or, if that kind of response is, from the point of view of the subordinate, strategically unwise, then we could use the language of 'negotiation' and 'exchange'. In any event, performance as a discourse of power will have less chance of reaching beyond incorporated resistance and producing new sources of radicalism through excess, so long as it remains within the established theatrical estate, even as represented by such experimental spaces as the Glasgow Tramway. It follows that more fruitful domains for both the practice and analysis of the radical in performance might be found in areas of culture that are crucial to the control exerted by dominant formations, but which may also be more pervious to ideologically transgressive action. To explore this idea we shall turn from the studio to the street.

Post-modern performance in the streets

Glasgow All Lit Up!, directed by Welfare State founder John Fox, was the 'centrepiece' of the community programme of Glasgow's year as European City of Culture. The chief creative activity of the project was lantern making. For eighteen months Welfare State artists trained local

Figure 4 Margaret Thatcher lantern on a truck, *Glasgow All Lit Up!*, 1980

Note: This image was created by shipyard apprentices. Its scale is indicated by the rear lights of the truck at bottom left

Source: Welfare State International (1990). Photograph by Paul Tyagi. Reproduced by kind permission of Welfare State International

Scottish artists in techniques learned in Japan, and the local artists in turn worked with some 250 community organisations throughout Strathclyde – the greater Glasgow area. In the early evening of 6 October 1990, these groups converged in the city centre to form a single procession of 10,000 people carrying, wheeling and driving some 8,000 lanterns. The Scottish arts correspondent of the *Guardian*, Joyce Macmillan, described it as follows:

> There were the big floats, of course; a gorgeous white reindeer, a huge unflattering image of the Prime Minister (Thatcher) shoving a gunboat out to sea…a beautiful white Swan Lake float.…But in a sense, the big set pieces were beside the point; what reduced one or two of us cynical old observers to tears, was the children, thousands and thousands of them…every one of them clutching a little lantern.…There were boats and space ships and churches and mutant hero turtles, and lots of simple triangular lanterns with

nothing but gorgeous, blobby abstract patterns on....There were rock groups and pipe bands and brass bands and steel bands.... As the columns of light snaked...along towards the High Street, toothless well-oiled old codgers emerged from a sawdust-and-spit pub called the Right Half and cheered and danced on the pavement, to the kids' delight. The city beamed from ear to ear....

(Macmillan 1990)

The huge procession paraded to Glasgow Green, a mile and a half from the city centre, where it was greeted by a 200-strong community choir, and the smaller lanterns were hung on to towers that were gradually hauled up by cranes to form four glowing pyramids of light over forty-feet high. The end-piece to the gathering was a spectacle staged by Welfare State artists, in which giant images from the Glasgow City crest – a tree, a bell, a fish and a bird – glowed and burned and flew through the air in a surreal animation that freed them from the rigour of their usual heraldic setting. A final big fireworks display ended the evening.

The procession manifested many post-modern characteristics – the wild mix of lanterns undermined aesthetic and cultural hierarchy, the subject was decentred by the massed scale, the images represented a concatenation of disparate power discourses and so on, and – as with *L.S.D. (...Just the High Points...)* – its politics are by no means transparent. But I will argue, on the one hand, that while its excessive plurality of representational realms could contain many kinds of politics, some of them clearly contradictory, on the other hand, its total relation to its context was marked by a kind of radical coherence. My main contention is that its political action can be best characterised as one of exchange with the dominant through which the participants may have been empowered by engaging in a deeply liberationist, radically democratic process. Firstly, I will discuss how *Glasgow All Lit Up!* may have enabled even its most powerless participants to construct themselves as 'democratic subjects', and through that the issue of performative presence will return to prominence. Secondly, I will consider how the total event modelled crucial aspects of democratic processes and created a new space of radical freedom for its participants. I will suggest that its politics of representation, in the semiotic sense, were indeed resistant to dominant discourses. However, its politics of representation and phenomenological excess engaged with dominant cultural, civil and governmental structures in ways that were much more challenging.

Paths to autonomy

When the big procession finally reached Glasgow Green the orderly ranks fractured into a confusion of mini-processions, bands playing at the centre of small crowds (the punk Scottish pipers were a hoot), small groups eating or playing games or just wandering around enjoying the spectacle. Although the Green was poorly lit, the mood seemed generally to be light and cheerful. In the middle of the up-beat hubbub my attention was drawn by a most extraordinary sight. This was a procession of about forty children aged from around six to nine years old, each of them carrying a self-made lantern based on the images of the Glasgow crest. The first notable aspect of this group was that they had a few adults with them, but the adults were not leading. The second was that they were moving in complete silence, with none of the usual chatter of excited children. And the third remarkable quality was that they were still clearly processing, but not in a straight line towards one of the lantern-pyramids on which their lanterns would be hung. They were weaving their way around the sodden field, apparently with no particular direction in mind, but they were obviously not lost, nor directionless. Despite – or maybe because of – the lousy weather, the tiredness from the long march that they'd already done, the plethora of spectacular attractions around them, the confusion and near-chaos of thousands of people gathering there, they appeared to be happy and self-possessed enough to be enjoying their procession for its own sake. Apparently, they were processing for the enjoyment of the fact that it was their procession – not because they were part of some mega-celebration staged by Welfare State, not because this was a major civic happening that justified Glasgow as the European City of Culture. This was their event, they were staking a claim to their own creativity and, I think, through *their* procession they may have been empowered.

One way of understanding the quality of this little procession is through Victor Turner's notion of 'spontaneous communitas', which he defines as 'a direct, immediate and total confrontation of human identities'. Turner emphasises that spontaneous communitas may occur only in certain circumstances, but he also suggests that it is a common experience available to any group of 'compatible people' (Turner 1982: 47–8). In other words, such moments of 'compatibility' may produce an identity which is, as it were, beyond signification because its signs do not have referents for the participants and so cease to be attended to as signs. Moreover, such pre-conceptual communication may well become an implicit, subversively articulate 'commentary' on the dominant discourses, the *status quo*, of its environment.

> ...communitas does not represent the erasure of structural norms from the consciousness of those participating in it; rather its own style, in a given community, might be said to depend upon the way in which it symbolises the abrogation, negation, or inversion of the normative structure in which its participants are quotidianly involved.
>
> (1982: 47)

Following Turner, I would claim that the children's procession presented an inversion of the anti-democratic aspects of its context, such as the quasi-militaristic organisation of the total procession and the way that its route to Glasgow Green had been determined by the authorities.

To better understand how it may have achieved this we can turn to the contrasts that Turner draws between carnival and ritual, and the liminal and liminoid modes of communitas. At the heart of their difference, argues Turner, is the notion of *choice*, because 'the carnival is unlike a tribal ritual in that it can be attended *or* avoided, performed or merely watched, at *will*' (1982: 43). This difference, between choice and compulsion, is what then drives the distinctions Turner makes between the collective, anonymous processes of tribal ritual and the individuated, authored processes of 'industrial art, literature, and even science' (1982: 43). Moreover, at the heart of these processes lies a further difference defined by the ways in which a socio-cultural 'threshold' is crossed by the participants. Ritual produces a *liminal* experience because its participants, paradoxically, have no choice but to be 'betwixt-and-between' the normative structures of daily life, literally beyond logos and the law; whereas carnival – and related forms such as art and theatre – creates a *liminoid* experience because it 'is all play and choice, entertainment'. In these terms we might say that the processing of the children progressed from the *liminoid* mode of carnival when it was part of the main procession, to the *liminal* mode of ritual when they broke away to form their own procession on Glasgow Green. However, this formulation may risk an over-simplification of the relationships between liminoid and liminal experiences, between ritual and theatre.

Turner is very careful to stress the liminal/liminoid distinction, partly because he keeps the basic issue of *choice* in relation to collective autonomy in focus. He quotes the example of a Ndembu ritual, where despite being stripped of identity the novices emerge with marked individual differences, through which he detects, with typical resonant style, 'in liminality is secreted the seed of the liminoid' (1982: 44). From this he draws the extraordinary conclusion that in the liminality of ritual it may be possible to '...locate the incipient *contradictions* between communal-anonymous and private-distinctive modes of conceiving principles of sociocultural growth' (1982: 44 – my emphasis). What I find amazing is that such an insight should be saddled with such crippling intellectual baggage; that label of 'contradictions' is a dead give-away. Because, of course, there is no necessity that we should conceive of the communal, or the collective, as implacably opposed to the private, or the individual; nor that the anonymous – or as a recent theoretical fashion has it, the invisible – is inevitably exclusive of the distinctive, or the visible (Phelan 1993). We might, in many circumstances, detect at least a shadow of one in the other, and the children's procession may have been such a circumstance. In other words, both communal and individual identities were fostered by this little carnival-ritual.

If this analysis is sound, then we could claim the procession as, at least in potential, an embodiment of certain crucial democratic rights, particularly those relating to the concept of autonomy. David Held argues that this concept indicates an underlying principle of both liberal and socialist democratic traditions, and states it in the following terms:

> ...individuals should be free and equal in the determination of the conditions of their own lives; that is, they should enjoy equal rights (and, accordingly, equal obligations) in the specification of the framework which generates the limits and opportunities available to them, so long as they do not deploy this framework to negate the rights of others.
>
> (1987: 271)

Held also stresses that this general principle means little if divorced from the specific, pragmatic 'conditions of its enactment'.

Now it is obvious that the 'enactment' of the children's procession was constructed in conditions that the children could not have determined in any critical way. However, it does not necessarily follow that, in the moment of making the mini-procession their own, the children would inevitably fail to achieve any sense of autonomy. At the very least we might justifiably claim that their action can be read in retrospect as a *metaphor* for 'the determination of the conditions of their own lives'; but also the nature of the performative, at least as conceived by Victor Turner's theatre anthropology, strongly suggests that the significance of the metaphor may be, quite literally, embodied in the action, so that the participants do not so much interpret its meaning as live it.

We can draw on Derrida to reinforce this point from a post-structuralist perspective. In his discussion of 'invention' in *Psyché: Inventions de L'autre* (published in English as 'Psyche: inventions of the other') he considers the performative quality of a fable as follows:

> The very movement of…fabulous repetition can, through a merging of chance and necessity, produce the new of an event. Not only with the singular invention of a performative, since every performative presupposes conventions and rules – but by bending these rules themselves in order to allow the other to come or to announce its coming in the opening of this dehiscence. That is perhaps what we call deconstruction.
>
> (Derrida 1992: 340)

So the performative opens up a space of absence in which the other can appear, and it has an affirmative as its constitutive quality. For Derrida, a crucial figure for this is the 'Yes' with which Molly Bloom ends James Joyce's *Ulysses*: 'Any event brought about by a performative mark, any writing in the widest sense of the word, involves a *yes*' (Derrida 1992: 298). In this sense, the children were 'writing' a *yes* through their procession, creating a performative excess in the liminal-liminoid quality of the event. And perhaps this is what gave them the powerful sense of 'absence-in-presence' that had attracted my attention in the first place: maybe their determination of the enactment quite literally empowered them in the excessive creativity of the moment. In other words, the children – in ways not entirely unlike those used by the young woman performer in *The Reckoning* – could well have had access to a basic process required for the construction of the democratic subject.

New space for democratic discourse

So there was potential for radicalism in the micro-politics of *Glasgow All Lit Up!*, but what about the macro-politics of the total event? In what ways, if any, did the 10,000-strong procession break any new political ground in respect of radical democratic empowerment? It will be useful to approach these questions by considering the relationship of the event to one of the key problems for democratic processes produced by the paradigm shift between modernity and post-modernity, namely the tensions between cultural pluralism and political unity.

To begin with pluralism: on the relatively mundane level of the semiotics of the lanterns, the politics of representation, it is clear that they constituted what we may call a multi-vocality or, to adopt a term from Bakhtin, heteroglossia (Bakhtin 1981: 262–3; Carlson 1992: 313–23). They were excessively multi-vocal in the sense of having no overall fictional narrative line or thematic structure, there was no identifiable imaginative logic in their juxtapositions: brash but beautiful political propaganda trundled cheek-by-jowl with nostalgic images of unsullied nature that in turn gave way to primitive abstractions reminiscent of the great modernist traditions in painting! They were heteroglossic in that they did not subscribe to a single set of explicit enunciations, there was no dominant language of imagery or form: a school identified itself through a string of two foot high capitals (MILTON SCHOOL), shoals of tiny fish flew above a fleet of boats, inchoate blobs hovered between recognition as suns or lemons, smiles or canoes, trees or candy-floss. While many images were totally engaging, none of the voices represented was predominant; all were expressive of a plurality rooted in many local, distinctive communities. The power to resist homogenous readings, to provoke contradictory interpretations, that the Wooster Group achieved through sophisticated techniques of deconstruction, was in this procession secured by the simple stratagem of random, or at least unplanned, juxtapositions.

The heteroglossia of the lanterns may also be interpreted from a more politically dynamic perspective through their representation of the kinds of cultural diversity typical of global cities. It was obvious that the people were parading their own creations, statements of their own creative abilities and flair. Moreover, as they were clearly parading in groups, the lanterns signified a plethora of collective cultural identities. However, as Anne Phillips sees so clearly, the rich pluralism of such minority groups, whether defined in terms of race, class, gender, sexuality and so on, is a mixed political blessing.

> The new pluralism arises out of a radical tradition that sets its sight on future change. Because of this, it cannot rest content with a live and let live toleration that just enjoins each group to get on with its private affairs. But, inspired as it is by a far-reaching egalitarianism that wants to empower currently disadvantaged groups, it is also more likely to…validate an exclusive and fragmented politics of identity that blocks the development of wider solidarity.
>
> (1993: 17)

Yet there was a cohesion to the variety of the lanterns. This was partly phenomenological: the fact that they all had been made through greater or lesser elaborations of the same basic techniques produced a similarity of visual texture, and a repetition of structural style, which was unmistakable. In other, more abstract words, the lanterns, as well as signifying a multitude of differences, all shared in a common aesthetic domain, a common creative language that hinted at an underlying unity of purpose.

Hence, *Glasgow All Lit Up!* may have produced a kind of 'wider solidarity' in the culminating procession, signified by its visual and kinaesthetic integrity, without erasing any of the many differences developed in the making of the lanterns. It achieved this, perhaps, by being inclusive of cultural pluralism, but by also furthering difference through the development of what was for each group a new creative language, which could be called, to make a risky discursive leap, a language of quasi-citizenship. That is to say, the lanterns, through their similarity-in-difference, provided complementary realms of representation that fostered a formal equality within which all the participants gained a common identity as 'artists' or 'creative citizens'. In this way the project may have modelled processes for the formation of a new kind of direct democratic collective. This analysis links the politics of semiotic representation to a resistant politics of cultural representation, but in what ways did the procession insert radicalism into the politics of civil society, and into the systems of governance that shore up the politics of the State?

My argument roots out the radical in the event through the idea of democracy and the concepts of civil society and the State, and it takes as its analytical framework David Held's claim that:

> ...civil society can never be 'separate' from the state; the latter, by providing the overall legal framework of society, to a significant degree constitutes the former. None the less, it is not unreasonable to claim that civil society retains a distinctive character to the extent that it is made up of areas of social life – the domestic world, the economic sphere, cultural activities and political interaction – which are...outside the direct control of the state.
>
> (1987: 281)

In an important sense, then, the law mediates the interaction of civil society and the State, and in so doing variously defines the extent to which any particular activity may be in, and/or out of, direct State control. It follows that any exchange between the law and *Glasgow All Lit Up!* will indicate how the event dealt with the politics of State, how its excessive semiotic and culturally democratic processes may be related to the structures of political democracy in Scotland.

The quickest way to identify any exchange between the two processes of democracy – the civil and the governmental – is to look for signs of disequilibrium, and as *Glasgow All Lit Up!* wound its way through the city centre this took the form of disrupted traffic flow. Despite strenuous efforts of persuasion by Welfare State, the police had insisted that the roads of the route should remain open to vehicles, so that the procession had heavy Saturday evening traffic flowing in both directions alongside it. The roads crossing the route were to be kept open through the maintenance of agreed 'gaps' in the procession. Not surprisingly, given that this was the people's procession, most of the gaps disappeared once it was under way, and the net result was that traffic came to a standstill – for a time the procession became the dominant discourse in the public domain of Glasgow city centre during that damp Saturday evening. So, in David Held's terms, the law did not manage to mediate the interaction of civil society, as represented by the procession, and the State, as represented by the police and other authorities. Rather, the 'presence' of the procession, its excessiveness, was directly impacting upon the authorities and, for whatever reasons, the authorities gave way and the law was temporarily, in part, abated. So the symbolic discourse of the lantern procession was translated, as it were, into another discourse; namely, the kind we might identify as a radical, non-violent 'political' demonstration for egalitarian rights to individual and collective identities. In temporarily transgressing – rather than just resisting – the institutions of democratic government the procession opened up, metaphorically and literally, a new space of radical freedom for politically democratic action.

The politics of democratised performance

I have been discussing the possibilities of radically democratised performance in a post-modern world. So my account has assumed the growing predominance of a paradigm that, at first sight, may seem totally to destabilise traditional analytical perspectives on the politics of performance. We have seen, though, that such an image of acute rupture from older notions of 'political theatre' is probably a distortion. That is to say, even if the old structures supporting the political analysis of theatre are being demolished by the paradigm shift, it does not follow that the components used in their construction are now useless. The pluralistic politics of excessive moments in contemporary performance promote reflexive judgement, a process similar to Brecht's idea of 'complex seeing', with the difference being one of degree between apprehending binary contradictions or multiple perspectives of interpretation (Brecht 1964: 44). An up-to-date politics of performance should, in fact, recognise the contiguities between Brecht and Baudrillard, between, say, a vision of theatre as a dynamic arena for social experiment and a view of the social as an experiment so thoroughly imbued with the potential for a sense of reflexive performativity.

I have attempted to address some of the issues for the politics of the performative embedded in this new(ish) global situation by noting some of the positive political aspects of the post-modern. I mean, for example, the democratisation of systems of representation when traditional cultural hierarchies are undermined. I mean, too, what de Marinis calls the semiotic 'openness' of post-modern performances, which in Auslander's terms allows audiences to impose their own 'interpretive schema' (1997: 64) on the work, and which is obviously a potential source for democratic empowerment through enhanced control over the politics of representation, or more accurately, the politics of semiotic representation (de Marinis 1987). But also I have been arguing that much more needs to be taken into account, such as the nature of the commodity and commodification in post-modernity, if we are to construct a convincing description of performance as an effective radical force articulated to other kinds of political process: the processes of cultural, civil and governmental politics particularly. This, I think, is a prerequisite for the recognition that some approaches to making performance do not simply 'model' ideologies, or 'reflect' the politics of their context; but rather that they are actively engaged in widening the bounds of political processes, in opening up new domains of political action, usually through excessive performativity, the creation of resonant absences.

This is a project that performance in traditional or mainstream theatre venues is hard pressed to join, because the disciplinary forces at work in such spaces have been reinforced by the downside of the post-modern, its collusions with the logic of late-capitalism. There, the commodifications of consumerism foster a creative sclerosis that is the enemy of radicalism, and where performative excess struggles to appear it is invariably neutered by the operations of the market-place. So while theatre *is* both the first and last place we might expect to find democratised empowerment through the exercise of creative freedom, it is generally now rendered the end of the line for performance's powers of resistance and transgression. Performance beyond theatre has a much better chance of turning the trick of cultural production back against the commodifying depredations of late-capitalism. Performative excess untrammelled by theatre is much freer to create new domains for radically democratic practice.

Paradoxically, post-modernism's decentring stress on pluralism and cultural difference has helped to set the global scene for such acts of democratisation, but at the same time it has promoted an ethical relativism and practical pragmatism that always threaten, in theory and practice, to undermine democratic principles. This is the political burden of a post-modernity in which commodification and late-capitalist market systems shape every aspect of the social. In this context, democracy, radical or otherwise, appears to have no more claim on our allegiance than any other political programme, however hierarchical, oppressive or unjust it may be. Theoretically, though, there is a crucial flaw in the post-modern attack on universals, as Steven Connor has succinctly pointed out.

> ...the postmodern critique of totality has only ever amounted to the demonstration that totality and universality are regularly claimed dishonestly in the names of structures of power that are neither total nor universal; they nowhere build convincingly into an argument against the desire for a universal application of the principles of freedom and justice. Indeed, when inspected closely it becomes apparent that the postmodern critique of unjust and oppressive systems of universality implicitly depends for its force upon the assumption of the universal right of all not to be treated unjustly and oppressively....
>
> (Connor 1989: 243)

Of course, the issue of democratic rights is right at the heart of my account of the struggle between theatre and performance. This is why it seems to me to be so important to stay poised between Brecht and Baudrillard: for if we can determine ways to encompass the mutual refractoriness of modernity and post-modernity, then some progress might be made towards a better understanding and valuation of the contributions of performance to radical human endeavour in the contemporary world.

I have been focusing on performance and democracy because it seems to me that, with the demise of the old meta-narratives, any hope for a progressive prognosis for performance practice will lie in its attempts to grapple with the ultra-vexed global issues of inequality, injustice and servitude. If performance can illuminate some of the sources of world-wide oppression by exposing how the politics of representation, say, may be used to reinforce the marginalisation of minority groups, then it may contribute to a fairer economy of signs. If it can create fresh cultural space in which the silenced majorities might find a newly resonant and engaged voice, then it may lead to a wider liberation of humankind's most precious resource. I have concentrated on these possibilities in Western examples of performance not because they are in advance of practices elsewhere, but because when there is resistance to, and transgression of, oppression at the *heart* of the systems of global domination then that may give added impetus to parallel and complementary projects in other, less fortunate, parts of the world. In fact, there are many such projects on every continent, ranging from the famous ones of Augusto Boal to the relatively unknown ones of Zakes Mda, and from the liberalism of theatre for development to the radicalism of theatre for liberation (Boal 1979; Epskamp 1989; Mlama 1991; Mda 1993; van Erven 1992; Srampickal 1994; Breitinger 1994).

This international flourishing of contemporary performance beyond theatre in the past forty years in part signals a widespread reaction against the established political processes. Yet also the advances in the politicisation of performance can be seen as part and parcel of a potential re-politicisation of massive social formations everywhere. In the developed countries the emergence of new social movements, in all their performative variety, seems to be evidence of this. In the developing countries the struggle against neo-colonialism, in all of its guises, obviously is part of a related desire for autonomy and self-determination. And maybe a radical politics of performance can have an important place in the drive for equality, justice and freedom. Because performance that is culturally democratic – a celebration of difference and pluralism within an always provisional unity – may become politically democratic in almost the fullest sense of the term. At this point we will not be talking about 'traces of resistance' in performance, but about performative negotiation and exchange that can, under certain circumstances, constitute a radical inflection of dominant discourses, including perhaps even the discourses of disciplinary theatre, of a kind that furthers the evolution of effective democracy.

To discover the full potential of performance in such a project on the cusp of the paradigm shift, it is necessary to identify some of the kinds of radicalism that the excesses of performance can create in the contemporary world. Consequently, Part II of this book is devoted to a search for sources of the radical in performance.

Part II

Performance, participation, power

Chapter 3

Fighting in the streets
Performance, protest and politics

Another victory like that and we're done for.
Pyrrhus

On the road to an RSG

For many others besides me the late 1950s were jazz, hitch-hiking and protest. The jazz, of course, was a compulsory pleasure for the beat generation, especially in muggy old Manchester, the trad jazz Mecca of the North. This was our antidote to industrial history, to the dour black buildings and mucky canals, to the ingrained graft of the generations before us, to the bastard shop-floor foremen who liked to piss on youth. And the hitch-hiked journeys were always pilgrimages in search of a fix of ecstatic sounds or sights. The beat-up roads and the thumbed-down cars and trucks were our American dream, but somehow an Austin mini on the clogged-up streets of the Potteries couldn't match a Pontiac on the freeway, even when the point of the journey was to be a rebel with a cause.

To start with, though, protest was just part of the hip new scene, a style statement. So the elders on the annual Aldermaston marches of the Campaign for Nuclear Disarmament had their work cut out to stop the press from prying too closely into our overnight stops. Dire moral warnings were issued about squeezing more into a sleeping bag than was good for its seams. Of course these sensible reactionaries of protest generated a counter-force: by my third march I was super-tuned from the outset to any naughtiness that would relieve the boredom.

Rumours had been circulating from the first day that something big was going to erupt. Busy with a new companion, I gathered vaguely that it had to do with something called an RSG. I remember feeling a silly warmth toward anything that could be flagged-up in the image of a mighty metal support – for to an engineer an RSG is a rolled-steel girder. On the second day suddenly a lot of people started clambering through the roadside hedge and running across a field, so we followed them. After the slow slog of the main march the rush across a great green expanse of dew-glittering grass was just ecstatic. But at the third fence my duffle-coat got seriously snagged on barbed wire and we finished up at the tail end of the run, finally slowing as the big crowd in front came to a halt, spreading out to each side like the backwash from a wave hitting rock.

We wove our way forwards to where the action was, to be fazed by an amazing sight. In the middle of this ordinary field a great concrete ramp, as wide as a road, sloped steeply down into the ground. On each side of the ramp gradually rose enormous concrete walls, their tops level with the field. The surface of the ramp was corrugated so that vehicles could drive safely down, and at the bottom of the slope were a pair of huge doors, glinting steely grey in the thin morning light. It was as if someone had taken a great deep wedge of the earth away. I remember childishly thinking that the gates were like the entrance to some giant's private dungeon. Hundreds of people were standing on the ramp and more were ranged on the walls at the side and above the doors. No one was moving, everyone was just silently standing there bearing witness to something awful. And not knowing quite what it was made the thing for me totally awesome. But I soon learned that *this* was the RSG; we were gazing on the gates to a Regional Seat of Government. From this underground bunker the powers that be would try to control the country after a nuclear war. We had fallen from earth and were looking down at an obscenely silly bulwark against a man-made hell. From that moment, for me, protest became as crucial as breathing.

The dramaturgies of protest

Protest can instil the impulse of radical performance into the blood and bones of the body politic. At its best, protest is performance wrestling successfully with the entropic resistance of histories shaped by dominant socio-political forces. So the progress of protest in the post-war period can tell us a good deal about the soft underbelly of official power, about the inevitable flaws in the operations of authority on the cusp between modernity and post-modernity. An investigation into popular protest as performance could open up useful new vistas on the changing nature of civil autonomy and desire in its articulations to political tradition, social movements and cultural histories. Moreover, as protest has become an especially significant feature of the international political map in the past fifty years, a study of its evolving dramatic principles and tendencies could indicate fresh sources of radicalism in the contemporary world. A *dramaturgy of protest as performance* may be particularly appropriate to this task, because the idea implies a reflexive alertness to the aesthetic assumptions informing radical action for socio-political change. An aesthetics of protest must try to give a convincing account of the *knowing* performativity of direct political action.

I am talking about the dramaturgy of *performance* because protest is a type of cultural performance that has little or nothing to do with the theatre estate and its disciplines. But successful protest events have to confront a system of commodification even more virulent than theatre, in the voracious gaze of the media. Protest is locked into the disciplines of mediatisation by its prominence in the public sphere. Moreover, the growth of globalised media networks threatens to transform protest into a prisoner of its own need for exposure, its performances neutered by electronic representation and reproduction. Through this, as Walter Benjamin argued of mediatised art, 'the quality of its presence is always depreciated' (1992: 215). And of course in a global economy dominated by late-capitalism the mediatised industries are articulated to an international market in which nothing is beyond mutation into a commodity (Frow 1997: 130–217). If protest has survived as radical performance in this context, then its changing aesthetics may indicate sources for the radical in the social that might be impossible to identify in any other way.

The discovery of such sources, though, will require a fresh analytical methodology. I argued in Part I that the promiscuity of the political in post-modernity has thrown the traditional idea of 'political theatre' into crisis. To construct a more flexible notion of the politics of performance through an analysis of protest events we need to reverse the terms of that tradition. Rather than search for the political *in* theatre I will investigate performance *in* the political. A study of performative events that are recognised generally as political *and* radical – high-profile protests and demonstrations – will extend the politics of performance by linking the post-war growth of performance beyond theatre to civil sources of the radical in the performative society. Taking a lead from John Lahr and Jonathan Price's now largely forgotten *Life Show*, and picking up on some points that Richard Schechner originally raised in 1990, my argument will concentrate on an analysis of major post-war rallies, demonstrations, marches, sit-ins, peace camps, vigils and so on (Lahr and Price 1973; Prentki 1990; Schechner 1993; Kershaw 1997). Hence, I aim to identify a changing *dramaturgy of popular protest* in the past forty years and to anatomise evolving sources for the radical in the wider cultural histories of the period. From this angle we will see how, on the cusp of the paradigm shift, the symbolic and the real have been reconfigured by innovations in the performance of protest.

Popular protest and the post-modern hyper-real

So what can the changing dramaturgies of popular protest tell us about the cultures of their time? More precisely, what might such forms signify at moments of crisis in history, when radical social and political change is, or appears to be, immanent? How do the forms of popular protest embody their historical context through their location in identifiable traditions; and how do those same forms crack open traditions, disrupt socio-political expectations and produce new kinds of radicalism in an increasingly mediatised and globalised world?

I will address these questions through an investigation of a few selected events: the Grosvenor Square (London) demonstration of March 1968, the White House (Washington) demonstrations of May 1970 and the fall of the Berlin Wall and the Tiananmen Square occupation of 1989. I have chosen these because they seem to have a transparent relationship to their historical 'moment'; cultural and political historians commonly note that they indicate especially widespread or popular discontent, seeing them as signals of deep rifts and schisms in society (Hewison 1986; Feigon 1990; Chipkowski 1991). The relationships between micro- and macro-politics, specific events and general histories, can be framed in many ways, of course, but the version informing this type of analysis is one of *synecdoche*, as a part of the social (protest) is made to stand for the whole (society).

This is an appropriate perspective to take on protest events in the late twentieth century because, like terrorism, they have become integral to the production of the 'society of the spectacle' that Guy Debord identified in the late 1960s. The idea is central to the argument of this chapter and the book, for if we follow the logic of Debord's 'situationism' a couple of theoretical steps further it turns into Baudrillard's post-modern society of the simulacra and the hyper-real (Debord 1977; Baudrillard 1983). In these versions of the cultural economy, the synecdochic spectacle of protest challenges a system of authority *in its own terms*, because in such societies the *display* of power – its symbolic representation in multifarious forms of public custom, ceremony and ritual, and then their reproduction throughout the media – has become in some senses more important to the maintenance of law and order than authority's actual powers of coercion and control (Foucault 1977, Fiske 1993, and Strong 1984 indicate a long lineage).

In *The Most Radical Gesture* Sadie Plant demonstrates how the Parisian-based Situationist International of the late 1960s, represented primarily by Debord, was influenced by modernism/Marxism. The situationist theorisations of the society of the spectacle commonly pictured the commodifications of consumerism, amplified by the mediatisation of culture, as a screen of alienation placed by power between the people and reality. Disruption of the spectacle would expose the systems of domination and stimulate a revolution through which popular desire for freedom would be satisfied. From a starting point sympathetic to situationism, Baudrillard, through the late 1970s and into the 1980s, extended its premises through a logic in which the spectacle of simulation became the only reality. In works such as *Simulations* (1983) and *Fatal Strategies* (1990), he demonstrates a brilliant pessimism in arguing that the 'precession of simulacra' in the capitalist overproduction of commodities and images finally entirely banishes the real by representing nothing other than their own, simulated, reality (Baudrillard 1988). As Plant makes clear:

> This circularity, in which the image is engaged in an eternal return upon itself, marks not only the ends of reality, meaning and history, but also signifies the impossibility of critical thought and all political engagement.
>
> (1992: 162)

Of course, there is one obvious sense in which the global histories of popular protest in the post-war period makes a nonsense of Baudrillard's logic, but to stop at that would deny the power of his insights into postmodernity and their utility to radicalism. For we might accept Baudrillard's account of the processes of simulation in late-capitalism whilst disagreeing that they have finally achieved their completion.

For example, Baudrillard frequently portrays the world of simulacra as *flattened out* by the abolition of reference to the real, as if every sign is ultimately equivalent to the next, like pixels on an LCD screen. They achieve this state by passing through the different orders of simulacra – counterfeit, production and simulation – which have been in process 'since the Renaissance' (Baudrillard 1983: 83). But the apocryphal flatness of simulation, in which semiotic equivalence rules across all discourse, may be challenged by an ubiquitous – even inescapable – desire in humans to invest variable value in signs. A lot can be learned from Bourdieu's work on 'distinction' in this regard, by recognising that the universal drive to confer greater distinction on some signs rather than others always offers to throw the order of simulacra into reverse, as it were, and thus return us to a sense of the real in history (Bourdieu 1984). In addition, the multifaceted culture of the cusp of the paradigm shift paradoxically might deliver a kind of double vision, a reflexivity that sees through the apparently impenetrable flood of simulation to highlight, for example, unacceptable levels of exploitation, inequality and injustice in the local and the global.

In such a culture, the synecdochic nature of protest events may produce enormous political potency. For disruption of the seductive sweep of the spectacle, in any particular context, can double the whole social process back on itself, as it were, and present a reflexive critique of the machinations of authority; for example, by exposing the assumption of power by the State as based ultimately on nothing more substantial than the chimera of presumption or a predisposition to violence. Hence, a dramaturgy of protest events could prove an effective key to understanding major socio-political changes in the late twentieth century, around the cusp of the paradigm shift.

Grosvenor Square, 1968

I take this event as a starting point in my argument because it can be located in relation to two great modernist traditions of protest, and the contrasts between them will help to clarify the dramaturgic nature of mass demonstrations. It took place in March 1968, when, following a Campaign for Nuclear Disarmament rally in Trafalgar Square, 25,000 people – including Vanessa Redgrave and Tariq Ali – marched under the banners of the Vietnam Solidarity Campaign to protest against the war in Vietnam outside the American Embassy in Grosvenor Square. The demonstration is generally considered to be a watershed in the history of British post-war protest because it became very violent (Morgan 1992: 294). Certainly, media representations projected on to it a near apocalyptic significance. The following commentary from the Pathé News film report is typical.

> London: It started as an anti-Vietnam war demonstration in Trafalgar Square. About 10,000 gathered. Most of them were young, most of them were sincere – they wanted peace....Vanessa Redgrave, as usual, was in the vanguard of the would-be peace-

makers, but also there were troublemakers…a hard core with intentions to drag the majority of well-intentioned demonstrators down to their sickening level….And so they marched through the Sunday streets of London to Grosvenor Square, and the American Embassy. Riot was being incited. At Grosvenor Square, police…waited – their intention to keep the peace, prevent trouble. But at the head and in the midst of the advancing column the hate-makers were at work. This was how they turned a demonstration for peace into a bloody riot, such as Britain has never before witnessed…on a day when a demonstration for peace ended as a war in the heart of London.

(Pathé News 1968)

The similarities implied between the well-practised tactics of CND – the non-violent protest march – and the peace movement of Mahatma Gandhi are fairly obvious: examples of the march that gathers numbers to end in a rally with speeches were familiar to the British public from earlier Pathé News items covering, for example, the Aldermaston marches. The tone of guarded respect in the film's commentary on this part of the march – 'their motives seemed honourable' – indicates the power of this tradition of peaceful protest as an acceptable component of democracy. By contrast, the virulent condemnation of the events in Grosvenor Square suggest something much more disturbing to the conventional British psyche than a few bloodied heads, even if they do happen to belong to the friendliest of bobbies. The public is being warned off some imagined, far more sinister and fundamental threat to British society.

A brief consideration of the broad historical context of the demonstration will take us some way towards an explanation of this revulsion. Obviously, Grosvenor Square was chosen for the climax of the day's events because the American Embassy represents the United States, the world leader in developing what was commonly called by radicals the 'capitalist military-industrial complex' (Roszak 1969). The attacks on the Embassy were therefore, metaphorically speaking, not just aimed at American action in Vietnam, but also at the economic, social and political system that was the source of growing British affluence in the 1960s (Bédarida 1979; Marwick 1982). This was not simply a revolt against a foreign invasion of a far-off Eastern country, but a representation of the potential for bloody revolution at home.

The revolutionary implications of the event may have been reinforced in the popular imagination by recent songs by the Beatles –

especially 'Revolution' (1968) – and the Rolling Stones – especially 'Streetfighting Man' (1968) – as well as by the counter-culture's shallow lionisation of Che Guevara. In political circles the connections between the Vietnam Solidarity Campaign and far-Leftist groups such as the Socialist Labour League (which in 1969 became the Workers' Revolutionary Party) and the International Marxist Group were well-known. These links are a clear clue to the source of the demonstration's dramaturgy. Not long before the Russian revolution of 1905 Trotsky had written the following:

> To make the workers quit their machines and stands; to make them walk out of the factory premises into the street; to lead them to the neighbouring plant…to go thus from factory to factory, from plant to plant, incessantly growing in numbers, sweeping aside police barriers, absorbing new masses…crowding the streets, taking possession of buildings…fortifying those buildings…holding continuous revolutionary meetings with audiences coming and going…arousing their spirit…to turn finally, the entire city into one revolutionary camp, this is, broadly speaking, the plan of action.
>
> (1964: 48–9)

The Grosvenor Square protest, then, appears to have been based on a dramaturgy of total revolutionary opposition, in which the enemy – the antagonist – is *assumed* to be known: the war in Vietnam, American imperialism, Western capitalism (Ali 1978). But the march did not overtly identify these in its symbolism, except through the odd cryptic placard, as if its meaning for the protagonists, the protesters, was 'given' by its place in the traditions of protest.

However, the demonstration's dramaturgy significantly deviates from the last scene of Trotsky's scenario: if the protesters had ever intended to lead up to a 'revolutionary meeting', or even create a 'revolutionary camp', they were thwarted by the authorities. Paradoxically perhaps, the demonstration ended up as a pale reflection of its overt object: the actual confusion and chaos of the war in Vietnam, which the US government had fairly successfully disguised from the general public, was reproduced as 'bloody war' on the streets of London. The symbolic protest slips into a scaled-down version of the irrevocably real violence that it aims ostensibly to prevent.

This contradiction, together with the fact that the key antagonists for the protesters were not clearly identified in the symbolism of the march, makes it unusually open to deliberate mis-readings by commentators:

instead of, say, coherent politicians who know how to unite action and ideology – the Gandhi model – we have rabble-rousers, hooligans and opportunistic thugs. Sadly for those who were there, the uniform of duffle-coats and sandals adopted by many of the marchers lacked revolutionary resonance. The significance of the event may the more easily be turned against the authors because they have not clearly 'written' the central metaphors of the drama. In a sense, they lost control over the relationships between the symbolic and the real because they seemed to assume a transparency of meaning that could not be sustained in the face of the contradictions produced by events.

Methodological considerations

This analysis of the Grosvenor Square protest raises a number of methodological issues for the construction of dramaturgies of protest. First, the relationships between protest events and their socio-political context may turn out to be by no means as transparent as protesters might wish. This is not simply a function of *différance*, the undecidability of signification and the deferral of meaning identified by Derrida, but also – as we saw in Chapter 2 – a quality of the performative itself. Divergent interpretations of the wider cultural significance of the same demonstrations obviously bear this out. So while we may be able to identify dramaturgic sources for particular demonstrations – the Gandhian and Trotskyite in the case of Grosvenor Square – their destination, so to speak, may always surprise us through a fresh inflection of old, or an invention of new, forms. In these ways the messy excesses of performance – and especially cultural performances as *relatively* unprecedented as protest events – may produce an especially rich exchange between symbolic action and socio-political reality. Such a prospect seems particularly appropriate for an analysis of events whose outcome, as they were happening, was steeped in profound uncertainty.

Second, while the performativity of protest may always evade the closure of interpretation, the analysis of protest as performance may reveal dimensions to the action that are relatively opaque to other approaches. It is obviously an assumption of my argument that most forms of contemporary protest – excluding perhaps the most spontaneous outbreaks of violence – are in part shaped by performative considerations. Though they often involve a good deal of spontaneity, they also follow scripts or scenarios. Moreover, contemporary protest in a mediatised world almost always assumes an audience, onlookers for whom events are 'played out'. Contemporary protest therefore is always other-directed, and therefore often reflexively aware of the symbolic potential of its own, sometimes all too real, action. It follows that in the analysis of protest events we should always be alert to the particular ways in which they are reflexively articulated to their socio-political context. In this respect, at least, performance analysis may discover aspects to protest that resonate with their historical moment in especially telling ways.

Third, in discussing protest events we are likely to be dealing with mediations of those events, rather than the events themselves. However, for the kinds of event we are considering this is not necessarily a disadvantage, because in its desire to capture the high points of the 'news' the media may well play into the hands of the people creating the events. The media tends to pick out the performative precisely because the performative stages the dramas that the media considers to be the 'news'. Of course, since the late 1960s there has been a rich tradition of radical theory and practice that has celebrated this key characteristic of the society of the spectacle, beginning with Guy Debord and the situationists, and Abbie Hoffman, Gerry Rubin and the American yippies. Their ideas in turn relate to Marshall McCluhan's theories of the media, to Herbert Marcuse's socio-political philosophy, and beyond that to the theories of the Frankfurt School (Hoffman 1968; Rubin 1970; McCluhan 1964; Marcuse 1969; Bottomore 1984; Thompson 1990). This critical tradition focuses on the commodifying powers of the mass media, which the performativity of effective protest is always aiming to subvert.

My fourth point concerns the aesthetics of the performative in protest events. Clearly we are dealing with forms in which spontaneity and improvisation may often be very much to the fore. This is partly because large numbers of people in situations of conflict are very difficult to organise. But it is also because the unexpected and the surprising are especially potent weapons for disrupting the spectacle and challenging authority, even at the level of everyday experience (de Certeau 1988: 18; Lefebvre 1971: 35). So a general dramaturgy of protest events, an account of their performative structures, will probably look very unlike anything outlined by Aristotle, say. Even given examples such as Grosvenor Square, which mostly follows a linear modernist scenario, it would sound odd to suggest that protest is entirely organised to the principles of a unitary action, or that everyone involved is working from a *single* script, or its equivalent. There may be scripts, or at least quasi-scripts, but probably they will be related only loosely to each other. In similar fashion we should probably be talking about an interweave of actions, any one of which may dominate the event for a time – a charge at police lines, say – but which will inevitably be reabsorbed in a series of multiple actions that are running simultaneously.

In other words, we would be constructing a dramaturgy that stressed qualities such as multiplicity, discontinuity, abrupt eruptions of dramatic intensity, sudden shifts and changes of direction, tempo or focus. If it wasn't already an overworked theoretical seam, we might even be tempted, like Schechner, to draw on chaos theory in order to spot strange attractors, Mandelbrot sets and fractal boundaries in the swirls and eddies of your average demonstration, which often appears to incorporate random happenings within a disorder that is somehow coherent (Gleick 1988). Yet it is this paradoxical quality – order within disorder, disorder arising out of order – which is at the heart of protest events as potential paradigms for the socio-political economies of their times, because they aim to latch on to the cusp of major historical change at the moment of its happening. To achieve such historical resonance they must develop dramaturgies that draw on tradition to produce a recognisably *ordered* cultural performance, while never fore-closing on unpredictability, on the potential of *disorder*. It is that dynamic that may articulate protest to history in ways that are often unprecedented, thus making it a potent augury of change, perhaps especially when paradigms are shifting.

The White House, 1970, *via* Paris, 1968

Just two months after the Grosvenor Square demonstration, Paris was beset by an even more violent uprising. The *événements de Mai*, 1968, are usually seen as the high point of counter-cultural protest, combining ambitions of political revolution with desire for totally free expression (Cerny 1982; Reader 1993; Absalom 1971; Seale and McConville 1968). Protest graffiti coupled the personal and the political in symbi-otic and often erotically linked ecstasy: 'The more I revolt, the more I make love' was an especially popular one. Politics and art are supposed to have merged together as news-sheets, posters and banners prolifer-ated, and as Situationist slogans underlined the theatre in the events (Plant 1992: 133–41).

Yet the marriage of politics and art perhaps happened more in theory than in practice. It is true, of course, that Jean-Jacques Lebel, together with Judith Malina and Julian Beck of America's Living Theatre, led an attack on the Odéon Théâtre that was then occupied for the duration and became a focus for the whole revolt. But the theatricalisation of this particular protest was closer perhaps to costume drama than to the radical symbolic disruption of the spectacle envisaged by Debord. Richard Neville indicates as much when he points out that:

> The Odéon occupation...was the first time the revolt engulfed non-university territory. The wardrobe department was ransacked and dozens faced the tear gas dressed as centurions, pirates and princesses. The Theatre came into the streets.
>
> (1971: 37)

This implies that the overtly symbolic gestures of the Parisian uprising were less crucial to its dramaturgy than the actual fighting in the streets: the dominant images of the protest are the barricades, the petrol bombs, the torn-up paving stones and the wrecked cars – not the graffiti or the costumes. The scenarios of this revolt perhaps were rooted less in the exhortations of the Situationist manifesto, than in Trotsky's prompt-book for insurrection, his report on the Russian Revolution (1935). The Parisian uprising of 1968 was still, like Grosvenor Square, primarily located in the modernist traditions of radical dramaturgy, the main difference between them being that the *événements* for a while succeeded in turning parts of Paris, such as the Odéon Théâtre, into a 'revolutionary camp'.

For a contrasting dramaturgy of protest we can turn to the United States in the late 1960s and early 1970s, when the civil rights and anti-Vietnam movements coalesced to stage demonstrations that, at their best, had all the polyphonous eloquence that Bakhtin claimed for classic carnival, plus original forms of theatricalised spectacle that, true to Debord's recipes for symbolic revolution, fashioned new relations between the imaginary and the real. There are many examples, but I will focus briefly on one discussed by Richard Schechner: the occupation in Washington of the White House lawn by many thousands of demonstrators on 9 May 1970 (1993: 63–7). This followed the Kent State University killings of May 4th and the first bombings of Cambodia, and so had great potential for violence. However, all the conflicts that ensued were entirely symbolic, and it is precisely this contrast between the object of revolt – violence and war – and the style of the event, that marks it out as a significant moment in the development of new dramaturgies of protest.

The demonstration combined the identification of the 'enemy' – the White House and US government – as in Grosvenor Square, with the occupation of his territory – the White House lawn – as in Paris, but it lacked the directly violent confrontational tactics of those events. Rather, the protest was played out in the realm of the sign, sometimes in anger but mostly in an atmosphere of celebration. Schechner rightly links this celebratory ethos to the development of the so-called Woodstock Nation – the hippy movement – and he stresses its carnivalesque qualities.

> The frolic – with its characteristic whorling choreography, the dispersal of orderly ranks into many intense and volatile groups, the show of private pleasures satisfied in public places – subverted and mocked the neo-Roman monuments and pretensions of imperialist Washington.
>
> (1993: 65–7)

He is drawn to this interpretation mainly by the bathers – many of them naked – who took to the Reflecting Pool of the Lincoln Memorial. An *en masse* immersion in the waters that reflect the memorial to State-protected liberty generated popular pleasure: the collective body of the populace ironically obliterating an evanescent image of the State's false promise of peaceful freedom.

But it was also in the more direct encounters of the event that the principles of a new dramaturgy can be detected. Earlier in the morning, and amazingly from the perspective of the terrorised 1990s, President Nixon himself had come out on to the lawn to talk to the demonstrators. According to Schechner, he was greeted with shouts of 'Fuck Nixon! Trash Nixon!' and a few people lifted up dustbin lids with his picture stuck on their underside (see Figure 5 on p. 102).

The metaphor in this moment of high drama is both witty and sinister, as it rests on the ambiguous sign of the lids as shields and as ironic picture frames for the President's image: political elevation brought low through a comedy of dirt and darkness, we might say. Such parodic mockery is the stuff of the carnivalesque, but the context of the protest pushes the drama beyond carnival in at least two crucial respects. Firstly, the transgression of the demonstration (unlike in carnival) is decidedly *not* licensed. The protest represents more than just time out from the mundane and everyday, framed by the law and the State. Rather, it fashions new or, perhaps, stolen time – time (and space) taken on the terms of the demonstrators, not contained by the law but beyond the law (at least until the police and troops move in). And secondly, it is more precisely other-directed than carnival, for not only is it a face-to-face statement against the most powerful authority in the world, it is a gesture made for the media, an image that can be quickly

Figure 5 President Nixon in dustbin lids, Washington, 1970

Note: The real stars-and-stripes headband – often sported by counter-cultural urban guerrillas of the period – gives added irony to the image

Source: Reproduced by kind permission of Routledge

captured and transmitted through the world's airwaves, reproduced and read across many national boundaries. Hence, the drama of protest aims to utilise the processes of globalisation to magnify the wit, determination, bravery and tactical skill of the protagonists – the demonstrators. And through these processes the imaginary – the President in a dustbin – and the real – the President in the White House – are placed in new relationships for the spectator.

In the wake of this demonstration yet another dimension of the new protest dramaturgy was created in Washington. By 1971 some 1,500 supporters of the Vietnam Veterans Against the War campaign had set up a camp on the green around the Washington Monument. From there, small groups of veterans marched in double file around Congress and through the streets of the capital (see Figure 6 on p. 104).

They wore whiteface, carried toy guns and had their real purple hearts, silver stars and other war decorations pinned to their combat fatigues. According to Lee Baxandall, as they marched they shouted:

> 'Where are our dead brothers? We're looking for our 50,000 brothers. Have you seen them?'…(While…) other troupes of Veterans paraded mock Vietnamese prisoners, hands tied behind their backs, past government workers and visiting tourists. They did it for real. The prisoners were kicked, screamed at, slapped and shoved. At the end of the week, the Vets threw their medals and papers onto the steps of congress.
>
> (1972)

The combination of the camp and these enacted provocations shift this protest into yet newer dramaturgic territory. Relations between the real and the imaginary are deliberately distorted and confused; the fact that these are real veterans living under canvas much as they would have done in Vietnam validates the play-acting, yet some of the play-acting is also done 'for real'. The camp and the performances turn the Washington streets into metaphor, so they become both an extension of the Vietnam jungle and a limbo for ghostly soldiers searching for their comrades. We can characterise this as an imaginative hyper-realism that in a globalising gesture challenges the spectator with both the immediacy and the distance of the war, carrying an excessive intensity that makes the action paradoxical. This dramaturgy aims to make sense by bypassing the rational, subverting the logic of critical containment, in order to provoke an unprecedented response. Significantly, it is not recommending an action: it is giving opportunity for revulsion/fascination with one of the vilest wars in human history. But by confounding the real and the imaginary so thoroughly it leaves the nature of any subsequent action open to the spectator. This is a protest that leaves the future, even in the imagination, radically undecided. It is a post-modern protest.

Figure 6 The whiteface Vietnam veterans, Washington, 1971

Note: Note the ambivalence produced by the toy guns set against real medals
Source: Photograph: LNS Women's Graphic Collective

A new dramaturgy and its theorists

Sources for this new dramaturgy can be identified in the 1960s trend in America to create performance beyond theatre. The work of the San Francisco Mime Troupe, for example, combined Brecht and the techniques of *commedia dell'arte* to produce popular political theatre. In the mid-1960s the troupe's founder, Ron Davis, first used the term 'guerrilla theatre' to indicate an action that aims to 'teach, direct towards change, be an example of change' (1975: 149; see also Lesnick 1973; Sainer 1975 and 1997; Wiseman 1973). Guerrilla theatre was distinguished from traditional political theatre by being staged in the environment of political conflict – the streets of ghettos, the grounds of government buildings; hence the analogy to real guerrilla warfare – but it was allied to traditional political theatre by being mostly didactic in purpose. Equally influential was the Bread and Puppet Theatre, which introduced archetypal and satirical imagery to street protests, usually in the form of giant puppets. These combined the techniques of religious spectacle with ideas drawn from Artaud, and so had a less specific symbolic charge than the stereotypes of guerrilla theatre (Brecht 1988). Similarly, the Living Theatre aimed to subvert rational analysis by turning spectators into participants in excessive performative action, but working mostly in theatres. But whatever the venue, the group's ritualised, hieratic gestures of ecstatic or sublime experience were supposed to project a reality in which authority and oppression, the law and exploitation simply did not exist: a kind of pan-humanistic Utopia (Biner 1972; Tytell 1997).

These sources for the dramaturgy of late-1960s protest events variously combined Brecht and Artaud to produce a politics of ecstasy, fun or celebration. Brecht's notion of *gestus* (the moment of action that perfectly expresses social relations) can explain the penchant for the quickly read image; while Artaud's idea of cruelty (the transcendent disruption of received realities) may illuminate the forms of excess that were often on display. Moreover, both theorists (though in different ways) spoke of the power of the symbolic to penetrate the real, to intervene so fundamentally in the real as to render its hegemonic oppressions totally transparent and so subject to radical change.

Drawing on such sources, the central focus of protest dramaturgy shifted in the early 1970s away from the modernist notion of an attack on a known enemy in the name of revolutionary progress towards a more improvisatory and hyper-real style of scenario. Although protest, of course, was still directed against authority, increasingly it aimed to produce for both participants and spectators an image or an experience that gave a glimpse of the future as pure freedom from the constraints of the real, a hint of Utopia at the very moment in which it engaged in the messy business of street marches and peace camps. Hence protest, whether in the form of procession or occupation, became multi-vocal, polyphonic, as much an expression of difference as of unity. It could achieve this because, in a sense, the symbolic content of protest was repositioned in relation to the real: while earlier protests usually drew primarily on *political* sources for their dramaturgies, in the sense of political theory or ideologies, these later events derived much of their dramaturgical power from *performative* origins. This adjustment of focus opened up a much wider perspective on the potential of protest: in a sense the imaginary became more important than the possible, the visionary more persuasive than the rational.

We would expect such a significant reorientation to produce its own brand of theorist-practitioner, and the most outrageously funny ones, at least in America, were Jerry Rubin and Abbie Hoffman, leading members of the yippies, who variously advocated civil disobedience and violent revolution. (Richard Neville was perhaps their closest British equivalent.) Schechner notes how they were committed to the theatricalisation of political action. In *Revolution for the Hell of It*, for example, Hoffman wrote, in typical anarchistic vein, that 'Drama is anything you can get away with.…Guerrilla theatre is only a transitional step in the development of total life actors' (1968: 183; Schechner 1993: 64). In almost identical mode Rubin argues that 'Life is theatre and we are the guerrillas attacking the shrines of authority.…The street is the stage. You are the star of the show and everything you were once taught is up for grabs' (Rubin 1970: 250; Schechner 1993: 64). These claims take the sociological theatre–life analogy most fully developed by Goffman into a new dimension, where the symbolic and the real overlap to produce new forms of political protest and new arenas for action (Goffman 1959). In this increasingly post-modern dimension the ironic verbal aphorism, the parodic visual image and the paradoxical 'message' are crucial weapons, and Hoffman was a master of their use.

It was Hoffman who explained that a yippie is a hippie who's been hit on the head by a policeman. And he instigated one of the most resonant examples of non-violent protest action. In the early 1970s he and a few colleagues visited the public gallery of the New York Stock Exchange (Hoffman 1985: 134–40). Far below them the floor was full of busy buyers and sellers, market executives dressed in neat suits and wearing dignified ties. Hoffman and company proceeded to scatter real dollar bills from the gallery, which gently drifted down like leaves on to the heads of the marketeers. Within a minute trading had completely stopped as the executives jumped and scrambled for the bills. The Stock Exchange was shown for what it actually is: a grotesque dance of greed.

Carnival and protests

It has become an orthodoxy among performance analysts to associate performative excess with notions of carnival and festival – Bacchanalian riotousness! For example, in 'The Street is the Stage' Richard Schechner draws on Bakhtin to explain how both protest events and celebratory gatherings may activate the basic functions of carnival by (a) transgressing, up-ending, mocking and in other ways destabilising the images and structures of authority in society, and (b) returning the participants to a social order that, whether the same as before or modified, has been reinforced by the pleasurable 'time out', the holiday from law (1993; see also: Bakhtin 1968; Bristol 1985; Carlson 1992 and 1996; Gash 1993; Kershaw 1992; Roach 1996a and 1996b). In many events such action may be confined to the symbolic realm, in which case there is likely to be little, if any, change to the structures of power and authority in society. But in some events the irrevocable happens, in the form of 'violence...or the playing out of irreconcilable differences'. Schechner forcefully links this prospect to the idea of sacrifice and approvingly quotes Rene Girard, who argues that 'the fundamental purpose of the festival is to set the stage for a sacrificial act that marks at once the climax and the termination of the festivities' (1993: 47). It is then just a short step to the idea of ritual purgation, to the proposition that protest events that transcend the symbolic, whether they change society or not, operate as a kind of vent for the pressures of discontent, dissatisfaction, dissidence and radicalism itself. In this version of a dramaturgy of protest events we are not so far from Aristotle, and especially his claims for catharsis, after all.

Such totalising explanations are problematic, in two main ways. Firstly, they tend, of course, to gloss over difference; in particular they tend to usurp the creativity of practice by recommending a primacy of schema. Hence, Schechner's recourse to carnival and ritual leads to the simplification of many dramaturgic differences into a binary contrast between the 'swirls, vortexes' of protest events and the 'neat rectangles' of parades by official culture (1993: 88). This kind of contrast restricts the interaction of the symbolic and the real to a fairly limited repertoire, whereas the whole purpose of much contemporary protest has been to achieve efficacy by inventing unprecedented symbolic-real configurations. Secondly, Schechner's structuralist analysis downplays the ideological content, the political significance of particular events *as part of* a wider historical process. As a result, events as different as the New Orleans Mardi Gras and the occupation of Tiananmen Square are given a notional socio-political equivalence. Of course there are some similarities of form between the two types of event, but in Schechner's account the 'art' in the events appears to become more important than the purposes for which it was probably created; revolutionary and reactionary gatherings are contained by the same theoretical rubric.

These characteristics link Schechner to the 'ritualist' tendency in anthropology, identified by Clifford Geertz in his celebrated essay on 'Blurred genres', where he notes this approach to analysis '…can expose some of the profoundest features of social process, but at the expense of making vividly disparate matters look drably homogenous' (1993: 27). Geertz goes on to suggest that the underlying epistemological problem of the ritualist framework is revealed as a '…separation of data from theory'. He argues that as a result the methodology cannot '…prosper when explanation comes to be regarded as a matter of connecting action to its sense, rather than behaviour to its determinants' (1993: 34). Schechner's view of protest as ritual is not crudely determinist in this sense, of course, and he recognises that protest can contribute to profound socio-political change. But his claim that '…revolutionary street actions are rare examples of history in its molten state…' (1993: 86) reveals a curiously hypocaustic perspective on human action, which tends to separate it from its sense: how else might we understand a view of history as normally consisting of some kind of solid state?

In contrast, the argument of this chapter aims to articulate the dramaturgy of protest to the complex processes of global historical change creating the conditions of the cusp between paradigms in the past forty years. An approach which mainly stresses the aesthetics of protest, especially through an analogy with carnival, offers a useful model, but its concentration on *formal similarities* tends to detract from protest's contribution to the major ideological shifts of specific periods. Connecting 'action to its sense' in this way is not just a matter of noting the immediate and explicit purposes of particular protests – Grosvenor Square as a reaction to the war in Vietnam, for example – but of trying also to discern how they are a part of the wider socio-political histories under way in the moment of their happening. The relationship of late 1960s/early 1970s protest to the first of the major post-war counter-cultures offers some purchase on this problem: the tectonic shift of paradigms can be detected in Western democracies through the repositioning of generational formations *via*, for example, the increased educational opportunities and growing purchasing power of the young (Brake 1985; Hall and Jefferson 1976; Hebdige 1979). Hence, the contrasts between the protest march (CND/Grosvenor Square) and the peace camp (Vietnam Solidarity Campaign/White House) outlined above can be read synecdocally as 'evidence' of the gain in cultural power of the younger generation: the greater permanence of the camp provides the kinds of time/space needed to fashion new relations between the symbolic and the real.

Whether this might amount to a kind of active 'cognitive mapping', in Jameson's sense, through which the performativity of protest gives access to a meta-critique of late-capitalist post-modernity, is an issue that the following analysis is meant partly to address (1991: 408–18). Certainly a reflexive dramaturgy of protest would at least leave open the question of links between individual agency and global organisation, by appealing to the potential of performance to invent unprecedented prototypes for critical cultural action: in this respect the idea that performance can transcend dominant socio-cultural processes – including marketisation and commodification – is obviously crucial. But this type of theorisation needs to be tested against contrasting examples, such as the East-European protests which led to the fall of the Berlin Wall, and the cataclysmic events of Tiananmen Square in 1989.

Eastern protests in 1989

How much of the new dramaturgy of protest filtered through to the demonstrations that were crucial to the downfall of communism in East Germany and the reinforcement of hard-line brutality in Tiananmen Square? In the West the intervening years had seen a wide variety of successful experiments: from the Greenham Common Women's Peace Camp to the queer rights demonstrations of Gay Pride. How might the events of 1989 relate to these developments, and did they add any new dimensions to the dramaturgy of protest? I will address this question through a brief comparison between the East German demonstrations and the celebrations surrounding the fall of the Berlin Wall, before more fully discussing the occupation of Tiananmen Square. My purpose in this and the final section of the chapter is to suggest that in the last quarter of the twentieth century global protest has developed a new range of performative strategies. Through these strategies, protest has gained new kinds of synecdochic relevance to its socio-political contexts, and this suggests that it has drawn on new sources for radicalism in performance.

First, East Germany and the Berlin Wall. The fall of the wall was preceded by a series of mainly peaceful demonstrations in the chief cities of East Germany. These began in Leipzig in August–September 1989, following regular Monday evening 'peace services' in St Nikolai Church. Each week the crowds swelled in Karl-Marx Platz, but, according to a student organiser, they always were 'wondering what to do or say' (Chipkowski 1991: 77). Probably, too, the threat of violent retaliation from the armed police added to the crowd's uncertainty. A similar mood seems to have gripped other demonstrations, including one of the most significant in Plauen, on October 7th, the fortieth anniversary of East Germany, which was marked by a visit of Soviet President Gorbachev to East Berlin. Over 20,000 people, 25 per cent of the city's population, gathered in Plauen's central square. For some time they simply stood around 'unsure why exactly they had come' until a young man from a local school:

> ...climbed on top of a small stone statue next to a theater and held up a sign reading 'We want freedom!'. He was joined by another student who raised a black-red-gold West German flag. The crowd applauded and began to chant 'Germany, Germany!'. Suddenly a man dressed in a trench coat forced his way through the crowd, ripped down the flag, and punched its carrier in the face. At this moment, according to one spectator, the crowd became unified.
>
> (Chipkowski 1991: 80)

Such accounts of the demonstrations hint at a dramaturgy that is especially context-specific, and maybe a reflection of the lack of direct contact with the West imposed by the East German regime. Their immediate source in the Protestant Churches may help to explain the form of 'peaceful witness' that generally they adopted. This could be described paradoxically as a drama of inaction, a protest after Beckett, as it were, in which the straightforward presence of huge congregations with no obviously expressed immediate goal or target bears witness to a great unfulfilled need. So even the slightest signs of reaction – the single agent in the symbolic trench-coat – sparks off a process of extensive unification, a flood of yearning for an absent ideal. Maybe the dramaturgy here is rooted in the fabulous forms of Christian religion: the waiting for a sign through which a sudden conversion can be delivered?

What then was finally delivered was both stupendous in its symbolic charge and perhaps ironically trivial in its actual expression. The fall of the Berlin Wall marked the end of the cold war, the crumbling bricks and mortar signalled a possibly permanent postponement of nuclear armageddon. Yet the dramaturgy of the fall of the wall was remarkably undynamic. It was great to see people chipping it away with everyday hammers and chisels, but bulldozers and cranes with demolition balls would have signalled more resonantly the magnitude of the political collapse. So what the demonstration of freedom actually amounted to was a scramble to get on to the wall, and maybe the most memorable collective image was of a thin line of people holding hands and going nowhere (see Figure 7 on p. 112).

So the fall of the Berlin Wall produced a dramaturgy in which there is an enormous gap between the real – the means of surmounting and demolishing it – and the imaginary – the freedoms that its collapse appeared to promise. And maybe this is reflected in the gestures with which capitalist West Berlin welcomed the newly freed East Germans: free cinema tickets, bottles of booze and a hundred marks each to spend in the shops that were, for once, kept open all night. Such, perhaps, is the ironic outcome of a dramaturgy that quickly shifted from the structure of religious rite to the limited 'carnivalesque' free-for-all of the late capitalist market-place in post-modernity.

And what about Tiananmen Square? Even a short analysis of the tragic protest will show how its dramaturgical forms were designed to create maximum ideological impact in the briefest of moments. While the occupation lasted for over two months (April–June), many of its most potent political scenes took the shape of short dramatic 'dialogues', or exchanges, which resonated by contrast with the lengthening *duration* of the occupation. These theatricalised high points gave symbolic shape to the whole occupation through highly inventive experimentation with the radical performance of direct political action and imagery.

Joseph Esherick and Jeffrey Wasserstrom, in a thoughtful and thorough essay on the theatrical qualities of the occupation, argue that:

> As essentially non-violent demonstrations that posed no direct economic or physical threat to China's rulers, the power of the protests derived entirely from their potency as protests which could symbolically undermine the regime's legitimacy and move members of larger and more economically vital classes to take sympathetic action.
>
> (1990: 839)

Figure 7 Holding hands on the Berlin Wall, 1989

Note: An expression of unity before the Brandenburg Gate. An image of people going nowhere

Source: Reproduced by permission of Reuters

And they draw attention to three particular moments orchestrated by the students: the presentation of petitions, the dialogues arising from the hunger strike, and the entrance to the square of the Goddess of Democracy and Freedom. Each of these drew on Chinese traditions of political public action. For example, the presentation by the students of the petition that demanded an explanation of the resignation in 1987 of the pro-democracy General Secretary of the Communist Party emerged 'out of traditions of remonstrance and petition stretching back for millennia' (1990: 839). The image of three students kneeling on the steps of the Great Hall of the People would have profound resonance for the Chinese population, and so:

> The party leadership's failure to acknowledge in any way the peti-
> tion...was a major violation of ritual, and it significantly increased
> public anger against official arrogance.
>
> (1990: 842)

Esherick and Wasserstrom also note how a later visit to the hospitalised hunger strikers by party leaders was a more adroitly performed 'ritually required act of compassion', but one which was already negatively framed by the earlier televised dialogue between student leader Wuer Kaixi and Premier Li Peng.

> The costuming was important: [Wuer Kaixi] appeared in his hospital
> pyjamas. So, to, was the timing: he upstaged the Premier by inter-
> rupting him at the start. And props: later in the session, he
> dramatically pulled out a tube inserted in his nose (for oxygen?) in
> order to make a point.
>
> (1990: 841)

The guerrilla theatre-style inventiveness of this scene is reinforced by the fact that hunger striking was a relatively recent addition to the repertoire of Chinese protest, an introduction that also signalled 'how internationalised models for dissent had become' (1990: 841). But whether dealing in ancient or recent forms, the students demonstrated their superior control of protest dramaturgies in a highly mediatised world, both by ironically turning official Chinese political ritual back on itself and by extending the potential of direct action through globally tele-vised agitprop. Their grasp of these techniques of radical performance indicates a tactical order in their strategic disorder that delivers a clear political advantage over the interests of the State.

In describing Tiananmen during the occupation Richard Schechner adopts the language of the Chinese authorities to point out its links with carnival. He notes that the Chinese government labelled the occupation *luan*, or chaos, and he argues that 'Meaningful theatrical luan is a potent weapon' (1993: 63). He then uses imagery associated with chaos theory to make a contrast between the occupation and official uses of the Square, which generally take the form of geometric parades – such as military march-bys – and similar displays.

> This direct theatre [of Tiananmen Square] is always staged as, or ends in swirls, vortexes of activities...moving in spirals and circles without easy to identify centres or heads. Multivocal and multi-focus, a popular deconstructing of hierarchy....
>
> (1993: 88)

Obviously there was some of this celebratory action in Tiananmen; the students were there a long time and devised ways to amuse themselves, releasing the tensions of the situation. But Schechner's account tends to blur the historical and ideological achievement of the protesters in their highly controlled and imaginative uses of the symbolic to pose a threat that was ultimately felt as all too real by the Chinese authorities.

The traditional and the internationally innovative were combined stunningly in the most spectacular 'dialogue' of the occupation with the appearance of the Goddess of Democracy and Freedom. Constructed by students from the Beijing Academy of Art, the Goddess for three weeks faced the giant picture of Mao, symbolically blocking his view of the Monument to the People's Heroes. As the Monument is a 'sacred symbol of the Communist regime' (Esherick and Wasserstrom 1990: 841) the positioning of the Goddess offered a direct questioning of the validity of the Chinese government's power and proposed a revision of the nature of Chinese democracy for the future.

Ideologically speaking, the thirty-foot-high icon was appropriately multi-vocal: Esherick and Wasserstrom note its obvious allusion to the Statue of Liberty, which the Western media and the Chinese government tended to stress to the exclusion of other meanings. But they also point out that the image alludes to the rough-cut styles of social-realist sculptures of revolutionary heroes of communist tradition, and may well have been reminiscent of the giant statues of Mao that were paraded through the square in the 1960s. In similar vein it reminds Schechner of the Bread and Puppet Theatre effigies used in American anti-Vietnam war demonstrations of the 1960s. In fact, the Goddess is 'a potent pastiche

Figure 8 The Goddess of Democracy and Freedom, Beijing, 1989

Note: A multi-vocal image that spoke internationally, made by students of the Beijing Academy of Art

Source: Reproduced by permission of Sing Tao Press

Figure 9 Solitary man confronting tanks, Beijing, 1989

Note: The 'standard' version of individual heroism promulgated in the West

Source: Reproduced by permission of Associated Press

of imported and native symbolism' (Esherick and Wasserstrom 1990: 841), which participates in post-modern aesthetics to add a newly radical inflection to the performance of protest (Minzhu 1990: 342–8; Wasserstrom and Perry 1994: 140–7).

This makes the Goddess more complex than traditional agitprop imagery: it imports into that tradition new ironic and satirical inflections that link it to the more celebratory and carnivalesque aspects of late twentieth-century protest. But also it reflects a developing internationalisation and globalisation of protest, in two connected ways. Firstly, the discourse of the Goddess is international in its combination of signs drawn from both Eastern and Western cultures; secondly, it is globalised because it is clearly intended to speak cross-culturally through the media, and so become a focus for identifying the nature of the protest in relation to shifting global political formations. This was a demonstration for democracy, but not a democracy that would simply mimic Western models; this was a demonstration for a Chinese form of democracy. That democracy, as Esherick and Wasserstrom make clear, is much more wedded to notions of *unity* than those of the Western liberal democracies, which have tended to stress pluralism and reinforce the shift to the post-modernity of performative societies. For the Chinese, the gendering of the statue would almost certainly carry that extra charge.

The statue was smashed by the troops and tanks, and now maybe it hardly figures in the popular Western imagination as a symbol of resistance. The image that dominates representations of the Tiananmen protests in the West is resonant in quite different ways to the Goddess: this is one of enormous individual bravery, as a solitary man, shopping bags in hand, blocks the awful progress of a line of tanks on their way to the square (see Figure 9 opposite).

The moment is a wonderfully powerful one for the dramaturgy of protest, partly because it echoes earlier Western resistance to the colonising tendencies of communist states in the Prague Spring of 1968, and so reinforces the globalisation of protest. But also, as a mediatised image contending for the 'meaning' of the Tiananmen Square occupation it reflexively underlines the need for *continual* struggle for freedom and justice, as it is itself part of an international discourse through which the contending forms of democracy are shaped.

The two contrasting pictures of the solitary man facing up to the tanks gives an indication of the ideological issues at stake in the discourses of globalisation. The first image, which is the one most disseminated in the West, literally foregrounds the role of the *individual*

Figure 10 Solitary man confronting an army, Beijing, 1989

Note: There are over fifty tanks in this picture and two helicopter gunships can just be seen in the distance

Source: Reproduced by permission of Sing Tao Press

in the drama of protest, heightening modernist notions of heroism as a personal trait of the essentialised subject. The second image displays the awful context of that heroism, and shifts it towards quite different dramaturgical territory, raising questions about how the man could possibly have gained enough courage to confront a whole army alone (notice the helicopters in the background). The panorama of latent violence also implies the vulnerability of the State *and* the strength of many *invisible antagonists*, the decentred 'other' of the protesting students in Tiananmen Square that the lonely protester represents. This second image (see Figure 10 opposite) changes the ideological focus of this particular drama of the protest: without diminishing individual heroism it gestures towards a source of radicalism in the collective action of the students. On the global stage created by mediatisation, representations of the performance of protest become part of the struggle between different versions of the democratic process around the paradigm cusp.

In this new global context, the Goddess of Democracy and Freedom and the lone man facing the tanks together may suggest that radical resistance and transgression can thrive across space and time, however differently they are inflected by the circumstances of particular cultures: as male, female or some other gender; as collective, individual or some other formation; as modernist and/or post-modernist. Through globalisation, protest may become a phenomenon that partly transcends cultural difference and strengthens resistance as a universal possibility. Whilst we may gladly accept that there are no transcendental signifiers in the dramaturgy of protest, or any other discourse, it does not necessarily follow that where politics and ethics meet, post-modern relativism rules the world. The forms of freedom may be relative and the hold of justice tenuous, but, just possibly, the need for freedom and justice, like the need for food and company, may be edged towards the absolute.

New sources of radicalism

What, then, might an analysis of disruptive micro-events through a dramaturgy of protest tell us about macro-changes in cultures internationally in the past forty years or so? Does it tell us anything more than we could probably already deduce from general trends in cultural histories; for example, that anarchy and anti-structure were ideologically crucial to the 1960s counter-cultural 'revolution', or that the globalising thrust of international media networks in the 1980s contributed to profound unrest in politically sclerotic Eastern regimes?

In answering these questions we need to recognise that any response will be particularly susceptible to the ideological perspectives of the analysis brought to bear on such complex material. We also need to have constructed a kind of multi-focal methodology that will both take into account and counter the simplifications implied by the micro-/macro-binary. The problem with a ritualist approach is that it does neither: in mapping a schema on to diverse forms of street event it simultaneously elides their ideological macro-context and suppresses reflexive aware-ness of the values shaping its interpretations. But the difficulties of such a project are prodigious, because the writing of a general account, and particularly general histories around the cusp of the paradigm shift, always implies a meta-perspective that may invoke the spectre of meta-narratives. The main line of defence against that danger is a robust reflexivity, which can be developed through the cross-disciplinary tendencies of multi-focal methodologies.

In drawing on cultural studies and general social and political histories in my account of post-war protest I had to assume that *their* accounts have some valency. Hence, I chose not to challenge the usual associa-tions made between the events of 1968–70 and growth of the first counter-culture, which produced a supposed 'gap' between the value systems of the immediate post-war and earlier generations (Gordon 1986; Martin 1981; Musgrove 1974). Similarly, my account mostly took as read the common explanation that the uprisings of 1989 were the result of a chasm between the people and the State, between desire for individual freedoms and the oppressions of totalitarian communist regimes (Chip-kowski 1991; Wasserstrom and Perry 1994). However, the dramaturgical analysis of protest in this chapter has evolved a methodology and a theoretical perspective that differs from those generally informing inter-pretations of civil unrest in cultural studies and political histories, which seem often to rest on what we might call the *volcanic view* of protest. This view – which is a close cousin of the theorisations about the carniva-lesque in the social – usually posits that disruptive events are the irrepressible blow-out of a vast and usually invisible mass of turbulent socio-political material.

In this view, micro-events are still treated as synecdochic, as protest is seen as indicative of instability in the structures of society, but the implied function – condensed into the image of the volcano – suggests that protest is somehow always *within itself* out of control. The sources of radicalism in the performance of protest consequently are always by implication then associated with the irrational, the uncontrollable, the dark side of the human. In this respect, at least, such an approach to analysis implicitly allies itself with the dominant in interpreting disruption as in some sense always anti-structural, as in the Chinese government's interpretation of Tiananmen as *luan*. And this then has profound ramifications for the ideological interpretations placed on the relationships between particular micro-events and macro-structures. For example, for Bernice Martin the Parisian uprising of 1968 was mainly significant as a spectacular staging-post in an 'expressive revolution' that was anyway sweeping the whole of 'advanced' Western society towards greater liberation. So:

> The counter-culture of the 1960s looked revolutionary in its first flowering....Yet underneath the red clothing was a beast of a different colour, or perhaps a chameleon able to take on any political colouring.
>
> (1981: 21; quoted in Hewison 1988: 147)

While for Stuart Hall the disruptions were part of wider reaction to the fundamental contradictions of bourgeois capitalism, and therefore both inconsistent in themselves and constrained by their source.

> The point of origin within the crisis of the dominant culture may help to explain why the 'counter-culture' could not stand on its own as a political formation....This may account for why the 'cultural revolution' oscillated so rapidly between extremes: total 'opposition', and incorporation.
>
> (1978: 257; quoted in Hewison 1988: 148)

For both Martin and Hall, the counter-culture and its manifestations in the politics of radical protest were inevitably unstable and adaptive, and though they disagree profoundly about its liberatory potential for society as a whole, as Robert Hewison points out, they concur that it could not be 'political' in the sense of having a coherent articulation to the institutions of the State (1988: 150). Paradoxically, both liberal humanist and Marxist see this key feature as marking the ideological topography of this particular volcano. But in what ways is that the result of the assumptions that inform their analyses, which for example imply that the micro of protest is an *effect* of the macro of socio-cultural structural change?

In contrast, my argument suggests that what has been forged by the 1960s counter-culture and later global social movements is a new kind of radical politics, and that the sources for this can clearly be seen through a dramaturgical analysis of protest. Hence, the actions described by a dramaturgy of protest suggest the character of *civil autonomy and desire* through their negotiation of tradition and innovation in the forms of resistance. So the dramaturgy of protest, as a focus for cross-cultural study, may provide a kind of historical 'relief map' of changes in civil radicalism internationally. The development of peace camps, occupations, vigils, rallies and other spectacles of resistance suggests, for example, that the traditions of marching or processing were seen as inadequate for the expression of new forms of dissidence. In accord with the paradigm shift towards post-modernity in the socio-cultural sphere, and new critical theory in the discursive sphere, non-linear forms supplemented and sometimes supplanted linear models. Similarly, the semiosis of protest tended towards greater polyphony and heteroglossia, multiple referenced images were added to monologic slogans, and the slogans themselves often became more aphoristic and punning. Satire and caricature were welded to images suggesting desired ideals and Utopias. All of this signals that civil autonomy and desire was becoming more sophisticated, complex, multifaceted – more *reflexive* and flexibly organised. In general terms, as I argued in Part I, it is this kind of deep cultural shift that tended to render traditional forms of 'political theatre' redundant, because civil radicalism could, as it were, reshape itself through the post-modern, shaking itself increasingly free of the meta-narratives that had given those earlier forms their meaning and utility. The performance of protest, then, can be seen to embody new sources of radicalism in the changing cultures of civil society (Wark 1994).

Protest on the cusp

Contemporary protest, then, has broken new ground for the radical in performance, both in terms of disrupting the spectacle of hegemony and in terms of opening up new forms of ideological exchange between civil society and the State, new social movements and institutional power. However, given the determination to stay poised on the cusp of the paradigm shift, we cannot confidently conclude with a claim that the dramaturgy of protest in the late twentieth century participates synecdocally in a wider cultural transition from modernity to post-modernity. In staying poised between Brecht and Baudrillard, we must note that contemporary protest has always participated in modernist traditions to a greater or lesser degree, while at the same time increasingly being more or less aimed at creating new post-modern spaces for radical discourse, new sources of radicalism. This is achieved because the dramas of protest perhaps always aim for a radical liminality, in

Turner's sense of the term, and a radical freedom through the performative, in Derrida's sense of the term. By these means protest can draw authority into a new relation with the potential for change initiated *beyond its domain*. This can be seen most clearly, perhaps, in extreme forms of protest such as strikes, riots and civil disobedience: the Los Angeles riots that followed the beating of Rodney King, the British poll-tax riots and refusals that led to the downfall of Margaret Thatcher – such action aims always to be metaphorically and literally 'beyond the pale', outside the normative boundaries that the market, the law and the State would enforce.

More recently, the growing direct-action campaigns of the 1990s have provided some of the liveliest and most complex examples of resistance that aims for transcendence. The demonstrations staged by 'eco-rad' groups are a good case in point, best represented internationally, perhaps, by the more radical wings of Greenpeace, and in Britain by the anti-roads protest movement. Ecological radicalism may focus on a single issue in any particular protest, but its underlying concerns are inevitably multifaceted. For example, as George McKay argues:

> The anti-roads movement embraces issues of land ownership, environmentalism, health and pollution, technology, big business, regional and self-empowerment and self-development, the power of the law itself.
>
> (1996: 135)

Such comprehensiveness affects the way protest relates to life-style and cultural formation: the occupation of a proposed road-building site evokes long traditions of community cohesion forged from resistance – the Diggers and the Levellers of the seventeenth century, say – while simultaneously forming new alliances of class, gender, race and generation in the necessary negotiations between incoming protesters and the local population. Equally, there has been a growing sophistication in the eco-rads' use of the performativity of protest, no doubt based on a reflexive grasp of the new intertwining of aesthetics and politics in the post-modern. McKay quotes 'artist activist' John Jordan:

> Non-Violent Direct Action is a performance where the poetic and pragmatic join hands. The sight of a fragile figure silhouetted against a blue sky, perched dangerously high, on a crane that has stopped

work for the day, is both beautiful and functional. NVDA is deeply theatrical and fundamentally political.

(1996: 130)

The 1996 Greenpeace occupation of the defunct Brent Spar oil rig as it was towed out into the Atlantic for dumping was a remarkable amplification of the performative principles of contemporary global protest, showing the protesters had skills in the use of technologies of survival and communication every bit as sophisticated as those developed by the international corporations they were attacking (Rose 1998).

In an ironically homely way, a similar sophistication was demonstrated in 1997 by the tunnellers who dug live-in burrows beneath the planned paths of the Newbury Bypass and the second runway for Manchester Airport, adding, I think, a new aesthetic strand to the dramaturgy of protest. The dangerous extravagance of a subversion that was literally underground produced an *invisible spectacle* that seemed to set the British popular imagination running riot, perhaps in an excess of admiration for the inverted ingenuity and sheer resistant determination of the protesters. That one of the chief subterranean radicals turned out to be a quietly spoken, shyly inarticulate smiler who had re-christened himself 'Swampy', added an ironic gloss to the deep threat to the dominant represented by the subtle extremism of the protest's imperceptible performativity. If *he* could create a Temporary Autonomous Zone that even in its peace-ability carried unmistakable echoes of violent guerrilla operations, then anybody might (Bey 1991). The complexities of the Brent Spar and Newbury/Manchester occupations are a crucial part of their political power, especially when imaginative action transforms the self-defeat of contradiction into the piquant memorability of paradox. Then the global audience for protest may get a lasting glimpse of the engaged liminality of performance that breeds effective transgression, the potential of radical freedom.

Hence, it is through the radical in performance that contemporary protest may be seen to have gained a potent ideological transgression, beyond subversion, beyond resistance – because in the liminal-liminoid action of performative protest may be found the very figure of new notions of freedom, equality and justice. So the performativity of protest is a key index of its ability both to subvert the commodifying hyper-realism of the globalised media industry and to contribute effectively to the construction of future realities for a more democratic world. We may say that in doing this it pays due respect to Baudrillard's vision while refusing its delirious seductions, and it buys into Brecht's political pragmatism without wholly giving up on an idealism crucially inflected by reflexivity. Hence, as a form of performance beyond theatre, protest indicates widespread sources for radicalism in the civil societies of globalised cultures. And so a dramaturgy of protest may provide useful access, hopefully, to an active understanding of the kinds of global transformations that have changed the political face of the world in the past fifty years.

Chapter 4

The shadow of oppression

Performance, the panopticon and ethics

Trying to define yourself is like trying to bite your own teeth.
Alan Watts

Cell shocked

The cell was like a film set: whitewashed stone walls, bare wooden chair and table, metal-framed bed with sagging springs and stained mattress, a bucket for piss and shit, a window high in the end wall with small panes and thick bars. But in no way could any flickering image on a screen capture the infiltrating damp, the scum lines ridging out below the rim, the sickly tang of reused disinfectant, the scratchy threads and semen sniff of a stretched-thin blanket, the chilling, unavoidable draught through the broken bottom square of glass. Everywhere an archaeology of despair, etched into the grain of each object; everywhere a permeating sense of dread, hanging in the cold air like toxic fumes. I lay on the grim bed, back bent and soul stung, breathless with the pace of calamity.

As instructed by the Committee, I had already inspected my body for tell-tale signs of the day's roller-coaster decline. Nothing, except a couple of lightly grazed knuckles, maybe from being flung into the paddy-wagon. Under the surface of my skin, though, the body burned with layers of pain laminated into every subtle twist of the nervous system. When I closed my eyes consciousness was a pulsing recession, a go-nowhere implosion of wasted matter. Worst of all was the electric prickle of newly-short hair as my shorn head shifted under the canopy of the grotty blanket. Somehow, though, from out of this nowhere a fragile nugget of anger was dredged up, a slivery seed of resistance. Somewhere in the foetal curl something decided to grow a beard.

This was the avant-garde of early sixties protest. For me and my radical mates, the Campaign for Nuclear Disarmament had fallen even further from fashion as it fervently embraced the folk-song revival and continued to toe the line of the law. Now Bertrand Russell's Committee of 100 was the place to be. My best friend Frank and I signed our names as two of the first 100 members of the North West Regional Committee in a packed parlour somewhere in suburban Whalley Range. We were committed to Civil Disobedience in the battle against Britain's cold war insanity. We made a banner for the first ever sit-down demo in Manchester, outside the Town Hall in Albert Square, where we blocked the road with our bodies and sang 'We Shall Overcome' to the grim-looking police. The front-page of the *Manchester Evening News* showed Frank and me with the banner, trying to look suitably defiant despite our fresh-faced youth. Inside was another picture of me in the back of a police truck, my hand raised as if in a clench-fisted gesture of dancing revolt: but I recall that really I was reaching out to stop myself from falling over a woman who'd been flung violently at my legs by three big policemen. These images were seen by many before me, because like twenty or so others I'd pledged to go the whole hog with the Committee and refused to give my name to the police or in court. They had no option but to send me to jail.

So on a cold Saturday night in Strangeways Prison, the day before my birthday, I lay facing a sizeable stint of solitary confinement. The strip search and the cold shower complete with hard-bristle brushes was bad enough. The tray of cold food dropped on the floor right by the slop bucket was nauseating. I was terrified by the two huge warders who manhandled me dangerously down a steep flight of metal stairs to shave off my hair. But worst of all was having no name, just being a 'you', then a number, thinking that those in power liked it that way, because the mental torture of a vanishing self left no visible marks and might mean an early surrender. Of course, we had been warned by the Committee about this, but no one had mentioned how horrible the brutality in a warder's twinkling eye could be, how the slightest smile could be a stab of degradation, how much venom could be carried by a friendly voice. Those intimate exchanges nurtured the toxic seed of utter vulnerability, stripping away the last slivers of youthful self-knowledge, leaving only an infinite sense of absence. Of course, there were no mirrors in which to face up to the loss, but in the hollow that was left the beard *was* growing, a wispy down as fragile as a half-remembered dream, but definitely growing. The same beard is still growing now, as I sit here ironically stroking its greying hairs, considering how absurd it is as a sign for a lifetime of looking at the world turned upside down, as if forever in free fall.

'The only victory is surrender'

A barbed-wire mesh separates the stage from the auditorium, completely filling the proscenium arch, a constant ironic reminder of the invisible fourth wall. Behind it the bunkhouse of an American military prison in Korea is reproduced in exact detail: wire-mesh walls, metal bunks, slop buckets and narrow passageways with white lines painted on the floor at each end. When any of the numbered prisoners – they are never named – moves, it is done on the double, elbows and knees pumping the air like wildly driven pistons. Whenever they have to cross a white line they bellow: 'Sir, prisoner number XX requests permission to cross the white line, sir!' and the Guards bellow back 'Permission granted!' Or if the action is not performed exactly as the rules determine the Guard gets to punch the prisoner in the stomach. For two hours the fearsome regime of the prison is condensed into a brutal recreation of degrading military ritual. The audience is quickly taught to hate those white lines: negative thresholds.

When the Living Theatre brought Kenneth H. Brown's *The Brig* to London from America in 1964, at the start of their four-year exile in Europe, the reviews of the show could have described a real prison. Bernard Levin, for example, claimed it was 'horrifying, inescapable' in its portrayal of 'a place not easily distinguishable from Buchenwald', while Herbert Kretzmer saw it as 'undeniably hateful' because 'men… become so dehumanised that dignity is reduced to an obscenity, to a point where the only victory is surrender' (Gottlieb 1966: 68–70). Such powerful effects derive from the company's success in an almost total merging of the imaginary and the real onstage: the rehearsal regime was every bit as punishing as the brig itself and in performance prisoners and guards reversed roles regularly, in part to share out the injuries. Yet the audiences turned it into a triumphant sell-out, and it remained in the Living Theatre's repertoire for over five years.

However, the six-week run at London's Mermaid Theatre was cut short. The rumour was that the cancellation was caused by influence from the US government, which had only let the company out of America on the promise that the directors, Julian Beck and Judith Malina, would return to serve a real jail sentence for contempt of court (Gottlieb 1966: 2). The initial charge in the New York Trial was that they had evaded paying tax, but the theatre's landlord also sided with the US tax agents and allowed the Inland Revenue Service to seize the building, effectively banning performances of *The Brig*. In response, the company occupied the theatre and, in a last-ditch snub to the law, played the show under police siege after the audience had climbed into the building through windows at the rear. Twenty-five people were arrested. At the trial the judge was incensed by the company's ironic theatricalisation of court ritual: Living Theatre actors staged improvised scenes of protest inside and outside the courtroom. Beck was sentenced to sixty days; Malina to thirty days. Their view was that they were political prisoners (Croyden 1974: 92–4; Shank 1982: 11–13; Tytell 1997: 186–90; Sainer 1997: 285).

Clearly the success of *The Brig* in America and Europe was massively offensive to the American state. Written by an ex-marine, it exposed a rottenness at the heart of the so-called greatest democracy. The Living Theatre touched on a radical weakness in America's sense of moral superiority, to produce the absurd spectacle of a small experimental theatre company being attacked by the most powerful authority in the world. No surprise, then, that the company went on to ride the wave of the first counter-culture, developing a huge cult following in Europe, which is said to have enabled its members – amazingly – to travel without the passports they had torn up during the 1968 performances of *Paradise Now!*. Hence, the merging of the imaginary and the real in a new type of hyper-naturalist performance ironically scorned the established theatre, undermining its commodifying powers and leading to an inversion of the vast asymmetries of power between the company and the state. As if in mockery of the white lines in the brig, real borders were crossed freely in a blurring of boundaries that anticipates the anarchic processes of late-capitalist globalisation. This kind of radical survival in exile powerfully challenges Kretzmer's deeply pessimistic view that there can be a point where 'the only victory is surrender'.

Freedoms through oppression

Kretzmer's paradoxical motto – if we can call it that – indicates a kind of ground zero of the soul, a place producing the automatic reversal of any impulse of hope into despair. Here self-respect, even the self itself, vanishes in a hell of inverted ethics in which evil is good and we witness, to adopt Elaine Scarry's characterisation of torture, the 'unmaking of the world' (1985). I am focusing on such unmaking because something like this loss of self, the total instability and/or death of the subject, is a problem frequently found in the post-modern, which in turn links to two other crucial themes of post-modernism; namely, its commitment to pluralism and its doubts about the possibility of human agency.

The arguments raging around these components in theory are, as usual, complicated, but for our purposes we can risk reducing them to a couple of fairly straightforward formulations to do with ethics and choice. Full-blown pluralism spawns an ethics of relativism which challenges the possibility of universal value, because every subject's identity through difference provides the framework for their moral code. It follows that no culture, no individual, can say what is right for another, beyond saying that it has a right to define it for itself. Post-modernism's love affair with difference also means that identity cannot derive from any idea of an essential self, because if we all had an essential self then we would all essentially be the same. Hence the nature of identity becomes a problem – are we just hyper-real appearances? – and the idea of autonomous agency, freedom of choice, is shifted closer to the philo-sophical dustbin, for there is no identifiable *thing* which can do the choosing. It is this combination of the infinite choices of pluralism and the sense that there is no ground from which choices can be made which in large part inspires the delirium of Baudrillard's vision of post-modernity.

From this perspective, the determination to hover around the cusp of the paradigm shift entails an investigation into the plausibility of perfor-mance as a source for the creation of autonomy and agency in a plural-istic world. Hence, this chapter questions post-modernism's suspicion of the autonomous subject and raises the stakes in my interrogation of the ways that post-modernism would place a *limit* on creative radicalism, on radical freedom, by exploring the deepest recesses of oppression. Inevitably this will raise questions about the ethics of performance, because when performance directly engages with society's most virulent disciplinary systems inevitably it will end up wrestling, one way or another, with the major ethical issues of its time and place.

So the main topics of this chapter will be, first, performance in contem-porary prisons, and second, performance in the histories of slavery and colonialism. I am linking these together because they exemplify, in acutely contrasting ways, how disciplinary systems which are predicated on the production of pain aim for a kind of moral impermeability, a total self-justification that would, if it could, rule out anything that smacks of even the slightest opposition. This is the case whether the system is focused on a minority of citizens in tightly constrained spatial settings, as with prisons, or on whole populations spread across huge swathes of the globe, as with slavery and colonialism. Despite such contrasts, these systems may be said to operate according to what Foucault calls the 'panoptic modality of power', which aims:

...first, to obtain the exercise of power at the lowest possible cost (...politically, by its discretion...its relative invisibility, the little resistance it arouses); second, to bring the effects of this social power to their maximum intensity and to extend them as far as possible, without either failure or interval; third, to link this 'economic' growth of power with the output of the apparatuses (educational, military, industrial or medical)...in short, to increase both the docility and the utility of all the elements of the system.

(1977: 218)

Foucault has been variously attacked for seeing the start of a 'totalitarian blueprint' for our times in the eighteenth-century rule-bound bourgeois society of modernity (Merquior 1985: 90–9). But despite his detractors, for my purposes in this chapter there is a resonance in his favourite figure for the tentacular processes of the disciplines: Jeremy Bentham's idea of the panopticon, the radial prison in which, through surveillance, one person can exercise absolute control over many (1995).

For the panopticon may be taken as a paradigm of all the disciplinary systems in society where thought and practice are most firmly wedded to each other in an attempt to engender ethical conformity in the hearts of the resistant or delinquent, to bring the disaffected subject to society's heel by eliminating autonomy and reforming the 'self'. Inevitably, then, prison is an ideological and ethical hot-spot in all social systems because it attempts to raise the law above contingency by shaping its injunctions in stone. This shaping is what makes the prison inherently dramatic, because it is built on a contest between a supposed immutable rigour of rule and the infinite suppleness of the human soul – or at least, seeing as it is my intention to keep one foot in the camp of post-modernism, the human subject. The prison is also quintessentially *theatrical* because it stages the absolute separation that society seeks to impose between good and evil – or, to switch back to the mode of post-modernism, between acceptable and unacceptable forms of subjectivity.

Similarly, slavery has staged the arbitrary exercise of absolute power on a global scale in ways that still shape the contemporary world disorder. The histories of slavery, the ultimate form of commodification, as John Fiske and others have argued, are a continuing drama, through which the struggle for black peoples' identity and autonomy against racism can be strengthened or weakened (1993: 284–9). Particularly since the 1960s, black people in the West have begun to reclaim those histories, even though, as James Baldwin reminds us, they are stories of horror.

> This past, the Negro's past, of rope, fire, torture, castration, infanti-
> cide, rape; death and humiliation, fear by day and night, fear as
> deep as the marrow of the bone; doubt that he was worthy of life,
> since everyone around him denied it....
>
> > (1964: 84; quoted in Crow and Banfield 1996: 5)

Likewise, the histories of colonialism and its mechanisms are being reclai-
med. Frantz Fanon, for example, has firmly established connections
between the loss of self and the cultural denials of colonisation.

> Because it is a systematic negation of the other person and a furious
> determination to deny the other person all attributes of humanity,
> colonialism forces the people it dominates to ask themselves the
> question constantly: 'In reality, who am I?'
>
> > (1968: 250)

In the histories of slavery and colonialism the death of the subject was
commonplace, because when the *whole* of reality is panoptically shaped
in all of its details by malignant dominant forces then sometimes
Fanon's question cannot even be asked. So, whether in the physical
tortures of slavery or the psychological brutalities of colonialism, the
spectacle of global injustice is played out according to the performative
principles of the panopticon.

The extreme stringency in the operations of power in these contexts
will require us to develop a particularly reflexive approach to analysis,
so that we do not unwittingly collude in reinforcing oppression by
simply replaying its tropes in another key. What I mean by this is
signalled by the somewhat oblique critical angle that I shall take on the
question of racism in slavery and colonialism. As I am a white man,
and as a major purpose of this chapter is to explore the performative
implications of post-modern pluralism, obviously I cannot even begin
to aspire to speak from a black perspective about racial injustice,
however much I sympathise with that view. To do so would be to risk
reinforcing the very oppressions I wish to interrogate for their attack on
democratic principles. So I have chosen to study a *white* genre – blackface minstrelsy – for the light it might throw on the potential for
radicalism in performances that dealt more or less directly with slavery
and colonialism. In similar vein, to investigate performance in the real
panopticon I shall analyse a *screenplay* written by a prisoner, rather than,
say, one of the many prison performances I have seen. This is because
Western judicial systems are logocentric, so my attention to the written

word as used by a victim of such a system is an attempt to mitigate the ways in which *my* words might collude in that system. In short, I want to address the question of radicalism in obviously panoptic regimes through performative material that, at first sight, might seem to play openly into the hands of panopticism.

As in the last chapter, it will be helpful to reverse the conventional critical strategy in the effort to illuminate the processes of radical performance. So rather than dealing with representations of the prison in theatre I shall be searching for efficacious performance in the panopticon itself, and rather than discussing anti-racism in post-colonial drama I shall be investigating its potential in the histories of blackface minstrelsy. Through these strategies I shall attempt to answer two key questions: how might radical freedom exist at the moment of greatest constraint; and how can transgressive autonomy be nurtured in an exchange designed to destroy it? I am searching for what might be called, somewhat riskily, the creation of *freedom through oppression.* And as this formulation suggests, we will again be entering the territory of the paradoxical as a prime feature of perching around the cusp of the paradigm shift. The territory begins in the idea that to be oppressed we must enter *into* oppression, but also that – in Tom Stoppard's elegant phrase – every entrance is an exit somewhere else.

Performance in prisons

In the early 1990s I undertook a participatory performance project with postgraduate students in an English 'Category C' prison. The category signals a 'semi-open' establishment, in which some internal gates are supposed to be kept unlocked. We worked with a group of five men under the auspices of the prison's Education Department, so in the penal discourse of power their time was ours even before we met them, even though they volunteered for our ten sessions. Anyone who ventures into prisons to 'do' performance is, initially at least, bound to seem to the inmates to be party to the authorship of their oppression. Almost by definition, we were aligned with the criminal justice system that gave them a sentence, therefore we were in several senses potential enemies in class, possibly more dangerous than the jailers they already knew.

As usual we tried to negotiate our way past the group's reasonable suspicions and mistrust through typical group-building games (Boal 1992; Brandes and Phillips 1979; Brandes 1982). Unpredictably, the second session ended in a frantic bout of joke-telling that had the women postgraduates giving as good as they got in the way of sexist jokes. Their reward at the next workshop was to be presented with a short screenplay written by one of the group, a young man who, for reasons of confidentiality, I shall rename Howard Bond. He called it *The Rat Run*, though tellingly he would never write that on the script, which went officially by the title of *One Hour in the Semi-Open*. The screenplay portrayed an especially virulent system of control and demonstrated how the power to repeatedly name – or number – a person is essential to the rigorous 'grammar' of authority's panopticism. This, in turn, generates specialist languages of incarceration that mirror the rigour of the law but invert its formality. Hence, in the argot of English prisons, the prisoners are 'cons' and the warders are 'screws', and areas of the prison from which 'cons' are banned are called 'sterile' by the 'screws' (Thompson 1998a: 252).

The Rat Run dramatised the regime that the group claimed controlled individual journeys in the jail, though the prison authorities would neither deny nor confirm its existence. Beside the regular mass movement of men from cells to showers, dining hall to workshops, and so on, the prisoners could be ordered to move about the prison alone, and these movements often had a time limit set on them. If the prisoner took longer than was allowed his name would be recorded. Several such infringements could be counted against remission of sentence. And this particular prison occupies an historic castle, so that it is a warren of corridors, stairways, alleyways, balconies leading to steel-studded doors, barred gateways and huge-hinged portals. As a result there is always more than one route for a journey – sometimes there are three or even four – and at almost every gate you encounter a screw, who will be more or less inclined – depending on what he knows of you or how he feels or whatever else might be in his head or heart right then – to promptly let you through or make you wait. Hence, the screws have direct control over the length of each con's sentence. A wait at a gate may eventually add up to more time tacked on to the end of a prisoner's term. This system is an example of what Foucault calls the 'counter-law', the networks of semi-formalised, usually unwritten, rules that are developed by institutions and organisations to cover areas that the law proper cannot reach (1977: 222–3). So each gate was a threshold of negotiation – an invisible white line – in a domain more subtly tuned to the logic of punishment than ever the law alone could be.

The Rat Run

The screenplay presents the story of one con's typical expedition from the prison's gym to the education department. The high point of the play, its performative fulcrum, dramatises the subtle ontological weapons that have to be forged in systems like the rat run for the incarcerated to create a bit of their own space. Up to this point the con has had to negotiate his way through five gates, in the process flogging unnecessarily up and down several flights of stairs and failing to get through three other gates, either because they were locked and unmanned or because the attendant screw would not let him through. Getting close to his destination he eventually arrives at a gate where he is not supposed to be, a threshold in a 'sterile' zone:

YOU ARRIVE AT THE BOTTOM GATE, TWO SCREWS IN THE OFFICE OUTSIDE.

CON: Boss can you let us out please.
SCREW: Why?
CON: I'm trying to get to Ed.
SCREW: What wing are you off?
CON: 'A' wing.
SCREW: You're not allowed on this wing.
CON: I'm just trying to get to Ed.
SCREW: You're not allowed on this wing.

HE STILL HASN'T MOVED. ALL THIS IS DONE SHOUTING.

CON: I can't hear you.

THE ONLY WAY TO GET HIM TO THE GATE.

SCREW: Why didn't you use the other gate?
CON: Because it's locked and there's no one there. I thought I could get through this way.
SCREW: You're not allowed on this wing.

OPENS THE GATE.

CON: I'm only trying to get to Ed. If someone was on the other gate or if it was open as a semi open should be, I wouldn't be here now.

(Bond 1991: 3–4)

Now, why does the screw let the con through a gate that he is not supposed to use? The answer to this simple question, I think, has profound ramifications for the notion of radical freedom, and, by extension, for post-modernism's view of the subject as lacking autonomy.

The screw has to come to the gate, and the con knows it, because in such a tight system the screw must check why the con is pleading at a gate he is not allowed through or even supposed to be at. The con's insistence is the sign of some flaw in the operation of both the law and the counter-law: in concrete terms, that a locked gate that should have been open has forced him to be where he should not be. This is the logical reason why the screw lets the con through the gate: the agent of the law overturns it partly because it cannot conform to its own rules, its own perverse logic. At this point the con is, as it were, creating a new counter-law and hence making a space for his own autonomy, a partial empowerment.

But there are other, *performative* reasons why the con is let through. His performance turns the gateway into a liminal-liminoid space in Turner's sense, a kind of virtual doorway or entrance, a doubled threshold, through a technique that the script elsewhere calls 'blanking': to 'blank' someone is to refuse to negotiate an exchange on the terms set by the other. This refusal in the script, when the con absurdly pretends to be deaf, creates a new imaginary domain, turns the liminal rituals of the threshold into a liminoid performance that opens up an enormous fissure in the system of the counter-law.

Hence, viewed from the perspective of the rituals of the panopticon, the con on the threshold of the forbidden gate had entered a liminal zone, where he was 'betwixt-and-between' the normative rules of the prison's laws and the rat-run's counter-laws. The outcome of the exchange between him and the screw in that zone *could* have been the reinforcement of the unwritten rules of the society of the prison: the screw *could* have escorted him back whence he came – ritual complete. However, the creative moment of 'blanking' transforms the liminal zone into a liminoid one; the ritual of the prison is instantly translated into an excessive performance which gestures towards an absence that the screw cannot comprehend, nor therefore control, and which exposes the flaw in the system of the counter-law. In the process the autonomy of the individual, his/her ability to choose another framework and terms for negotiation, is exercised *through* the structures designed to eliminate it, and the achievement of such radical freedom cannot be denied, even though it might be reversed, because its creation is a transcendence of the disciplines inscribed in those structures. The 'sterile' zone is transformed into fertility by performance.

As Victor Turner argues, in liminality is secreted the seed of the limi-noid (1982: 28). At the moment of 'blanking', the con may have achieved a radical freedom that allowed him, so to speak, to rewrite the rules to his own advantage, hence producing a degree of autonomy and empowerment in this particular panoptic system. The light of freedom can be discovered in the deepest shadows of oppression.

Theoretical reflections

The notion of the counter-law is developed by Foucault to explain how the vast inequalities of power are sustained at the 'capillary' level in contemporary societies, including the liberal democracies, despite any apparently egalitarian commitment to justice and the ethics of human rights.

> ...although the universal juridicism of modern society seems to fix limits on the exercise of power, its universally widespread panop-ticism enables it to operate, on the underside of the law [as counter-law], a machinery that is both immense and minute, which supports, reinforces, multiplies the asymmetries of power and under-mines the limits that are traced round the law.
>
> (1977: 223)

Translated into the terms of the democratic theory touched on in Chapter 2, the counter-law is authority's way of extending control over a civil society in which there are areas that are bound to be beyond the law (Held 1987: 281). From this perspective, the system portrayed in *The Rat Run* operates to the principle of a fine-tuned counter-law that aims to produce an impermeable panopticism. But my point is that no system of surveillance and control can ever entirely succeed in this ambition, because paradoxically the more prodigious the effort devoted to filling in every conceivable loophole in its operations, the more it will produce new ingenuities of subversion. This is a theme developed by de Certeau in his discussion of the practices of everyday life, by Lefebvre in his analyses of social space, and by Deleuze and Guattari in their flights of fancy through the disciplinary structures of Western civilisa-tion (de Certeau 1988; Lefebvre 1991; Deleuze and Guattari 1984). In the rat run the intensified, intimate conjunction of everyday disci-plinary routine and the grand architectures of the law is subject to the creation of a deep ideological fault-line that exposes the vulnerability of sclerotic panopticism. What prizes open the fault-line is the con's ability to improvise deafness, his unpredictable leap into the excessive *perform-ance of absence*.

The mode of awareness constructing this liminal-liminoid moment is one of *ironic reflexivity*, as the con is adding to his stock of autonomy through an imaginative *subtraction*. The technique of 'blanking', as the word itself suggests, is, to risk a theoretical heresy, pure Derrida. It is the performative equivalent of Derrida's use of the word crossed out, which he adopts, as Philip Auslander succinctly explains, 'to indicate... the inescapable use of terms the validity of which he denies' (Derrida 1982: 26–7; Auslander 1995: 66). Hence, the con's sudden switch to ~~deafness~~ enacts the arbitrary relation of signifier to signified, illuminating the absence that is *différance*, and demonstrating that power can emanate from a performative playfulness that may be accessible to all. The technique relates to Grotowski's idea of the *via negativa* in acting, which he defines as 'not a collection of skills but an eradication of blocks' (1968: 16–17). But there are more *via negativas* than are dreamt of in Grotowski, for the semiotics of any disciplinary system, its symbolic capital, as every comedian knows, is always ripe for picking, so long as its subjects can ironise its assumptions or in some other way turn them upside down and inside out. The best of the joke in *The Rat Run* is that, to the audience for the screenplay, the absence – the blanking – is clearly an invention, a *performative ruse*, which potentially puts the con in control of the situation. The reflexivity of acute dramatic irony then places the audience on the con's side and exposes what the panoptic system would prefer to keep hidden: arbitrariness in the distribution of authority and power.

Through these means, the con may well have created for himself, in a way similar to the children processing in *Glasgow All Lit Up!* and the demonstrators in Tiananmen Square, access to a basic process required for the construction of the autonomous democratic subject. So his action can be seen as not simply *resisting* the dominant ideologies written into the prison regime but also as *transcending* them. We can express this by saying that while it mimicked the counter-laws by pretending a failure to grasp them, it also created a cultural space in which it could exercise a *modus operandi* of quite another order, producing an altogether different ontology. This process opens up an ethical domain through which injustices can be challenged, even within the most rigorous system of justice. This domain does *not*, of course, excuse the prisoner his crime, but it does give him access to democratic rights. It is a cornerstone of my argument that these kinds of liminoid-liminal spaces – Turner calls them 'the seedbeds of cultural creativity' (1982: 28) –

provide common sources of radical freedom to which performance, even when sometimes staged in theatres, even in the theatre of the panopticon, can give access.

Hence, *The Rat Run* demonstrates how the mechanisms of discipline can sometimes be turned inside out to produce resistant and transcendent empowerment. It achieves this because those mechanisms generally hinge on an act of performance – in legal systems the law court is paradigmatic of this. And at another level of ideological negotiation, *The Rat Run* as a creative linguistic artefact also demonstrated the self-reflexivity available to its author by signalling to us, the workshop members from 'outside', and then to the prison authorities, that Howard Bond could 'see through' the disciplinary mechanisms in such a way as to subvert, or perhaps even to negate them. When the inmates in the workshop group first read the screenplay they immediately grasped this significance, and they were very enthusiastic to produce it. They were particularly taken, I recall, by the final moments of the script, when the con turns to the imagined audience:

YOU ARRIVE AT THE CLASSROOM BUT YOU'RE NOT EXACTLY REFRESHED, RELAXED AND READY FOR A DAY'S WORK. A FAG, A CUP OF TEA AND A PUNCH BAG ARE MORE THE ORDER.

THIS IS JUST ONE HOUR, ONE EXAMPLE OF THE FREEDOM, REHABILITATION, RELAXED ATMOSPHERE OF [this particular] SEMI OPEN NICK. WHICH DOES ITS BEST TO GET YOU READY FOR THE OUTSIDE WORLD. LET'S HEAR IT FOR THE SCREWS AND THE SYSTEM, COME ON, ONE BIG CHEER. NO? OH WELL, I UNDER-STAND.

(Bond 1991: 5)

The implied silence from the audience is another form of ironic blanking, wittily drawing them into participation in the main dramatic strategy of the play. The individual perspective of the con is reflected in the collective (non-) response of the audience, which was positively echoed in actuality by the workshop group. What started as an individually authored exercise became a force for strong cohesion in the collective, as the group went on to create an audio-tape of the script. The recording was an especially apt form of production: the silence called for in the play's final moments resoundingly demonstrated a *shared* ironic reflexivity that comprehends how injustice can be built into the whole *system* of judicial incarceration from within, placing it in a bitterly critical light by creating yet another absence, a cheer that will never be heard.

From micro- to macro-politics: blackface minstrelsy

'The degree of civilisation in a society can be judged by entering its prisons', wrote Dostoyevsky in *The House of the Dead*, but one obvious objection to my account of a performative source of radicalism in the panopticon could be that the story is not really open to that much generalisation. The creative antics of one small group of prisoners might conceivably throw light on the opportunities for autonomy available to the rest of the 60,000 people in Britain's prisons in 1998, but the prison, despite Foucault's vision of the disciplines, cannot so easily be made to represent the regimes of power in all types of society (Merquior 1985: 106). It may well be that in dictatorships prison *is* a model for the carceral society; but in liberal democracies the converse is the case. In democratically free societies, the panopticon plays a special institutional role, and while it might well produce its own perverted structures of power, that very perversion distinguishes it *in kind* from the world outside its walls, where authority has been created through representation to act on behalf of the common good.

Yet it is a historical commonplace that democracy was founded on slavery, the most extreme form of subjection, delivered through the commodification of the human. Given this, what David Held claims for classical democracy may just as well be applied to modern democracies, with their roots in the eighteenth century: 'a growing number of independent citizens enjoyed a substantial increase in the scope of their activities with the expansion of slavery' (1987: 14). In the twentieth century, of course, outright slavery as such has been much reduced, but the conditions of what Held calls 'nautonomy' – 'the asymmetrical production and distribution of life chances which limit and erode the possibilities of political participation' – still obviously shape the world disorder (1995: 167–72). It follows, that to understand more fully how the interdependence of oppression and freedom forms the conditions for the creation of radical emancipation, it should be useful to look into the performance arts that were generated by slavery. Of these, the blackface minstrelsy of the nineteenth and early twentieth century provides an especially testing example, because the spectacle of a white person blacking-up his (or her) face and pretending to be a person of colour appears as inevitably racist, an expression of white supremacy: an unambiguously oppressive misuse of cultural power.

It is one consequence of post-modernism, as we have seen, that the freedom to adopt multiple subject positions that devolves from the death of the soul problematises the ethics of representation in the realm of identity politics: who has the right to speak for whom? I shall argue that blackface minstrelsy is, in a sense, a spectacular forerunner of this problematic, and so if it had any potential for radicalism at all then its history could be especially instructive to our central concern in this chapter with individual autonomy and the ethics of performance. For, of course, blackface minstrelsy was part of the wider histories of Empire, colonialism and slavery, of global systems of oppression that for black peoples turned reality itself into a panopticon. Yet it was in part *through* this appalling system that the radical sources of emancipation for subjugated peoples had to be created in order to lay the socio-political foundations of human rights in present-day democracies. Could blackface minstrelsy have contributed in any way to democratic emancipation?

Blackface histories

From the perspective of contemporary democracy the slave narratives of the seventeenth and eighteenth centuries, as legacies of a global outrage that eventually fostered new freedoms, are shot through with the profoundest ironies. And the stories of blackface minstrelsy are among the most astonishing and ironic of those legacies. Starting in the American Deep South in the 1820s, significantly as slavery was coming under increasing attack, the spectacle of white men with blackened faces pretending to be black men quickly spread across the continent. The genre reaching an initial culmination, after many years of solo acts, in New York City in February 1843, when the Virginia Minstrels put together the first full evening of 'oddities, peculiarities, eccentricities, and comicalities of the Sable Genus of Humanity' (Toll 1974: 30).

The solo form had already been exported to England in 1836 by T. 'Daddy' Rice with his famous 'Jim Crow' song, quickly to be followed by the Virginia Minstrels themselves in 1843. The genre reached its heyday on both sides of the Atlantic between 1850 and 1880, when there were many hundreds of troupes in both countries, followed by a long, slow decline into the first half of the twentieth century, the last traces in Britain being BBC Television's weekly *The Black and White Minstrel Show*, which lingered, remarkably, into the early 1970s. Since then the rare examples of its use in performance, such as in the Pip

Simmons Theatre Company's *The George Jackson Black and White Minstrel Show* (1973) and the Wooster Group's *Route 1 and 9* (1981), have been greeted with intense controversy (Ansorge 1975: 33–5; Itzin 1980: 73–4; Savran 1986: 9–46). Of course, this thumbnail historical sketch vastly oversimplifies a rich and remarkably varied performance tradition. For example, in the 1880s American and English blackface troupes simultaneously occupied one of the smartest of London's West End theatres and the roughest of outdoor fit-up stages in seaside towns: the American Haverly's Mastodon Minstrels opened at Her Majesty's Theatre in Haymarket, London, on 31 July 1880, while Uncle Bones Margate Minstrels were playing their shows on the sands (Reynolds 1928: 203–6; Pertwee 1979: 8). But the historical elision has the benefit of pointing out the awful global irony of a trade that exported real black families as slaves from East to West and simulated 'black' *men* as free artists from West to East. How can anything of the radical be embedded in such a bitterly vicious system of economic, social, political and cultural exploitation?

To answer this question we have to try to understand particular examples of the genre in their specific contexts. In the southern states of America, for instance, the solo blackface performers of the 1820s and 1830s, according to musicologist Dale Cockrell, were a carnivalesque force for subversion. This was not simply because they produced a rough and ready inversion of the norms of *ante bellum* gentility – all noise and viscerality against refined good taste – but also because skin colour was a distinctly *subsidiary* mark of difference among the poor to whom they made their greatest appeal. Poverty and the struggle to survive ensured that working-class blacks and whites did much more than rub shoulders together, and the high energy and sometimes overtly satirical blackface of Rice's 'Jim Crow', for example, commonly spoke for both in a world where justice was scarce and equality hardly even a dream. Cockrell demonstrates the ideological ambivalence of 'Jim Crow', but concludes that it is '...at base a political song...', so much so that '...some verses are even staunchly anti-slavery' (1997: 73).

> Should dey get to fighting,
> Perhaps de blacks will rise,
> For deir wish for freedom,
> Is shining in deir eyes...
> I'm for freedom,
> An for Union altogether,
> Aldough I'm a black man,
> De white is call'd my broder.

The figure of blackface could achieve such paradoxical effects – and sometimes other, much less palatable ones – in *this* context because its meaning 'was slippery – all contestation and ambiguity' (1997: 89).

Such slipperiness was generated in part by the ubiquity of the solo form: its songs were sung by black and white, female and male, and it was performed as much in the streets as in bars and public halls. Here was an example of popular performance beyond theatre, not dissimilar to English music hall in its earliest stages (Bennett 1986b: 3–6). But even when the blackface carnivalesque was partly domesticated by the Virginia Minstrels, who set the genre in America firmly on the path from raucous roustabout to harmonic concert party and from do-anywhere entertainment to indoor theatrical fare, it still perhaps sometimes carried the resistant seed of its low-life origins. So although American blackface made the transition from a 'performative culture of the ear [to] a mediated culture of the eye' (Cockrell 1997: 141), its entry into representation – framed by the proscenium arch – may have been in terms that could not be contained entirely by the commodifying cultural economy of the new context. This is because, according to Cockrell's witty reading of blackface's politics of representation, it enacted an 'inversion' of inversion; that is to say, the lowly performers – white common people – symbolically lower their status – partly identifying with black common people – to produce a vulnerability that participated in the marginality of both and simultaneously promoted their combined strengths. In the process blackface minstrelsy became: '...one of the most powerful means developed in the century for working out the problems that follow from the magnetic attraction of marginal opposites' (1997: 161). Yet more crucially, we might add, the blackface itself signalled a blurring of racial identity that destabilised the modernist binaries upon which racist oppression depends. Hence, the aesthetics of the carnivalesque could be inflected by a more precisely focused radical charge, with the power to generate an ethics of cross-racial solidarity even at the corrosive heart of the white supremacist project.

Cockrell draws on Turner's theory of liminality to reinforce his argument, and he also points out that working-class blackface performers were the cultural equivalent of what biologists call an *edge* phenomenon: highly energised forms of life that prosper when two eco-systems rub up against each other, such as sea and shore, or river and land – a kind of threshold between racial identities. But he is also careful to note that the greater the separation between the opposites, in effect the more that minstrel performance became primarily a *theatrical* phenomenon, the more it was transformed into a weapon of racism. Hence, its loss of radical potential corresponds to its incorporation into a standardising system of capitalist production, so that in the second half of the nineteenth century minstrelsy flourished on both sides of the Atlantic precisely when its aesthetics consolidated into highly predictable stereotyping, formulaic staging and programmatic dramaturgy.

Blackface troupes performing in London venues, such as the long-running Moore and Burgess Minstrels, could have over thirty-five performers, while troupes offering seasonal seaside entertainment commonly would have only six or so; but scale hardly affected the stage lay-out, which invariably had the performers sitting in a half-circle with the master of ceremonies, Mr Interlocutor, in the centre and the two chief comedians, Tambo and Bones, at each end. Similarly, the shows virtually always had a three-act structure, with the First Part being an introduction to the troupe through a song medley, followed by the variety-format Olio that drew on music-hall conventions, and concluding with a dramatic sketch, often satirical, called the Afterpiece. And the stereotypes conformed to a narrow repertoire, including the 'city slicker coon', the carefree plantation hand and the big-footed 'mama' (Reynolds 1928; Toll 1974; Paskman 1976; Pickering 1991). The more popular blackface minstrelsy became, the more it would have to play to audience expectations, reifying the image of the black man (and woman) as a commodity and growing 'more nasty and brutish', binding the performers into a creative straight-jacket that reflected the colonialist need to control at all costs and the capitalist need to exploit for every ounce of surplus value (Pickering 1991: 213). From this perspective, the increasing formalism spells out a rich recipe for the fixing of black identity as ultimately subordinate, in the end a popular nostalgic hankering for the dead and gone days of slavery.

This interpretation ensues from the assumption that blackface minstrelsy in Britain may be seen *generally* to have had racist objectives, despite the multiplicity and variety of its practitioners and whatever its specific context of performance. Hence, any contradictions and conflicts emanating from the semiotic slipperiness of the doubled sign of the black mask are subsumed in the grand modernist narrative of empire. This perspective also tends to assume that in some ways the racist views of the powerful in Victorian England, as expressed in legitimate theatre, literature, newspapers and other media, can be mapped on to the working-class oppressed (Bolt 1971; Said 1993: 73 *passim*). However, although the views of the majority of those who had control of these media were profoundly racist, at the capillary level of day-to-day exchange among the lower classes there was probably plenty of scope for contrasting responses to the absent black other. Such scope would even have been enhanced by the likelihood that, in the words of V.G. Kiernan (1969: 316), 'Much of the talk about the barbarism or darkness of the outer world, which it was Europe's mission to rout, was a transmuted fear of the masses at home.' In other words, colonialism cast its oppressive shadow backwards, as it were, across the poor in the cultures that produced it, creating conditions in which more positive responses than racism might emerge.

Blackface and theories of colonialism

To discover if English blackface minstrelsy had any radical potential we will need to delve briefly into the question of how colonialism works, how a minority of white people can dominate an overwhelming majority of black people. There are many eminent theorists in the field, the more prominent including Stuart Hall, Gayatri Spivak and Edward Said, but Frantz Fanon and Homi Bhabha provide some of the most resonant formulations about the colonial, and post-colonial, subject (Ashcroft *et al.* 1995; Williams and Chrisman 1993). Fanon and Bhabha write from the perspective of the colonised and in the process shed a good deal of light on the nature of the oppressive procedures adopted by colonisers. For example, in *Black Skin, White Masks* Fanon asserts that 'to speak is to exist absolutely for the other' and 'to take on a language is to take on a world, a culture' (1986: 17–18). So the imposition of the English language, say, on the colonised goes hand in glove with the rout of their culture: the colonising culture imposes a white mask on the black soul to produce a pathology of subjugation. But, as the mask metaphor implies, it may be that the pathology cannot entirely eliminate the culture of the subject, and this is a possibility that Homi Bhabha brilliantly exploits in his account of the ambivalence that is constitutive of the hybrid cultural forms that inevitably are produced by the colonial nexus.

> If the effect of colonial power is seen to be the *production* of hybridisation rather than the hegemonic command of colonialist authority or the silent repression of native traditions, then an important change of perspective occurs. It reveals ambivalence at the source of traditional discourses on authority and enables a form of subversion, founded on that uncertainty, that turns the discursive conditions of dominance into the grounds of intervention.
>
> (1994: 112)

Bhabha identifies this ambivalence as a product of the unavoidable interdependence of binary opposites, whether of 'black' and 'white' or 'oppressed' and 'oppressor', because neither can exist without some recognition of the difference in the other – so the ambivalence serves to break down the binary and to usher in greater complexity, a potential multi-vocality, in the power relations fostered by colonialism.

Bhabha defines the notion of hybridity in relation to an 'in-between space' that combines two or more cultures, not so much to produce another homogenising, third and different culture, but rather to represent a process that creates new forms of knowledge about the relations between the combined cultures. Hence:

> Hybridity is a problematic of colonial representation and individuation which reverses the effects of the colonialist disavowal [such as the denial of the black person's humanity] so that the other 'denied' knowledges enter upon the dominant discourse and estrange the basis of its authority – its rules of recognition.
>
> (1994: 114)

In this sense, blackface minstrelsy was a paramount hybrid type of performance because the black mask could never just represent the 'other', for the white face always showed through it. This is a point that Joseph Roach makes in an excellent essay about hybrid performance on the Atlantic rim:

> ...in the doubling accomplished by blackfaced minstrelsy, one actor wears two distinct masks – the mask of blackness on the surface and the mask of whiteness underneath [and so] the doubled African American remains ventriloquised.
>
> (1995: 54)

Hence, blackface performance spoke, as it were, in at least two voices at once in a complex exchange between the dominator race that had partly effaced itself and the dominated race whose image performed the effacement. So, in Roach's formulation, white blackface performers ended up 'speaking in tongues not entirely their own' (1995: 61).

In the English troupes such doubling would carry an especially resonant semiotic charge, because, as we have already noted, for the vast majority of its audiences generally one of its terms had no immediate referent in Victorian social reality. English blackface therefore performed an absence in much the same way, say, as the figure of the clown performs an absence (it is no accident that many blackface costumes were clown-like). Like the deafness of the con in *The Rat Run*, the black person is both there and not there; in Derridean terms we are talking about ~~black~~face. This is the source of the genre's carnivalesque energy, its creative freedom. But also blackface minstrelsy embodies a crucial difference from the figure of the clown, in that it always implied a real, if usually distant and only vaguely known, global system of oppression. And for English working-class audiences there were, of course, corollaries in their own social experience, as colonialism was refracted back from the Empire to reinforce at 'home' the oppressions that, in turn, produced increasing demands for democracy.

These were the social and aesthetic conditions that could have enabled blackface minstrelsy to do more than simply reinforce a racist and imperialist world-view. But the sources of radicalism in blackface – say, its power to stimulate a questioning agency, or to unpack the corrupt ethics of absolute oppression, or even to generate a sense of resistant community – are, I think, intrinsic to its performative structures. As a quintessentially hybrid form it represents a special case of performance's power to promote the unique ontological confusion that Bert States claims may cause the audience to exist in 'a new dimension' (1985: 47). In blackface this dimension is all ambiguity and uncertainty, a kind of doubled instability, which could have allowed its English performers to speak both *from and of* global oppressions because the form placed them 'betwixt-and-between' races. Hence blackface performers had the resources, like Kate Valk as Tituba in the Wooster Group's *L.S.D.*, to give audiences access to a liminal-liminoid zone, a performative threshold that spoke of a way through the binaries of colonialism and emancipation, slavery and freedom, black and white.

No doubt blackface minstrelsy was less likely to enter this radical territory when playing behind the proscenium arches of the established theatrical estate of Victorian England, but also it was staged frequently as performance beyond theatre, particularly in the flourishing seaside resorts that welcomed the new mass of steam-train trippers from the burgeoning industrial centres. On the sands and promenades there was almost certainly scope for the performers of blackface minstrelsy, many of whom were probably of working-class origin, to strut some radical stuff. No doubt scholars will continue to argue about whether or not, or the extent to which, any radical opportunity was actually seized in the performance of blackface. So in the final part of this chapter I will explore a remarkably exceptional practice that may at least suggest a partial proof of the theoretical rule. The example will demonstrate, I hope, that sources of radicalism might indeed have been found through blackface even in the most unlikely places of performance, even in the cradle of the British Empire.

A bit of the practice

From the castle ramparts of the prison you can just see the edges of the burial ground. There you can find a rough-hewn headstone which reads 'Born under southern skies, Sailed the seven seas, At anchor in the town he loved.' The name carved in the stone is 'James Herns (Jimmy Cooney)'; the date of death is given as 5 March 1932. Reports in local newspapers inform us that the headstone was paid for by many hundreds of Morecambe's residents, who raised a subscription to honour the memory of the man. Besides memories, he left behind a short and colourful account of his life (Herns n.d.) that goes some way to explaining how this black man ended his days in friendship with the people of a Lancashire seaside town (*Morecambe Visitor* 1932).

He was born in Virginia in 1867, two years after slavery was abolished, as James Herns, but his mother told him many stories of slavery's horrors, including the sale of five of his brothers and sisters. In 1879, following his mother's death, he set out on a series of adventures that took him all over the world, eventually finding work sometime in the mid-1880s as an 'assistant to the clown' in Hengler's Circus in Liverpool. Shortly after this he joined the famous Bohee Minstrells (*sic*), staying with them for four-and-a-half years. He arrived in Morecambe sometime in the very early 1890s, to join a troupe of Afro-American black men who had set up as entertainers on the sands in 1889. Several of the original group died, not being used to the climate, but James Herns took up their mantle. There is scant information about the three or four troupes that he subsequently led, but they always had black men in them and they outlived the majority of English minstrel groups, which were mostly replaced by whiteface pierrots in the early years of the twentieth century (Rose 1960: 59–65; Pertwee 1979: 5–14). Several postcards of 1909 picture the 'No. 1 Troupe' of Morecambe, an integrated group of four Black and three white men, with James Herns always present. There is no record of when he gave up performing, but he spent many of his later years as the commissionaire – or doorman – at the resort's Royalty Theatre before he died, aged 62, of pneumonia.

The scant information about James Herns/Jimmy Cooney's style of performance describes him as a comedian and a singer with a 'still small voice' (*Morecambe Visitor* 1932), but judging by the company he

Figure 11 James Herns and the No. 1 Troupe, Morecambe, c.1909

Note: James Herns is on the right in the back row, looking dignified despite the raffish angle of his ur dersized top hat

Source: Reproduced by kind permission of Doreen and John Read

kept before arriving in Morecambe it was without doubt of good quality. The Afro-American Bohee Brothers were originally a banjo duo who came to Britain with Haverly's Coloured Minstrels in 1881. They are credited by Harry Reynolds as starting a banjo 'craze amongst society folk', which included giving lessons to the future Edward VII, when he was Prince of Wales (1928: 201). By 1889 they were successful enough to set up a thirty-strong company under the name of the Bohee Brothers' Operatic Minstrels at the International Hall, in London's Piccadilly. It is possible that James Herns was in this company, or perhaps he left before this, when he learned of the Bohees' plan to settle in a London venue. In his memoir he claims never to have liked working indoors. What he performed after his arrival in Morecambe is mostly lost to memory, though the original company he joined there seems to have had an extraordinary programme for the period. Besides singing 'negro spirituals', their 'leader used to tell the story of their life in captivity and carried a whip which he displayed as one used by their leader masters (*sic*) upon them if they slacked in their work' (Mellor 1966: 70). Certainly, something of this kind of showmanship seems to have been carried on by James Herns/Jimmy Cooney in his own companies: his catch-phrase was 'Raise the Roof', a suitably ironic shout for a man who preferred the open air and who in Morecambe always performed alfresco, or outdoors.

Clearly one must be cautious about the kinds of inferences that might be drawn about English minstrelsy from the story of James Herns. However, there is little doubt that the minstrel companies of Morecambe were very exceptional, if not unique, among seaside troupes, in including black men and being led by one. It is likely that the presence of real black people was a singular reason for their survival as a troupe well into the period when whiteface pierrots were taking over the resorts. This could be seen as a case of orientalism, the exoticism of the real black men, especially when working alongside un-blacked white performers, continuing to draw attention when the mock-blacks had gone (Said 1991). While we have few details about what was performed by Herns, it is unlikely that it would have differed much from the fare of the other troupes, and have all its usual potential for stereotyped racism. The fact that James Herns became Jimmy Cooney, even to the point of writing his memoir as the latter, resonates as a racist syndrome, and his final destination as a mere commissionaire opening doors for others – for the whites – would seem to clinch the argument for a life of denigration. It is obvious that this was a nothing if not contradictory life and art.

Yet there is no doubt that many people of Morecambe were fond of the man as a result of the pleasure he gave them, and perhaps of the income he helped bring into the town. It would seem churlish to put the subscription for his headstone *wholly* in the category of 'guilt money', even as we must acknowledge that, as for many years Herns was the only black man resident in Morecambe, he could not have posed much of a threat. The extent of his incorporation into white culture may be indicated by the fact that in 1896 he married Emily, a white woman from Penrith, with whom he had two children. But the local conditions for a more generous response than racist patronisation, both from Morcambrians and more importantly from holidaymakers in the town, were well established by the late nineteenth century. For Morecambe was a working-class resort, known locally as Bradford-by-the-Sea, because whole communities from the Yorkshire industrial towns would go there for their 'wakes week', the annual holiday when the factories shut down.

Tony Bennett makes a cautious case for the survival of disruptive carnival impulses in 'wakes weeks', even when they were faced by the heavy civic management of mass pleasures in nearby Blackpool (1986a: 147–52). But Morecambe, in comparison to Blackpool, was always more sedate, so carnival excess cannot be high on the agenda of explanations for any radical effect that may have been produced by James Herns's act. Rather, perhaps we should be looking to the ways that the actual black face of James Herns historically (roughly up until the turn of the century) first 'shadows' the fake-black of the white minstrel performers then (up to the First World War) 'highlights' the flat whiteness of the subsequent pierrot make-up. The effect for audiences of these contextual contrasts, I think, could have been to emphasise the inescapability for Herns of his black skin and to render its 'presence' phenomenologically powerful. In other words, the actual black face paradoxically both summons up the inter-racial threshold of blackface minstrelsy and replaces it in the relationship between the performer and his audience. The white spectator is then 'in' a threshold relationship with the black performer and has to negotiate a response that cannot ignore the black skin nor project on to it the spectre of whiteness. This response may then constitute a radical encounter with the right of the other to his own racial identity, an encounter of ethical equals.

But perhaps such knotty theoretical analysis is not necessary to the case, for might not these working-class audiences simply have recognised in James Herns and his compatriots something of their own rough deals in life? Could the unusual combination of shared perspectives on oppression, between American black and English white, somehow have shrunk the distance between these white audiences and the black people of the Empire, to mark a common plight? Certainly, the spectacle of an integrated group of black and white performers working as an ensemble, with each individual given equal performative space, projects a clear image of racial harmony. And could this have happened had there *not* been dozens of *white* blackface groups in other seaside resorts ringing the changes on the conundrum of power posed by the hybrid form?

There is at least a possibility that the genre could carry this kind of charge, and so, that the message of the former slave with the master's whip might have been continued in James Herns's performances. For reinforcement to this, one could call up the circumstantial evidence of some English blackface stump speeches. These were short burlesque lectures directed in mock edification at the audience, full of puns, malapropisms and *non sequiturs*, apparently designed to make the black stereotype look stupid and inept. But also they provided opportunities for a kind of extreme verbal clowning, in which the pratfall was replaced by self-denigrating illogicality and the flight of fancy by wildly improbable self-justification. The latent racism in many of these speeches is patent, but equally, like 'Jim Crow', they often dealt with important social and political questions. The following is not untypical of the kind of passage that is frequently embedded in the dubious stereotyping, from a stump speech called 'Police, Patriotism and Taxes':

> I turned up being a patriot and joined the police force. We have all heard much about the police. Some people think we hear too much of them. Some people think we don't hear enough of them – when they're wanted....I shall never forget when I captured my first criminal. I was in Trafalgar Square when I saw the man coming along. I went up to him, and tapped him on the shoulder. 'Hillo!' he said, 'who are you.' I said, 'young man, I am justice.' He said, 'there don't seem to be much of you!' I said, 'no; justice is a poor thing people never do see much of.'
>
> (Sands 1891: n.p.)

The conventional view of stereotyping would see this kind of radical social comment as being negated by the racism of the blackface image, yet this perspective does not take into account the doubleness of black-face in performance, and how it performed an absence in the context of nineteenth-century England. The key point here is that the ambiguity and uncertainty in performance may appear, paradoxically, as a *constant*

characteristic, so this passage when played in blackface could simultaneously operate as a social truth stumbled upon by an idiot – white
satirising black – *and* as the revelation of a truth that needs the special
condition of ironic disguise in order to be voiced in public – white
recognising the power of black, as it were. This is the performative
structure that, in the particular contexts of late nineteenth-century
cultural production, may have enabled blackface minstrels sometimes to
access sources of radicalism.

We can only guess at how James Herns might have handled such
material, but that it – or something very like it – was almost certainly
available to him should at least make us pause before we condemn
minstrelsy in its entirety as racist. Like many a blackface seaside
performer, Herns was extremely popular with children (Rose 1960: 61;
Pertwee 1979: 11; *Morecambe Visitor* 1932). Ironically, he didn't need to
black-up to get them, and their parents, on his side. So what would they
have seen in the spectacle of his performance? The surviving
photographs show a person of some pride, undermining the idea that
they were attracted by the sight of a black man abasing himself. Might
it not be more likely that the familiar doubling techniques of the white
man's blackface minstrelsy was both evoked and denied by the face of
James Herns? Could it not be that, paradoxically, the convoluted tropes
of blackface would have enabled him to entertain the working-class
holidaymakers in terms that made them equals, so setting a radical
example at the heart of the colonialist Empire upon which the sun
never set?

The performance of absence

> Prison, then, is a metaphor for the post-colonial space; for even in a
> country where there are no military regimes, the vast majority of
> people can be described as being condemned to conditions of perpe-
> tual physical, social, and psychic confinement. The state performs its
> rituals of power not only by being able to control exits and
> entrances into the territorial space – its entire performance space – but
> also by being able to move people between the various enclosures
> within the national territorial space. But the aesthetic of resistance
> that survives in both the smaller prison and the territorial one may
> force the state to try other measures.
>
> (wa Thiongo 1997: 25)

Ngũgĩ wa Thiongo was imprisoned for a year by the Kenyan post-colonial government in December 1977, not just for writing novels and plays that celebrated resistance against colonialism but also for his part in building an open-air community theatre for the people. Subsequently, in 1978, he was exiled, which is one of the 'other measures' he considers can turn the whole globe, for some, into something like a panopticon (1993: 88–95, 102–8). Ngũgĩ's insight, extending Foucault, is that the carving up of space by power itself generates an 'aesthetic of resistance that survives' (wa Thiongo 1997: 25).

I have been arguing that performance can significantly contribute to the creation of resistant autonomous subjects, especially through an engagement with systems of formalised power in an effort to open up space for radical freedom. Such freedom can be achieved through performative actions that combine resistant *and* transcendent ideological dynamics, which oppose dominant ideologies and also at least gesture to possibilities beyond them. Post-modernism is useful to this project because its pluralism opens up a rich range of approaches to the staging of resistance. But post-modernism cannot give an adequate account of transcendent action or thought because it tends paradoxically to make relativism an absolute, destabilising notions of identity and in the process undermining the possibility of the autonomous subject. However, I am suggesting, equally paradoxically, that when such ideological action is grounded in the contingencies of histories – in the particular spaces of prisons or in specific periods of colonialism – then it may achieve a transcendent perspective in relation to those contingencies.

Hence, radical performance may be generated by a performative reflexivity that embraces and comprehends, in the sense of taking in, the contradictions of its context. The sources of such reflexive, performative knowledge can be found at the heart of the very disciplinary processes that aim to eliminate it. Even Foucault, in a relatively rare moment of (admittedly very guarded) optimism, seems to admit to this possibility when he writes:

> ...the prison with all the corrective technology at its disposal is to be resituated at the point where the codified power to punish turns into a disciplinary power to observe...[this is] the point where the redefinition of the juridical subject by the penalty becomes a useful training of the criminal....
>
> (1977: 224)

From this perspective the old notion that prison is a training ground for criminals may take on a significant new inflection. For the socio-cultural structures linking the criminal to the merely rebellious, and then to the dissident and the revolutionary, operate according to similar principles of attempted control and determined resistance. This is not, of course, to assert an inevitable identity between criminals and revolutionaries, nor to collapse moral judgement into political romanticism: from various particular, historically situated perspectives, the criminal can still be considered ethically *wrong*, or even wicked, even as he or she shares the same pedestal as the revolutionary heroine in the best post-modern mode. This is why radical performance is always dealing in the ethics of aesthetics. But I *am* arguing for a recognition that in panoptic systems, whether we define them in local or global or temporary or more permanent terms, the force of these varied forms of resistance and transgression – from the revolutionary to the recidivist – may be generated in linked sources, in the reflexivities of performance. Such reflexivities are embedded crucially in the paradoxical doubleness of performances, whether achieved aurally – as in the ~~deafness~~ of the con – or visually – as in the ~~black~~face of the minstrel – and always created through the liminal-liminoid dynamics of performative thresholds. Hence, the radical in performance derives in part from the fact that performance cannot exist without entrances and exits, and of course ever entry is an exit somewhere else.

What has changed for radical action in the late twentieth-century intensification of post-modernity, at least in Western societies, is that the reflexivities of performance increasingly have become a principle of cultural processes in the performative society. In other words, the post-modern potentially is fertile ground for radicalism in its challenge to sclerotic social processes. Through the examples of resistant and trans-cendent performance discussed in this chapter, I have aimed to demon-strate how radical performative action may be variously articulated to crucial disciplinary structures in its specific socio-cultural environment. So between the law and the counter-law, between the legislator and the jailer, between the coloniser and the cultural instruments of colonialism, in any disciplinary system designed by some to control others, even in those that aim to be totally panoptic, there will probably always be a 'space' for resistance, a 'fissure' in which the subject can forge at least a little radical freedom. Such 'spaces' and 'fissures' are not best seen as openings into which performance can be inserted, like a scalpel used to dissect the body of ideology. Rather, we should see them as crucially *constituting* the dramaturgies of freedom because they present an absence that creativity seeks to grasp, like the phrase on the tip of the tongue that you sense will become the *mot juste*, or that vision of Utopia hovering tantalisingly on the edges of a nightmare. These 'spaces' – or times – these absences are inherently dramatic, paradoxically because they cannot be perceived, or created, as apart from the oppressive systems – the prison, the *logos*, the nightmare of enslavement – which seek always to eliminate them. That is why performance work that produces and exploits them is always an unwelcome challenge to authority, an unpredictable disruption of norms, a kind of playing with fire.

Of course, there is no case for assuming that all hybrid performances in liminal-liminoid zones will always have radical effects. Blackface minstrelsy obviously was viciously racist and reactionary in many, possibly most, of its manifestations, and participatory prison theatre can as easily become a creative sop to the panoptic system even as it grows in strength as a movement in European and American prisons (Peaker 1996; Thompson 1998b). However, if the performance of absence can sometimes, if only very occasionally, shed some emancipatory light into the darkest recesses of oppression, then there may be grounds yet for pathologies of hope even as we contemplate the ground zero of the soul. For nothing is more open, perhaps, than such absence and, as Ngũgĩ wa Thiongo writes, 'the more open the performance space, the more it seems to terrify those in possession of repressive power' (1997: 26).

Chapter 5

The death of nostalgia

Performance, memory and genetics

They spend their time mostly looking backwards to the future.
After John Osborne

The buildings

I was called as key witness to the trial at Manchester Crown Court. The mutilated body had been the plaintiff's, and he was lucky to be alive. When the examining doctor read out the list of injuries it took him five minutes. The assailants were two young deaf and dumb men from the day-care centre where the plaintiff worked. The three of them had been celebrating Christmas Eve in the city pubs and the lads missed their last bus home. They ended up sleeping on the plaintiff's floor and they claimed he'd made a sexual advance so they beat him up. But I thought that even if he had, the extent of the hurt done to him was surely out of all proportion to his 'crime'.

This was the first time I'd been a witness in a jury trial. The counsel for the defence focused on the gas fire. Did I think the two lads had deliberately turned on the gas in order to finish the plaintiff off? I glanced across to them in the dock. They were not much younger than me, with the look of people dealt a truly unfair deal in life. No, I didn't think that; probably the rubber pipe that ran from the gas outlet to the fire by the bed had been fallen on in the fight, the fire had gone out and when the pipe was released the gas resumed its flow. What kind of people lived in this building, that they would put up with such a dangerous arrangement? I described my friends as caring and tolerant. Did any of them smoke? Several did, but not the plaintiff. Did any of them smoke cannabis? The prosecuting counsel objected, but the damage had been done. The defence proceeded to construct a picture of 'the scene of the crime' as an appalling den of illicit drugs and kinky sex intolerable to normal society.

I have a powerful memory of the big front door on Oxford Street opening into the sickly smell of cheap sweets. The philanthropic land-lord had his business on the ground floor. Narrow and well-worn wooden stairs climbed steeply up past dark brown walls to empty offices on the first landing, where the only lavatory was located. Above that was the heart of the place: two floors of single rooms for the creative oddballs of the dirty old town. I spent my first six months there, sleeping on a mattress on bare floorboards, paying half of the ridicu-lously low rent to an artist who used the room to store his work, excitedly soothed by the oily aroma of freshly applied paint, thinking I'd finally found an innovative nest. It was a community whose talk fostered wild visions of a better world, every other weekend there was a party, and a constant flow of visitors dossed down on the dusty boards – people hitch-hiking the world, working the networks of the new bohemia, dog-eared copies of Ginsberg, Kerouac and Burroughs in their bags. The place was alive with new ideas and bright imaginings. We made the buildings a Manchester hot-spot, a place to be.

Then our little urban utopia was totally wrecked that Christmas Eve, when almost everyone was away visiting family or friends. A girlfriend of my American partner had arrived in the afternoon and in deference to her jet lag we went to bed early. We were woken by the heavy thumps and thuds, sounding like they were coming from upstairs. There were no cries or shouts, so we figured it was Clint the rock climber fooling around with one of his macho friends. But it went on for too long and then a door slammed and heavy feet rushed across the wooden floor outside.

My torch showed a door on the other side of the landing was ajar. I went barefoot into Bill's room, stepping immediately into wetness on the cold linoleum and the smell of gas. The beam of my torch glinted red as I shone it from my feet to the middle of the room. There was the body lying by the rubber pipe, its face so pulped that I couldn't tell who it was. Paddling through blood, I turned off the gas and ran back to our room. The women agreed to do what they could while I went to summon an ambulance. I ran up Oxford Street for half a mile to the nearest phone and by the time I got back the police were already outside. One of them pushed me violently up against the wall and his sergeant started firing questions at me as if I was a killer. The counsel for the defence got me to describe this in court, but the judge said it was a routine and reasonable assumption for the police.

But the damage had been done, and now memory floats free, unan-chored from time. What were the *real* buildings? Were they a hope-filled haven of creative friendships? Were they a squalid, unhealthy and dangerous slum? Were they just a cheap shelter for unconventional people provided by a kindly sweet merchant? Were they a pit of illegal drugs, driving tenants into a twisted take on reality? Were they all of these things at once? I remember the quickly disguised look in my mother's eyes during her one and only visit to my room when I was seriously ill: disgust and horror combined with care and love. The past was never together, even then. Remembering that the young men with blood up to their elbows went scot-free, as if innocent of their crime, puts the real itself on trial again. What use now, or ever, to trawl through memory in search of the grounds of value?

A poacher in time

The Poacher is playing its typical venue, a small village hall in rural England. Crowded into the well-used multi-purpose space there are about a hundred people, most of them sitting on chairs set out semi-formally in a shallow curve around and on the same level as the set: a low, slightly raked rostrum, ten feet square, with one corner jutting towards the audience to create a thrust stage. The back two sides of the set are lined with a broken wooden fence and hints of foliage, and it is covered with artificial grass: clearly the corner of a field. In village venues the familiar rural setting reinforces the intimacy of the general layout, undermining any sense of separation between stage and audience. The fact that usually the audience *owns* the space as common ground for the community also works to place performer and spectator on a par, in acute contrast to the hierarchy of privilege that 'good' theatre buildings always construct (Mackintosh 1993: 160).

The friendly hubbub of the audience quickly subsides to silence when Lloyd Johnston, as the poacher James Hawker, carefully stalks across the grass to the field's corner: sharp face, Victorian sideburns, battered felt hat, long and well-worn brown overcoat, muddy boots, shapeless canvas shoulder bag, gleaming rifle. He focuses intently on something over the hedge. A pheasant calls in the distance, beyond range, so he settles himself into the upstage corner of the set and quietly begins to sing to himself, without acknowledging the audience in any way, despite their close proximity. For the first five minutes he speaks a kind of internal monologue, a projection of private thoughts into an assumed void.

> There is no man in England who runs more risks, been in more dangerous scrapes than me. Yet the only time I have been in prison was not for poaching but for getting a poor old widow woman a

bundle of sticks as she had no coal. A man who still lives told the
keepers I had a gun. It was a long piece of ash, and they knew this
Oadby man had told a lie. But they sent me to Leicester jail for
seven days. They just thought it was time I was there. Ever since then
I have poached with more bitterness against the class. If I am able,
I will poach till I die.

(Manley and Johnston 1981: 13)

This initial sequence, closely based on Hawker's nineteenth-century
journal, quickly establishes the broad outlines of his character and his
views about the nature of his vocation. For example, we learn that he is
teetotal (drink being the enemy of the people, reinforcing a working-class
servitude that he abhors), acutely attentive to the signs of the natural
world, and respects the rural environment. He is vitriolic about the unfair
legal system of Victorian England, which can deport or hang the poor,
who are driven to desperate remedies – such as poaching – to stave off
hunger. Finally, he presents us with an ironic view of the class system:

> My father had tried to better our position lawfully and had failed.
> So I was determined to try some other means. I was surrounded by
> every temptation. The class that starved me certainly tempted me
> with all their game and fish.

(1981: 5)

All this is communicated with great economy, presented as plain information about Hawker, but, crucially, with no eye contact between Johnston
and the audience. The technique places a distance between character
and spectator, as if he is in another world, another time. History and the
hardships of the class system are rendered remote, relieving the audience
of any responsibility for what the play portrays. Apparently, and reas-
suringly, this is heritage industry theatre: the performance of nostalgia.

The end of narrative history

At the end of the twentieth century, history is not what it was. Telling a
true tale about the past, whether at the micro-level of performance practice or the macro-level of global culture, has never been more difficult.
This is mainly because new critical theory, and post-modern theory in
particular, has eliminated all the familiar historiographic markers and,
as it were, left the historical field newly unmapped. Theatre and performance historians sympathetic to post-modernism are, of course, well aware

of the difficulties involved in attempting to write post-modern histories. Not only do they have to deal with the key problem of theatre and performance historiography – how to create histories of a cultural form that is, in its most crucial aspects, wholly ephemeral – but also they have to privilege the multiplicity of the past and its traces – which makes 'history' profoundly volatile and a matter of acute contestation. So for analysts more or less in tune with the pluralistic music of the post-modern paradigm, 'Western theatre history' becomes a doubly dangerous concept, full of assumptions that marginalise or erase many dimensions of the theatrical past.

In view of this, one of the first authors to address the issues of post-modern performance at any length, tentatively writes:

> ...one might come to consider the postmodern in terms of the interaction of different histories and the various descriptions of the modern and postmodern which they construct.
>
> (Kaye 1994: 21)

Kaye goes on to applaud Umberto Eco's view of history as necessary to the existence of culture, and therefore unignorable, though it has to be approached with irony in order to subvert its potential for repression through, for example, the construction of dominant traditions (Eco 1985: 67). In similar but more direct vein, Linda Hutcheon argues:

> How can we know the past real? Postmodernism does not deny it existed; it merely questions how we can know past real events today, except through their traces, their texts, the facts we construct and to which we grant meaning.
>
> (1988: 225)

For Hutcheon, historical knowledge is a 'problematic' that has to be always put to question. Historians cannot presume to create a continuous story out of the traces of the past without violating the nature of those traces, which is characterised primarily by discontinuities, gaps, lacunae, ambiguities and uncertainties. From this perspective, there is not much difference, if any, between the writing of history and fiction.

The collapse of the distinction between history and fiction that is a crucial part of the wider movement of post-modernism drives Baudrillard into some of his most challenging claims.

> History is a strong myth, perhaps, along with the unconscious, the last

great myth....The age of history is also the age of the novel. It is this *fabulous* character, the mythical energy of an event or of a narrative, that today seems increasingly lost. Behind a performative and demonstrative logic: the obsession with historical *fidelity*..., the restitution of an absolute simulacrum of the past...[is] substituted for all other value.

(1994: 47)

He is writing about the extraordinary commitment to the appearance of the past in films such as *Chinatown* and *All the President's Men*, but he wants us to consider these as paradigmatic of a contemporary cultural trend that produces 'the disappearance of history'. Hence, around the cusp of the paradigm shift, there are acute problems posed by post-modernism for the ways in which performance might relate to the past in any effort to produce a radical effect. At the Baudrillardian extreme, the past is totally out of reach and therefore cannot be a source of radicalism. From the more moderate standpoint of a Hutcheon or Eco, the traces of the past are so fragmented that one must always adopt an ironic attitude towards history, always already undermining its pretence to authority. From the more antagonistic viewpoint of Fredric Jameson and Robert Hewison, as we shall see, performance in post-modernity is bound to lose touch with the past, not because history is an impossible or already compromised project, but because it is swallowed up in the logic of late-capitalism and loses all its radical force in becoming a mere commodity.

So in this chapter I will explore the tension between, on the one hand, a history that is at best rendered unstable, at worst made unavailable by post-modernity, and, on the other hand, the possibility that the past may be drawn on by performance as a source for a resistant critique of the present, or even for a trenchant radicalism. My method will be to stage a kind of double-take on the approaches to history that are common in the debates that I have briefly reviewed. Firstly, as they talk mainly about the *writing* of history, I want to discuss how the past might be *performed*; and secondly, as they usually discuss history that is written by professional *experts*, I want to consider how history might be authored through performance by *almost anybody* at any time. To develop this approach means shifting our focus of attention from history to memory, and from historical research through documents to processes for recalling past events. The material I will draw on includes a show by an English community theatre company produced in the early days of the 'age of Thatcher', performance at heritage sites, and the performances of reminiscence theatre. How can the performance of memoirs, diaries and journals of people now dead best produce a radical critique in the

post-modern present? How might reminiscence be used to create performances that stimulate radical re-visionings of 'history'?

The question of *repetition* is central to such issues, because it is
through repetition that histories, and performances, are made. The
stories of the past are repeated to make history. Memories are repeated
to bring reminiscences into being. Contemporary theatre, in the argument of this book, is mostly a machine for transmuting the liveliness of
performative repetition into a reified commodity. So how might repetition figure in the creation of the radical in performance? I will consider
this question by extending Richard Schechner's idea that performance
consists of what he calls 'restored behavior' (1985: 35). Following that I
will analyse the possibility of radicalism in the performance of reminiscence. But first I shall continue to anatomise *The Poacher* because it
produced performances that clearly depended on several different types
of repetition – of stories in history, memories in time, rehearsals of the
past – to create a potentially radical effect, again in a form and context
that would seem to be dead set against radicalism.

Poaching in Thatcherland

For a small company like EMMA, founded in 1972, a determination to
be both popular and to 'become part' of the English East Midlands area
in which it was based would seem to make the prospect of radicalism in
its work at the start of the Thatcherite 1980s especially remote. The
group's venues included 'village halls, community centres, church halls,
school halls, social clubs, hospitals, leisure centres, prisons, colleges, art
centres and theatres' (EMMA Theatre Company 1981). These were located
in a remarkable variety of communities, from working-class pit villages in
the north, through well-off commuter villages in the central area, to relatively inaccessible agricultural settlements in the east and south. By the
early 1980s EMMA was staging an astonishing 295 performances a
year in order to meet its objectives. The high level of output was achieved
through touring a mixed bag of shows, ranging from the nostalgic John
Burrows and John Harding's *The Golden Pathway Annual*, through a
Brecht/Weill compilation called *The Threepenny Cabaret*, to the one-man
documentary memoir, *The Poacher* (Hawker 1961).

My analysis concentrates on *The Poacher* because it toured mainly to
conservative villages – in the sense of conservative-voting communities
– down the winding lanes of rural Northamptonshire and Leicestershire,
and because it used nostalgia for a lost local folklore in an attempt to
engage critically with 1980s neo-conservatism. In terms of my developing

argument, then, the one-man show risked a kind of double jeopardy. In using a standard nineteenth-century 'low life' autobiography as its main source, in which a linear narrative invests a unified subject with a sense of psychological progress, it is clearly located in the modernist paradigm. Moreover, in framing that narrative in a nostalgic perspective, the show risked becoming little more than a heritage commodity in the capitalist cultural market-place of post-modernity. As a radical project, it would appear to be a non-starter wherever one is perched around the cusp of the paradigm shift.

To assess *The Poacher*'s radical potential in performance it is necessary to unpick its subtle uses of *doubled memory*, the embodiment of memories remembered. The opening section of the show, as already noted, separates the present from the past to produce nostalgia. In the second section, though, the actor Johnston begins to address the audience directly, shifting into a storytelling mode to construct an overt distance between past and present. This section seems designed to ensure that the audience finds Hawker *and* Johnston attractive, as the actor relates a series of witty and compelling stories about how Hawker became a poacher. These establish Hawker as an endearing rogue and Johnston as a skilful mimic, as the rhetorical conventions of storytelling are stretched to include impersonations, with Johnston switching roles to play other characters beside Hawker, in true Brechtian street-accident fashion (Brecht 1964: 121–9).

The perspective on 'history' and its uses developed by the show in the context of conservative-voting rural villages in the early days of Thatcherism was straightforwardly radical. As such, *The Poacher* risked outright rejection by the majority of its audiences. For example, in the second act 'Hawker' tells a series of stories about how he managed to evade or trick a variety of gamekeepers. He presents the relationship between the poacher and the keeper as a game with mutually acknowledged rules. However, he also makes it clear that the class system produces the poacher:

> Many times four of us would take the train for Weedon and then walk three miles to Badly Wood. Do our netting....I have often thought of the man who owned Badly Wood. He was a red hot Tory who travelled sixty miles to the House of Commons to trespass on my liberty. So this was tit for tat. I was getting a bit of my own back on Sir Charles Knightly Bart., who sat in the House of Commons for thirty years and never opened his kisser.
>
> (Manley and Johnston 1981: 33)

And the oppositional stance asserts itself at almost every turn, especially towards the end when Hawker modulates into undisguised political statement.

> Now let me give you a political tip. If every man who wants to better his position and at the same time benefit me and every man who toils, vote for the labour candidates – not only at the next general election but as long as you live. If you have no other reason not to vote Tory, this one is sufficient. The class tried to prevent you from having the vote.
>
> (1980: 37)

It is clearly a high-risk strategy to pile on the ideological pressure in this way, though the overall structure of the show aimed to soften the offence at sensitive points. The interval was framed by less critical material, as Hawker shared his wily knowledge of long-gone country customs. And the final sequence of the show also returned to the less threatening nostalgic mode, implying that Hawker is an entertaining and ultimately innocuous anachronism.

But there is a radical purpose built into the central performative techniques of the show, through its use of the many voices and subject positions that Johnston brings into play. For example, Hawker tells us of his admiration for Charles Bradlaugh, the nineteenth-century radical reformer and Liberal Member of Parliament. With great enthusiasm he describes the widespread and determined working-class support for Bradlaugh, which kept him in Parliament despite massive efforts on the part of the political establishment to throw him out. So pleased seems Hawker with this story of successful resistance that he ends up impersonating Bradlaugh at the hustings.

> I put it to you that the pretence that is made to you that good times are coming, is the vilest pretence that can be made. If the present government goes on, there must be more misery in the country.
>
> (1980: 12)

The conventional view of the performative construction here, found particularly in analysis of Renaissance drama, is that an actor is playing a character playing a character. Of course, that view derives from a modernist conception of the subject, in which there is a stable and essential 'self' – the actor's – upon which to build layered impersonations. This is the performative epistemology that informs the Brechtian claim that the aesthetics of Epic Theatre, through techniques such as historisation, enable the actor 'to criticise the character portrayed' (Brecht 1964: 139).

But the doubling of memory in the *The Poacher* confounded that reassuring perspective, for the dramaturgy produced a growing potential for slippage between the various subject positions available to Johnston the actor, established through the playing out of different modes of *remembrance* in performance. This was achieved mainly, I think, by the constant overlaying of two frames of reference, that we might best distinguish for the moment as the *performance of reminiscence* and the *memory of performance*. Hence, the subject positions 'Hawker', 'Bradlaugh' and other 'characters' from the nineteenth century were produced through the imaginative framework of 'Hawker' *reminiscing* about his past, representing memories of 'his' own and others' real past 'performances'. This *performance of reminiscence* brings into play the first sense of *memory in performance* that is part of doubled memory, the performance of a transcribed memory from the past. So a fictional reminiscence in the present (fictional in at least the sense that it was clearly being performed by Johnston) mimics the processes of memory in the past to the point where 'memory' appears *now* as a variety of performed subject positions. And this is achieved through the performative exercising of the actor *Johnston's* memory *of* performing the fictional:real reminiscence in the past, in rehearsals and earlier performances of the show. This *memory of performance* brings into play the second sense of *memory in performance* that is part of doubled memory, in this case performance of a memory of a memory from the past. To put this cryptically: memory *of* performance plays performatively with memory *in* performance, *in both its senses*.

We can represent the complexity of this doubling of memory in performance diagramatically as shown in Figure 12 opposite.

This performative structure enables the actor paradoxically to 'exist' in two time zones simultaneously, another liminal-liminoid threshold of performance. In *The Poacher* this doubling of memory then subtly ironises the whole performance, because it reflexively problematises the processes of memory at work *in performance itself*. This can be best grasped by asking: what is happening to the actor Johnston's memory through the performance? The simplest answer, perhaps, is paradoxically that it is both present (in use in producing the performance) in the performing, and not present (supplanted by the performed fictional reminiscence) in the performance.

The trope of doubled memory is an especially reflexive dimension in the doubleness of all performance and creates a highly complex

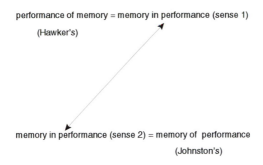

performance of memory = memory in performance (sense 1)

(Hawker's)

memory in performance (sense 2) = memory of performance

(Johnston's)

Figure 12 Diagram of memory in performance

disjunction of ontologies: in effect a limit case that paradoxically asserts both the difference between and the identity of past and present in all staged performances, between (to leap into the Derridean frame) writing – memoir, journal, autobiography – and speech – the onstage voices (Fuchs 1996: 69–91). Just as the con in *The Rat Run* was both within and beyond the law and counter-law, and the Goddess of Freedom and Democracy was both contained by and transcended the mediatised spectacle, and the children in *Glasgow All Lit Up!* were a part of and apart from the incorporative carnival, so Johnston is both in and out of the present.

It is this performative structure that *The Poacher* used to introduce radicalism into conservative contexts, because it allowed the performer to adjust the balance of nostalgia and ideological attack through the ways he modulated between past and present in response to the audience's reactions. In the intimate setting of the village hall, the show became a negotiation between performer and audience 'about' the significance of the radical historical material in the present. So the paradox of doubled memory indicates another type of performative liminal-liminoid zone, a threshold between past and present through which audience and performers together might explore the potential for radical freedom in the future. Doubled memory is a further source of the radical in performance.

Post-modernism and memory

Post-modernity can be described, in some key respects, as a process of forgetting. In the more extreme versions of post-modernism, nostalgia tends to replace memory as the reign of simulation collapses the differences between past and present, as well as fiction and history. The threatened debilitation of history as a source of radical value in post-modernity has caused cultural critics to issue dire warnings about its effects. We noted in Chapter 2 that Walter Benjamin predicted the new detachment of past from present in mediated societies as early as 1936 (1992: 223), and more recently Fredric Jameson has reinforced this by claiming famously that post-modernity fosters:

> …the disappearance of a sense of history, the way in which our entire contemporary social system has little by little begun to loose its capacity to retain its own past, has begun to live in a perpetual present and in a perpetual change that obliterates traditions of the kind which all earlier social formations have had in one way or another to preserve.
>
> (Foster 1985: 125)

In similar vein, Robert Hewison pins the disappearance of history in Britain during the past forty years or so on the obfuscating nostalgias generated by what he sees as the false pleasures of the heritage industry.

> Post-modernism and the heritage industry are linked, in that they both conspire to create a shallow screen that intervenes between our present lives, and our history. We have no understanding of history in depth, but instead are offered a contemporary creation, more costume drama and re-enactment than critical discourse.
>
> (1988: 135)

Hewison sees performance as sucked into the overwhelming simulacra of post-modernity, in the process losing all its critical edge. But it is Baudrillard, as usual, who provides the most haunting sense of the power that performance and the other arts may gain in creating the 'myths' of the new disorder.

> When the real is no longer what it used to be, nostalgia assumes its full meaning. There is then a proliferation of myths of origin and signs of reality, of second-hand truth, objectivity and authenticity.
>
> (1983: 12)

This could well be a description of the heritage industry at its recreative busiest, where environments from the past are restored and/or reproduced in meticulous detail to give a sense of the density of days long gone.

In Britain most major heritage sites now have this type of environmental reconstruction, such as the Victorian Schoolroom at Wigan Pier, or the Pit Village Street at the Beamish Centre in County Durham. These aim to immerse the visitor in 'authenticity', to produce an erasure of the time difference between the material world of the past and contemporary consciousness. The techniques used in the effort to produce this effect hinge on a kind of doubling of the commodity process, in which people-made past objects have to be remade in the present (even when they are 'originals'), with the result that the environments ironically become especially lifeless, as if doubly arrested, like refurbished old mannequins in a department store window. Often then, to counter this flaw in the reconstructive method, performers in period clothes – in costumes – are introduced to re-inject a sense of the sentient, to bring the objects and the environment 'back' to life.

Now performers at heritage sites offer a new way of 'writing' history because they are differently positioned in relation to the past than, say, an actor in Shakespeare's history plays or Lloyd Johnston in *The Poacher*. This is because the theatrical frame is downplayed or removed entirely in a drive to enhance the 'reality effect' of the past; there is a prodigious effort to create performance that is so far beyond theatre that theatre and its effects, especially its commodifying effects, are totally forgotten. But then in the moment of performance the actors are situated at a point where the seamlessness of simulation offers its greatest challenge to the possibility of meaningful history in post-modernity, because they have only performance skills to prevent them becoming sucked into a heritage Gestalt that aims to make its own commodifying processes completely invisible. The processes of performance at heritage sites therefore have a singular relevance to the issue of how recreated memory might supply an opening for radicalism, how it might revitalise a critical sense of history.

The performance of heritage

In what has become a very influential essay in performance theory, 'Restoration of Behavior', Richard Schechner writes about the Plimoth Plantation in Massachusetts (1985: 80–98). At this heritage site there has been an attempt to fully recreate the type of village that seventeenth-century Pilgrim settlers from England would have built, though inevitably the layout and architectural details of the settlement are an approximation of the originals, as their exact design is not known. To make the village lifelike, performers are employed throughout the tourist season to represent thirty of the 200 early inhabitants of the colony. These actors are assigned characters based on long dead individual settlers, using biographical details drawn from historical letters, diaries and so on. The characters 'live' in the village every day, starting before the first tourists arrive and finishing after the last ones have left. They are expected to talk to the visitors, answering whatever questions are put, filling out details of their life 'as' settlers. Clearly, this type of performance potentially gives the performers a good deal of latitude for improvisation, constrained only by a sketchy biography, their sense of localised history and an inevitably inaccurate environment.

What are we to make of this attempted time travel? Under what conditions might the actors best transport us through simulation to give us insights into the actual past? What are the formal performance characteristics – the conventions, the signs – which would open up the instabilities of 'history' at such a site and make it available for radical purposes? Schechner develops a notably ambivalent response to these issues. On the one hand, he wants to claim that:

> ...the 'first-person interpretation' technique [of the performers] has a kind of authenticity that the Plimoth architecture lacks.... Thus, while the buildings and furnishings are 'typical' of the period, the people are 'actually from' 1627 – as much as good acting can make them so....Performers who've been at it a long time identify closely with their roles.
>
> (1985: 88)

Clearly, this 'actually from' effect in large part will be the result of a growing knowledge of how best to represent the period for various types of visitor, balancing creatively between any assumed accuracy of representation and the freedom to improvise. On the other hand, though, Schechner doubts that this type of creativity can have any kind of efficacy beyond the deathly touch of commodification.

> And at Plimoth nothing (new) is going to happen; life there is finished. These restored behaviors are very much like theater in a theater; the script is fixed, the environment is known, the actors play set roles....Plimoth Plantation either continues as it is or it ceases to be; its very existence is knotted into its specific historicity.
>
> (1985: 94)

He arrives at this conclusion because he thinks the future action of the heritage village is predictable, as it can be little more than a repetition of its past. But this analysis obviously does not sit comfortably with his previous claim about the power of the acting: people who are 'actually from' the past are unlikely just to repeat themselves. Nor does it take into account the ways in which the close interaction between spectator and actor might make the past available for the construction of 'histories', a range of different interpretations, including radical ones, about its relevance to the present.

The point, perhaps, would not be worth labouring, but for the implication in Schechner's analysis for performance generally, and for the performance of 'history' specifically: namely, that this type of event cuts us off from the past at the very moment it attempts to recreate it. In the particular case of heritage sites, Schechner puts this down to the 'obvious fakery of a restored village', a point that chimes with the negative view of simulation in post-modernity projected by Jameson and Hewison. But he also argues that: 'Each production of aesthetic theatre is like Plimoth…', and by *aesthetic* theatre he seems to mean the whole of Western theatre. So Schechner's view seems to be that the performance of the past *as theatre* is bound to be a failed project as a source of knowledge, radical or otherwise. In his theory, as we saw in Chapter 3, it would seem that performance can only achieve proper efficacy when it gains the status of ritual. Hence, he contrasts performance at the Plimoth plantation and similar sites, as well as productions in the theatre, with the restored rituals of Bharatanatyan and Chhau in India, claiming that the latter 'have healed seamlessly into their cultural surround; they are living arts' (1985: 94).

The dead art of commodified contemporary theatre would seem to add weight to Schechner's line of argument, as would the reign of simulacra in post-modernity. But why should the analysis link heritage performance necessarily to that *type* of establishment theatre, and so see it as always carrying the aesthetic baggage of cultural traditions that, in some significant respects, it seems expressly designed to avoid? The example of *The Poacher*, and of other historically based work, such as Peter Cheeseman's documentaries at Stoke-on-Trent and Anne Jellicoe's community plays, suggest that this view is somehow missing a crucial dimension of how memory can work creatively, especially through performance beyond theatre (Cheeseman 1971; Jellicoe 1987). Moreover, the ambivalence in Schechner's analysis suggests a difficulty in his theory about the way performance works generally, and that difficulty, I think, stems from his central concept of 'restored behavior'.

Restored behaviour and memory

> ...restored behavior is the main characteristic of performance. The
> practitioners of all these arts, rites and healings assume that some
> behaviors – organised sequences of events, scripted actions, known
> texts, scored movements – exist separate from those who are
> behaving, the behavior can be stored, transmitted, manipulated,
> transformed. The performers get in touch with, recover, remember,
> or even invent these strips of behavior and then rebehave
> according to these strips, either by being absorbed into them
> (playing the role, going into a trance) or by existing side by side
> with them (Brecht's *Verfremdungseffekt*).
>
> (Schechner 1985: 35–6)

This key passage in Schechner's essay on 'Restoration of Behavior' sets
out a fundamental tenet of his theory of performance, namely, that
performance cannot exist without repetition. Another way of putting
this is that it is rooted in the past. Hence, restored behaviour depends
entirely on some kind of transmission from what has gone before,
whether it is directly learned from a master, or copied from some kind
of document, or restored by the performer from something she previously invented in her imagination. In other words, the medium of
transmission of the behaviour is secondary to the act of transmission.
Presumably this is why Schechner uses the metaphor of the 'strip' of
behaviour as a key term in his system: he wants to signify all possible
media of transmission.

At first sight, this account may appear to be unproblematic, as it
seems eminently obvious that a performance (even in the very broadest
sense of the word when, say, it is used to refer to the performance of
everyday actions, such as riding a bicycle) depends on the repetition of
something already more or less done before. It seems also sensible to
define it in terms of behaviour, because that is the observable aspect of
human action and it would seem nonsensical to claim that performance
is characterised primarily by something we could not observe. Accordingly,
Schechner's essay throughout stresses what he calls the 'objective' dimensions of performance. He says, for example, that restored behaviour can
be put on like a mask or costume, and its shape can be 'seen from the
outside'. He also says that it is independent of the person doing the
behaving. Of course, there is a sense in which this is true: images of
actions can be abstracted from identification with particular individuals,
and it is possible to stage such abstractions in live performance – as the

wonderful pictures of Bauhaus performances and the dance theatre of Alwin Nikolais, say, demonstrate (Gropius 1961; Roose-Evans 1984). But *equally* it seems obvious that – as Schechner himself suggests – each particular act of restored behaviour will have its own characteristics deriving from the unique circumstances of its production, and in particular who it is that is making the restoration. To problematise the idea of restored behaviour aphoristically, we might reverse W.B. Yeats's dictum: how can one tell the dance from the dancer?

Hence, the definition of performance as restored behaviour raises a huge question mark against just *how* behaviour may be restored. Schechner aims to answer this through describing what he claims are the universal characteristics of the performance process – 'training, workshop, rehearsal, warm-up, performance, cool-down, aftermath' (1985: 99) – but he does not analyse to any significant degree the *processes* that enable the performer to move through these stages. What is singularly missing in his account is significant attention to the *interiority* of performance, and particularly any sense of the centrality of memory to its processes.

To put the case bluntly: without memory there cannot be any 'restored behavior'. Memory is the process through which performance is transmitted in time, whatever the medium for that transmission might be in space. Hence, the processes of recollection are the invisible component of restored behaviour; or we might more accurately say – given that I am arguing that ultimately we cannot separate the dancer from the dance – restored behaviour is memory made manifest. I would argue that this is a useful description in at least two senses. First, performance is created through an act of memory *in* performance. At its most common, and quite simply, this can be indicated as a repetition of what was done in rehearsals. A more sophisticated frame of analysis would have to encompass the ways in which, say, memory may be said to be inscribed in the dancer's physicality as 'body memory', or in the Stanislavskian actor's psyche as 'emotion memory', or in the Brechtian performer's self-image as 'gestic memory' (Zarrilli 1995; Stanislavski 1937; Brecht 1964). An argument for the differences between such memory systems could form the basis of an explanation of the kinds of recall operating in what would in all likelihood be a limit case, namely, unrehearsed improvisation.

Second, performance always draws on memory *of* past events, at least in large part, for its codes and signs. Aesthetically speaking, we might claim that performative genres and forms encode a kind of general memory of past performance sequences. Culturally speaking, a case could be made for the inscription of cultural memory in the varieties of *mise-en-scène*: the cluttered stage of contemporary high-naturalism still carries echoes of its genesis in late nineteenth-century European drawing rooms, whereas bare boards with a few carefully positioned props fronting a painted or projected panorama hark back to between-wars frugality, and the incommensurate contrasts between, say, Victorian costumes and onstage video monitors in post-modern montage suggest, maybe, the dominance of conflicting information channels in late-capitalism. It is these kinds of correlation that Raymond Williams argues for, admittedly at a high level of generality, in his discussion of how '...certain forms of social relations are deeply embodied in certain forms of art' (1981: 148). In the field of theatre semiotics, Marco de Marinis mounts a similar argument in an entirely different critical language, when he writes that:

> Performance codes are codes from the general [cultural] text trans-formed (to a greater or lesser degree, or sometimes not at all) by the effect of theatrical conventions.
>
> (1993: 122)

But whatever might be argued in the different critical traditions of per-formance analysis about the detail of how memory works through acting styles, *mises-en-scène* or genres, I want to suggest that all performance depends on the *doubling of memory*, on memory *in* and *of* performance, for its character of uniqueness. Or to put this differently, exactly *how* perfor-mance plays with the doubled past is what gives it its particular nostalgic resonance, or sense of veracity, or ironic distance or radical edge in the present. Exactly how the past is doubled through performance therefore determines the kinds of access performance has to 'history'.

An exception to highlight the rule?

The example of the Wooster Group in *L.S.D. (...Just the High Points...)* provides, I think, a telling test case that highlights the significance of the interdependence of doubled memory and a sense of history in performance. It also uncannily exemplifies some of the problems raised by Richard Schechner's notion of restored behaviour as 'living behavior treated like a director treats strips of film', because this is exactly what the Wooster Group did in devising Part 3 of that show (1985: 35).

In Chapter 2 I described how the group staged a meticulous recon-struction of a rehearsal of *The Crucible* that had been videotaped when they were high on LSD. The technique ensured that the rehearsal was not directly accessible to them as memory, in effect short-circuiting half of the doubling of memory in performance through the introduction of a self-referential feedback loop – the imitation of the videotape – thus producing a kind of hollowing out of the perspectives that performance can provide on 'history'. Expressed through the key terms I have intro-duced: memory *in* performance was cheated of direct memory *of* performance. According to Philip Auslander the result could be described as a 'disinvestment of the self' because:

> The audience was…deprived of the ability to assume that it could read the imprint of the actor's self back through her performance; this blurring of identity nullified the possibility of charismatic proj-ection.
>
> (1997: 63)

But the disinvestment of the self also undermined the connection of the whole show to the past, not just in relation to the reproduced rehearsal but also to the parts of American cultural history represented both by Arthur Miller and *The Crucible*.

David Savran resonantly suggests the degree of this disruption in his analysis of Part 3 of *L.S.D.*:

> It performs the inability of historical discourse to comprehend and describe the feelings aroused during several hours of unfamiliar experience [both for actors and spectators]. It performs the fact that history, like theatre, is always a dance of absence and substitu-tion, a dance of death.
>
> (1986: 203)

While it would be easy to take exception to the claim that history is 'always' any one thing, Savran's general point is a telling one: the enfor-ced break in the chain of transmission from the past has profound ramifications. Just how profound this may be tempts me, I hope unchar-acteristically, into an area of high speculation.

Michael Stumm was one of the performers in *L.S.D.*, and he reports the reactions of its audiences as follows:

Many people mention to me that during the third section, whether they get it or not, they feel a little tingle in the back of their heads, as if they'd taken LSD. At a certain point, it looks like a bunch of people had taken LSD.

(Savran 1986: 203)

The 'back of the head' in this construction usually indicates the brainstem, an essential channel of transmission for the neuro-chemical disruptions of the normal functioning of the brain caused by hallucinogens. That functioning is structured by genetic imprint. Could it be that the Wooster Group were producing the performative equivalent of LSD: a disruption – an expansion, a confusion? – of the established deep structures of performance in its connections to the past. If so, might we discover a kind of genetics of performance by investigation of the ways in which memory works through its processes?

Reminiscence and performance

In the final sections of this chapter I will consider one way in which memory might be seen as constitutive of a genetics of performance, through a brief investigation of reminiscence and reminiscence theatre. Reminiscence itself occupies a paradoxical cultural territory in Western societies. The dominant view is that, especially when done by the elderly, it is an exercise in nostalgia, a retreat down a golden memory lane to visit idealised good old days that never actually existed. Reminiscence is thus one of the last cultural practices in which we would expect to find a motor for change or a source of radicalism. In relation to progressive social development, say, the encouragement of democracy, it is therefore a marginal activity best left in the ghetto of age. Yet in all developed countries, as is well known, the elderly as a proportion of the population is steadily on the increase: in Britain, for example, it has been estimated that by 2001 some 9.2 million people, out of a total population of 59.2 million, will be aged 65 and over, and by 2020 a third of the people in the European Union will be over sixty (Tinker 1992: 260; Mulgan 1997: 214). Also, all the empirical evidence indicates that there is a 'reminiscence peak' in old age, when we tend to recall mostly events from our teens and twenties, and when the exercising of long-term memory improves its performance (Conway 1990: 35–42, 151–6). It is the case, too, that the majority of elderly people engage in a 'life review' which uses reminiscence as a major technique (Garland 1994).

Hence, reminiscence should be of particular import both for the practice of democratised performance and for a theory of performance that accounts for potentially radical uses of 'history' in the quotidian, because it is a common cultural practice that imbricates memory and enactment. It achieves this mainly through repetition, even if the reminiscence is communicated only once. To understand this, it is useful to make a distinction between first-time reminiscences, those that are translated from memory to utterance or enactment just once, and repeated reminiscences. The distinction can be explained in terms of rehearsal and performance: first-time reminiscences may be rehearsed many times by memory before they are performed in public; repeated reminiscences are rehearsed through more or less numerous performances in public. We might call the activity of repeated reminiscence *performed history* because it is a form of (popular) historiography.

Using the frame of reference developed by Raphael Samuel in *Theatres of Memory*, performed reminiscence can be linked to oral histories and popular re-enactments of past events, such as battles and seasonal celebrations, which produce the resistances of 'unofficial knowledge' through new forms of historiographic hybridity. Samuel even suggests that the spread of these activities might infect the writing of history, so that:

> It is possible that politics will be studied as a species of performance art, religion as liturgical drama. Photographs, if in the spirit of postmodernism they are dissevered from any notion of the real, might be studied for the theatricality of social appearances....
>
> (1994: 39)

So I am particularly interested here in how the hybrid aesthetics of performed reminiscence may transcend nostalgia, to give access to new ways of 'knowing history' critically around the cusp between modernity and post-modernity. I will use the example of reminiscence theatre to argue that as an everyday cultural practice reminiscence-as-performance – performed history – may reconfigure a sense of history in the present, and that this may be empowering not just for the reminiscer but also for the audience. Such reconfigurations may be radical, and when they are they might just give us a glimpse of a genetics of performance.

Reminiscence theatre

Reminiscence theatre drew its first inspiration from a therapeutic practice – reminiscence therapy – which aims to improve the psychological
and social health of older people (McMahon and Rhudick 1964; Lewis
1971). Reminiscence by the elderly is held to be appropriate to this
objective because, as we have noted, long-term memory improves with
the ageing process: thus memory increasingly becomes a powerful tool
for the enhancement of identity, self-esteem and self-confidence in the
present. In Britain, since the Second World War, this kind of enhancement has been a much needed compensation for society's treatment of
many old people, who are ghettoised through dependency in residential
homes, or isolated in their own homes through individually focused
community care. The simple idea underlying the early stages of reminiscence theatre, in the late 1970s, was that reminiscences collected
from elderly people could be used as material to create shows that
would then be played back to the people who had provided them in the
first place. In theory, the status conferred on the memories by performance would empower the individuals who 'donated' them, while for
others the shows would help to redress the cultural deprivation imposed
by the conditions of care.

In the past twenty years reminiscence theatre has become an increasingly common practice, particularly in Britain and Europe, but also in
America. Currently in England two professional companies have policies
that focus exclusively on the genre, Age Exchange and Bedside Manners,
both based in London, and there are many other groups that incorpo-
rate it into their programming (Schweitzer 1994a, 1994b; Basting 1995).
The first reminiscence theatre company, Fair Old Times, was founded
in 1978, following successful experiments in reminiscence through performance by its Exeter-based parent community theatre company,
Medium Fair. Between 1978 and 1982 Fair Old Times produced some
fifteen shows and projects, mostly under my direction, which toured
mainly to local authority homes for the elderly. This was performance
that was particularly apposite to its cultural context, because Devon has
an unusually high proportion of retired people, a fact that has earned
its wonderful coastline the local tag of 'the Costa Geriatrica'.

In its short life-span the company evolved a complicated mixture of
presentational and participatory techniques in its shows. In the intimate
context of the residential home lounges, with performers in the same
light as the audience, acting within a horseshoe shape formed by the
old-people's easy chairs, it was natural for the audience to interrupt a

Figure 13 Reminiscence theatre in action, Fair Old Times, 1979

Note: Intimate and multi-focused contact with the audience encourages participation. Performers: Peter Bendall, Roger Beaumont and Peter Burford

Source: Medium Fair Theatre Company. Photograph: Dave Gill

performance, especially if it was about something they remembered well. Fair Old Times incorporated such give and take as a fundamental element of its style, so that its most effective shows almost always appeared superficially shapeless. Nick Sales provides a neat description:

> Discussions and scenes and songs and slides follow each other in what appear to be no logical sequence at all. Sometimes songs and sketches are announced, sometimes they just emerge from the general discussion and take off, but always one or other of the performers is acting as co-ordinator, picking up comments from the audience and relaying them back into the discussion....
>
> (Langley and Kershaw 1982: 15)

Traditional aesthetic rules (mostly drawn from popular theatre forms) were crucially inflected by the conventions of semi-structured social situations such as, on the one hand, parties, receptions, house warmings and, on the other hand, debates, arbitrations and political meetings. At best, then, reminiscence theatre as practised by Fair Old Times could incorporate a rich dialogic of cultural conviviality and socio-political criticism. Moreover, as the company progressed it discovered that there were powerful connections between emotionally and psychologically 'dangerous' material – stories and situations with the potential to produce trauma – and key ideological issues that were embedded in the reconstructed times.

Reminiscence theatre in action

Fair Old Times staged a story from the First World War told by an 85-year-old woman in Kingsbridge, South Devon. One spring morning she was taking a regular walk along the South Devon cliffs near the village where she then lived when she passed a woman that she didn't recognise who was looking out to sea. There was nothing unusual about this as people still took holidays there, even in wartime, but she did note that the woman's skirt stretched down to her feet, a little longer than the current fashion. During her walk a breeze got up, and on the way back she was surprised to see the woman still standing in the same place, still looking out to sea. And as she passed, the breeze lifted the woman's skirt slightly, to reveal a pair of heavy army boots. When she was out of sight she ran to the village and found the local bobby, who with a couple of mates managed to arrest the 'woman', who turned out to be a German spy. According to the storyteller the spy was subsequently hanged in the Tower of London, though she had no proof of that event.

Fair Old Times made a scene based on this story that used a range of styles (in typical post-modern mode) – naturalism, melodrama, silent film, slapstick comedy – and which was full of 'gaps' both in its narrative structure and its aesthetic codes, deliberate pauses and eye-catching appeals to the audience, and as usual the performance produced lots of interruptions. Often these interventions developed into discussions, even debates, which tended to centre on the treatment of the spy. Not many people, it seemed, had ever heard of spies being hanged in World War One, least of all in the Tower of London. The storyteller was just making it up for effect. But then even if it *had* happened it would not have been reported in the press anyway as it would have been bad for morale, and so on. Frequently, the discussions were about the suppression of free speech, the ways in which information may need to be controlled in the interests of democracy, the rights of authority to determine opinion, the writing and rewriting of history from different points of view: such issues were grist to the ideological mill of this particular scene.

It is important to note, firstly, that the undecidability of the story's outcome – was it 'true' or not – freed the audience in the making of its own interpretations, and secondly, that the form of reminiscence theatre as practised by Fair Old Times gave space to the many voices of the audience to have their say if they wanted it. To be sure, the story determined the starting points of the discussions, but as they dealt with such crucial questions of justice and freedom the debates could, and often did, range well beyond that origin to engage with questions of representation: for example, does the press have the right to represent only what it sees as in the public interest, or should groups that have little voice in society, such as the elderly, have the right to space in the media? In speaking, and listening, to such questions, audience members were, I think, constructing themselves as interrogative subjects, as people with the right to participation in the uses of 'history' for the making of democracy and its meanings in the present. Hence, what was discovered in the intimacy of the small lounges of the old people's homes, using stories from a past that the audiences were bound to know better than the performers, was that it was utterly natural for them – in fact *they had a right* – to interrupt, to correct, change, discuss, ask us to repeat, whatever was performed.

Sometimes the parallels between the situation of the spy and the audience became the main focus of discussion, and the bitter ironies of such parallels were by no means missed by people who experienced direct oppression, albeit in the form of care, daily. Hence, the performed past in reminiscence theatre may become an imaginative scalpel for opening up assumptions about the uses of reminiscence and its significance for the present, challenging the cultural framework that would reduce it to 'nostalgia'. By engaging audiences in the creation of 'unofficial knowledge' about the past, the techniques of reminiscence performance, at their best, encouraged participation in the development of reflexive autonomy, producing a performative aesthetics that sometimes created a potential source of radicalism.

A genetics of performance

The examples of doubled memory in performance that I have explored are small-scale and localised, taking place in cultural zones that can seem at first sight insignificant – or in the *lingua franca* of post-modernism: marginal, peripheral, sunk in the creases of society. I chose these examples also because they started with an apparently simple linear story, operating in the modernist paradigm – a life story, a death story – only to splinter out into many potential meanings, some of them incommensurable, when they enter the ground of negotiation between the performer and the spectator. This splintering of signification was achieved by the use of the first stage of doubled memory – performance of memory (reminiscences, memoirs) – to collapse historical distance, to make the past forcefully impinge on the present, whilst *simultaneously* using the second stage of doubled memory – memory of performance (rehearsals, past performances) – to variously deconstruct the historical material in play, to make the present interrogate the past. Hence, they aimed to recreate the past in the present, not as mimesis or exact imitation – the Plimoth Plantation showed this to be impossible – but as a negotiation about its meanings in the present.

The chief performative risk in this strategy is the production of nostalgia, a loss of the 'reality effect' that the performed past holds in potential. The chief safeguards against nostalgia are the deconstructive processes that the performer can create in the intimate context of the village hall, restored village or old people's home. Barbara Myerhoff, an American practitioner/theorist who has worked extensively with the elderly, provides a useful description of the general process.

> Cultural performances are reflective in the sense of showing ourselves to ourselves. They are also capable of being *reflexive*, arousing consciousness of ourselves as we see ourselves....At once actor and audience, we...watch ourselves and enjoy knowing that we know.
>
> (1992: 234 – my emphasis)

Paradoxically, in these performances audience reflexivity could be achieved through a replacement of the usual frames of 'theatre', producing performance beyond theatre, by the hybrid forms of documentary memoir, heritage drama and the theatre of reminiscence. Such hybridity transforms the processes of performances into a negotiation between performers and audience about how explicit the problematisation of the present by the past might become. If the problems are subdued, as in most heritage performance, nostalgia and the commodity reign; but if they become explicit then a fresh relationship is created between present and past because history is being newly created, as multiple histories come into play.

The rich resonances that such shows sometimes create across time invite speculation about the possibility of a genetics of performance. Is there anything in the ways that doubled memory works through performance that is akin to the transmission of genes from generation to generation? In animating cultural memories from the past might performance in some ways be shaping the future of the social through a process similar to genetic ancestry, in which some 'lines' die out while others flourish? Such questions might seem to belong more to the science fiction branch of performance theory and analysis than the empirical textbooks of theatre historiography. Yet in crucial ways they might throw light on major issues in the debates between modernism and post-modernism, they might be centrally relevant to the culture of the cusp in explaining, say, some of the reasons for its deep instabilities. A new genetics of performance might even identify the cultural equivalent of the mutation of the genes, '…an innate property…that ensures their survival even as it damages their hosts' (Jones 1997: 247).

A genetics of performance would inevitably engage with the key issue of cultural value and its transmission, and therefore with deeply political questions about how we might best account for the structure of cultures. Are there inevitably, for example, such entities as dominant cultural forms that carry forward the information of history in ways that are bound significantly to influence the future? Or are cultural forms better thought of as like so many elements in the common pool of genes, uniting us all in our differences? Such considerations have certainly impinged crucially on the science of genetics itself, which frequently has been embroiled in ideological dispute. Adherents of the melanin movement have argued for the supremacy of black-skinned people on the basis of the superior qualities conferred by the genetic transmission of the chemical that produces dark pigment. On that account, the cradle of civilisation is not in Ancient Greek whiteness, but in the black riches of the African continent (Jones 1997: 182–7). The Human Genome Diversity Project aims to rewrite histories from a genetic perspective by discovering the 'hidden links between nations', but it has been plagued by legal and political arguments (Jones 1997: 126–7; Frow 1997: 152–62). Hence, genetic transmission has been claimed for both hierarchical and egalitarian versions of the human, so we should expect similar tensions to appear when culture is thought of in terms of genetics.

Lucien Goldmann's theory of *genetic structuralism*, for example, provides the possibility of automatic dominance for cultural forms that comply to an *a priori* set of formal features. Although these features may have been gained through a historical evolution, say, in the different phases of capitalism, they assume the status of having immutable inherent value, so that other forms become by definition ephemeral, culturally negligible. Hence, the long-run West End musical – such as *Miss Saigon* – will be *automatically* more valuable culturally than a rough and ready community play that involves a large proportion of its constituency in creative work for over a year. So starting from a Marxist political analysis, Goldmann's genetic structuralism ironically fails to give a convincing account of potential sources of radicalism in post-war art, because he sees the structure of art as generally determined by society in much the same way as genes determine appearance (Laing 1978: 83–8). Raymond Williams expresses a severe reservation about Goldmann's theory because '…any form of *a priori* exclusion of know-able areas of culture is as unacceptable as the more evidently arbitrary exclusion of "history" or other "peripheral" concerns', which would rule them out as significant to the creation of cultural forms (1981: 144). In other words, the hierarchical shadow of high modernism, in which art can be entirely detached from society, still falls over genetic struc-turalism like the threat of a genetically engineered master race. For Williams, this is an 'unacceptable' account because it capitulates in the struggle for a more egalitarian and democratic cultural dispensation.

Similar genetically-inflected concerns have more recently animated the debates surrounding post-modernism. Consider, for example, the following view offered by Fredric Jameson about why the historical novel (in the tradition of Sir Walter Scott) has been supplanted in the early post-modern period by science fiction. According to Jameson, the generic shift makes it:

> …interesting to explore the hypothesis that science fiction as a genre entertains a dialectical and structural relationship with the historical

novel – a relation of kinship and inversion, of opposition and homo-
logy (just as comedy and tragedy have often been supposed to do...).
But time itself plays a crucial role in this generic opposition, which is
also something of an evolutionary compensation.

(1991: 284)

The 'speculation' is resonant not just for its obvious genetic metaphors,
but because it forcefully implies Jameson's wider purpose, which is to
reconnect art to changes in the material world – to the past and to
histories – which post-modernism in its most virulent forms would
render inaccessible. It may be objected that genres are not organisms
and may only in a fanciful sense be said to participate in an evolutionary progression. But even at the heart of the post-modern project,
or at least of the post-structuralist project, the question of genre transmission is a troubling, well, presence. Hence Derrida, taking the novel
as his general category of analysis, and Blanchot's *The Madness of the
Day* as his specific example, at the end of his demonstration *against* 'The
Law of the Genre' writes:

> The genre has always in all genres been able to play the role of
> order's principle: resemblance, analogy, identity and differance,
> taxonomic classification, organisation and genealogical tree, order
> of reason, order of reasons, sense of sense, truth of truth, natural
> light and sense of history. Now, the test of 'A *recit?*' brought to light
> the madness of genre.

(1992: 252)

'A *recit?*' (story, narrative) is the sub-title on the title page of Blanchot's
text which, of course, refuses to conform to any acceptable definition of
'A *recit*'. And because, as Derrida's editor says, 'genre always potentially
exceeds the boundaries that bring it into being' (1992: 221), and so
produces the constitutive quality of both belonging to and not belonging
to itself, Derrida is able brilliantly to show '...the inability of a law of
genre to maintain absolute purity, and the productiveness of this apparent
failure of the literary institution' (1992: 222). The close linguistic link
between genre and genetics is very telling in this context, but even
without it the parallels between this account and the descriptions in
genetics of the mutation of genes through time would be remarkable.

But, of course, genres are not genes and so any notion of a genetics
of performance currently has to be treated as metaphor, with the
patterns of doubled memory standing in for the transmission of genes

between generations. However, the metaphor may not be as far-fetched as it seems at first sight: there could well be a connection between the proven improvement of long-term memory in the elderly and the ageing process (Conway 1990: 151–7). According to the 'error theory' in genetics, that process may be inexorably caused by mutations in cells as they are replaced throughout life (Jones 1997: 269), but the performance of reminiscence suggests that the outcome may not be necessarily all on the side of deficit. Reminiscence performance, and by implication the other practices investigated in this chapter, can produce a paradoxical outcome from the realm of nostalgia by creating a reflexive 'dialogue' between past and present through a critical use of doubled memory. This parallels the ways in which ironic parody and pastiche create a problematised take on 'history' in post-modernism, with the difference that the performance of reminiscence may have a 'genetic' component that reanimates 'history' as a practice available to all. In this sense, the performance of memory may be part of a genetics of performance that is profoundly democratic, and therefore perhaps a source of radicalism that is potentially ubiquitous, within the creative reach of virtually everyone.

These comments are meant as no more than suggestive pointers to the potential significance of a genetics of performance, however conceived. My chief purpose in this chapter, rather, has been to raise the more modest question of what might be gained from thinking of performance as a kind of theatre of memory, using events that explicitly draw on the traces of the past in an effort to create a sense of history, even in the moment of post-modernity. Any success those events had in achieving this derived from the fact that doubled memory is constitutive of performance, and because they managed to deploy doubled memory in ways that were especially reflexive. So whilst retaining a kind of immediate hold on the past they had the potential to problematise it in the present, in the process transforming it into a shared 'history' that could encompass as many histories as there were people present at the performance events. Through this, the performance of memory may become a highly accessible and potentially a strongly democratic process. In these forms we may consequently find yet another source of the radical in performance – a radicalism of doubly restored memory – just where we might least expect it.

Chapter 6

The sight of the blind

Performance, community and ecology

A man may see how this world goes with no eyes.
King Lear

Falling into the net

The factory floor was nothing if not tribal. From the pillar drills I was moved on to small switch-gear assembly, a fiddly job where I found out the function of the pins I'd been drilling for the past three months. They were at the heart of an intricate mechanism, no bigger than a two-gallon can of oil, which stored the movement of a pull-down lever to produce energy high enough to drive a half-inch diameter rod forwards for an inch-and-a-half at the speed of a bullet. It took a week to learn how the switches were put together from the small and wiry middle-aged man who had been in charge of this work-bay for a long time. When he told me, on the second day, that he kept racing-pigeons for a hobby I barely managed to hide a snigger – the callousness of youth considered it a pastime for sad old men – and I wasn't sure if he'd noticed. But I soon learned to respect his scrawny hands, which were incredibly strong from years of squeezing pliers to compress the springs that held the power of the switch until the release button was touched.

On the third day he sent me for the first time to the stores. I had to collect a 'long weight' that he needed to teach me something new. The stores were at the end of the shop-floor, a lengthy walk past many different assembly bays in which hundreds of men and women were working. As I passed I had a vague sense that they were turning away. At the stores counter I asked the old man who worked there for a long weight and he grinned and disappeared into the labyrinth of shelves. I turned to look back up the long barn of the fitting shop with its clinky music of metal being screwed, bolted, clamped and riveted together.

Nothing happened. The old man was taking ages to find the weight and I started to worry that he might have had a heart attack or something. Maybe when someone else came to the stores they'd ring the bell and he'd reappear and I could ask him how much longer I would have to wait, but the long path down the shop-floor was deserted, and slowly I realised that its usual noise had quietened and all the workers were looking at me. They saw the penny drop – I'd already had my long wait – and their laughter washed along like the swirl of a rising flood as I trudged red-faced back to my bench.

I didn't fall for the 'sky hook' a few days later, but soon after I over-heard a rumour that it was my turn for the drubbing. I'd seen it done to one of the other boys who'd started at the same time as me and it was obviously horrible. A gang of older apprentices pounced on you, dragged off your overalls, pulled off your underpants, painted your genitals with red-lead paint and then paraded you around the shop-floor. Sometimes, I was told, this was done to two newcomers at once if the gang thought they were a pair of weaklings. You were supposed to put up a struggle and then submit, so when four older lads appeared in my bay and grabbed me I followed the script and writhed about as they dragged me to the junction of shop-floor paths where the drubbings took place. But when I saw that another group was bringing in someone else from another direction I really lost my temper and started to shout to the other lad that we'd better get out. We both went wild, immersed in angry resistance, and somehow managed to break free together and a great chase started up with us dodging in and out of the maze of machines and benches and piles of metal, and the pack after us and the workers cheering at the unexpected fun. We arrived at the ladder to the gantry crane and the cab was empty so we scrambled up and before the gang got to it we'd got the motor whirring and were smoothly sliding over their heads along to the other end of the shop. As we got back our breath, the sight below was scary because they'd all stopped work and were looking up, some cheering us on, some gawping in glee, some looking worried but we were in it up to our necks and there was no turning back, so we drove the crane to the end of its track where there was a high-up window we could clamber through. It was a fifteen-foot drop into the mucky canal but the reeds and mud would break the fall, and we were out of there utterly smothered in foul-smelling slime but with our balls intact.

The drubbings were always a Friday event, so I had the weekend to stew over getting the sack and dad said the music had to be faced. Monday morning came and it was smiles all round. The gang had decided our dip in the cut was embarrassment enough, the workers mostly thought our caper was a hoot and put the gang in its place, and the foreman said the bosses would only threaten the sack because they wanted the drubbings to end. Later that day my pigeon-fancying chief in the fitting bay said he wanted to show me a real foreigner. The only ones I'd heard of on the factory floor were some Polish refugees from the Second World War who worked in the panel-beating shop. But he led me just to the end of his bench where he crouched down to show me on the shelf below something covered with a long oily sack. He pulled it aside and there I saw the most amazing scale model of the steam train known as the Flying Scot, at least two-feet long and perfectly done. A foreigner was something that got made on the firm's time as a gift for someone else, and this one he proudly said had parts made for it by people in every part of the factory. He covered it up and stood up straight and reached out his hand. I took it and shook it, and I could feel that it was as strong as steel but the grip was as gentle as pigeon's down.

Into the labyrinth

Ithaca

When you start on your journey to Ithaca
then pray that the road is long
full of adventure, full of knowledge.
Do not fear the Lestrigonians
and the Ciclopes and the angry Poseidon…
You will never meet them…
if you do not carry them in your soul,
if your soul does not raise them up before you…

Always keep Ithaca fixed in your mind
to arrive there is your ultimate goal.
It's better to let it last for long years…
and even to anchor at the isle when you are old,
rich with all you have gained on the way…

(Cavafy 1961: 36–7)

You read the words of the 'Ithaca' poem sitting alone on a rough wooden throne in a small curtained antechamber. To your left is the narrow black gap that forms the entrance to the labyrinth itself. A white hand appears and beckons you into the pitch darkness, where invisible fingers guide you around turns in the narrow passage of curtains before a whispering voice asks you to take off your shoes. Moving forwards, your stockinged feet tread gravel, and as you approach a glimmer of light, gentle hands stop you from behind and offer you a quarter-moon-shaped mirror. The hands guide yours to hold the mirror horizontally across the bridge of your nose. The hands urge you firmly forwards into a winding, narrow, lit passage and an illusion of walking through solid shapes that glow like mountains at sunset, hovering lozenges of glittering rock, diaphanously bright crisp stalactites. Your mind knows that you are seeing mirror reflections of skilfully sculpted hangings above, but the artifice is so entrancing that you have no desire to break the spell of the simple visual trick. The visual become visceral as your senses build up imagined resistance from the appearance of solid objects that you tentatively walk through. You can feel the rocks and mountains giving way like water as you walk through them.

The lit passage tapers off to darkness again, and invisible hands relieve you of the mirror and guide you into a dimly glowing chamber that smells of fresh wet leaves and slightly dank clay. There are two swarthy men clad in russet and fur crouching over a low mound, but you have only a moment to register the primeval scene before a whisper in your ear asks you to shut your eyes. Darkness descends and you nervously give yourself up to whatever might happen next in this warp of a cave. Firm hands take one of yours and help your extended index finger to trace across the ridges and runnels of slightly slimy clay and softly cool moss. Is this the outline of the maze you are in, or a relief map of some mountainous country, or the fragments of a complex rune? There's no time to decide before your finger is moved onto and up the damp arm and across the wet back of the body of your guide. The flesh becomes a new landscape that you are to follow. Whispered instructions are planted gently in your brain: 'Your eyes are in your shoulders; your fingers are your nose; you can taste through your toes...' (though this last is probably my fancy rather than accurate report). 'He who risks, loses something; but he who risks nothing loses everything.' You open your eyes to find you have been left alone in another pitch-black narrow corridor with apparently no option but to proceed.

Your mind fumbles for orientations and suddenly grasps the ironic lack of substance produced by the brilliant trick that has been played. You may think you know where you are but you've no idea where you are going, yet you may never know for sure where you are for however long you keep going. The 'unique ontological confusion' wrought through being in the maze as both metaphor *and* reality exploits the central paradox of performance with extraordinary force: one is, often simultaneously, subject and object, active and passive, performer and spectator (States 1985: 47). Within the pressures of the paradox, the interpretative intellect may sometimes give way totally to sensation, sometimes it may hone itself to ever more acute insight and understanding, but always the doublenesses of performance, its mirrors-within-mirrors structuring, its especially high quotient of reflexivity, will effect unsettling oscillations between self-consciousness and absorption, memory and desire, discomfort and pleasure, even agony and bliss. This is the special pleasure of performance.

The black maze places you at the heart of the paradox as, performer and spectator of yourself-as-performer, you grope warily along thinking you've got the whole thing sussed as a sophisticated trip down a memory lane, when the fabric roof begins to lower and press down on your skull so you have to stoop until you're crawling on your hands and knees into an ever shrinking claustrophobia of narrowing tunnel. Panic twists your throat into knots of rope, shortening your breath to pants, made worse by having now to scrabble in a desperate wriggle up steepening soft steps as the tube you're in tightens into suffocating waves of fear. Suddenly you squiggle free and out on to a smooth cool narrow platform. You crouch, curled on the brink, to explore beyond the edge where there's a steep slope slipping away into nothingness. What the hell, fuck it, let it go, yes and fly with a smile and a hugely relieving slither wholly out of control to land ragged and doll-like in a huge pile of soft gravel. *Soft* gravel? You hear its gentle clatter as someone else in there stirs slowly, so you go absolutely still. The silence stretches for ages before the other body shifts and the gravel is shifted towards you. A quick and sexy hug with your welcoming friend – an inhabitant of the maze – and you are crawling on, then standing again, and breathing deeply and calmly in the next black corridor of the lengthening labyrinth. Beginning to have fun now, body light with exhilaration, apparently reborn, knowing you are not alone.

Community coming to an end

> *Community* can be the warmly persuasive word to describe an existing set of relationships, or the warmly persuasive word to describe an alternative set of relationships. What is most important, perhaps, is that unlike all other terms of social organisation (*state, nation,*

society, etc.) it seems never to be used unfavourably, and never to be given any positive opposing or distinguishing term.

(Williams 1976: 64)

It is a measure of the destabilising effects of post-modernism that this history of 'community' finally has been dislocated. In the post-modern, notions of the common good are frequently viewed, paradoxically, as potentially coercive. Anything that smacks of collectivism, whether in the 'traditions' of conservative thinking or in the 'communes' of left-wing Utopias, is treated with suspicion, so that sometimes even the slightest hint of 'community' becomes a disease of the imagination, a nostalgic hankering after a shared sense of the human that never actually existed. Stephen K. White puts the point colourfully when he argues, *apropos* Foucault, that post-structural theory attacks 'the "soft collar" of our community's traditions' because they foster an illusion of shared meanings that forces people into conformity. So any project that claims to act on behalf of a common good 'may easily be…extended in ways that so tighten the bonds of community as to suffocate diversity'. From this point of view it is all too likely that 'Soft collars [can] become garottes' (1991: 125 and 127).

A common defence against such extreme attacks on the idea of the collective, by theorists on both sides of the paradigm shift, has been to reduce the scope of the claims made for the cohesiveness of community or the unifying powers of communitarianism. The terms of these reductions have tended to be mainly temporal and spatial. For example, in the growing emphasis on identity politics fostered by post-modern diversity, alliances are frequently framed as necessarily impermanent: 'community' lasts for only so long as participants need it to reinforce an identification that is bound eventually to shift and disappear. So Lyotard talks of how:

the temporary contract is in practice supplanting permanent institutions in the professional, emotional, sexual, cultural, family, and international domains, as well as in political affairs.

(Lyotard 1984: 66; see also Mouffe 1992: 108–25)

In post-modern political theory the retrenchment has often been expressed spatially, not surprisingly perhaps, given the central role of territory in politics. Terry Eagleton points out that post-modern political philosophers as different as the neo-conservative Richard Rorty and the communitarian Alasdair McIntyre consider 'the self is at its best when it belongs to a set of *local* cultural practices' (Eagleton 1996: 86 – my emphasis). David Harvey calls this tendency the 'progressive angle to postmodernism which emphasises community and locality' (1990: 351). However, Harvey also notes that the urban spatial practices which can result from community conceived in this relatively localised sense are fraught with a frightening potential.

> The dramatic spectacles of the sort the Nazis organised certainly brought space alive and managed to appeal to a deep mythology of place, symbolising 'community', but community of a most reactionary sort.
>
> (1990: 277)

In this reading, the newly negative view of 'community' in post-modernity follows almost automatically on from an incredulity towards master-narratives – fascism being, of course, one of the worst daddies of them all.

Moreover, the issues surrounding the idea of 'community' are intensified by the globalising processes set in train by the late twentieth-century internationalisation of capital and communication networks, brought about particularly by the spread of new digital technologies, such as the World Wide Web and the Internet. The compression of global space and time resulting from instant communications and high-speed travel serves both to underline the finiteness of 'our' world – gesturing towards the dream of a 'global community' – and to highlight the dangers flowing in the wake of technological proliferation. The whole world gets to know that the globe is inevitably threatened by irreversible ecological damage, producing what Anthony Giddens calls 'manufactured risk' and Ulrich Beck calls 'the universalisation of hazards' (Giddens 1994: 152; Beck 1992: 36). These aspects of post-modernity paradoxically produce a pressing need to reverse the ways in which post-modernism tends to reduce the cohesiveness of community to the temporary and highly localised.

Viewed in this fraught theoretical and practical context, how might performance provide radical responses to the crisis of community in post-modernity? What are the most effective ways for performance to redress the collapse of confidence in collective action, especially on a global scale? Might there be an *ecology of performance* that engages with the new world disorder to produce radical insights into its dilemmas?

To address these far-reaching questions, this chapter will explore the potential for radicalism when spectators or audiences become *full* participants in *ready-made* performances that are part of the international theatre network. This type of participatory performance mirrors the relationship of humans to the potential for global ecological crisis, because the post-industrial societies of the world have ensured that it is already being ready-made for everyone and that humankind is by definition fully immersed in its future progress. I am interested, then, in the dynamics of an *aesthetics of total immersion* in performance, through which spectators become wholly engaged in an event which they, as it were, inherit as a complete environment. Clearly such environmental performances, like the ecological crisis itself, have the potential to make participants extremely vulnerable, to disempower almost completely. But if, paradoxically, such performances can somehow create access to new sources of collective empowerment, especially through the forging of a strong sense of community, then they may indicate the potential for a radical response to the ecological nightmare promised by the postmodern world. In other words, the types of participatory performance that this chapter investigates are particularly relevant to the issue of 'community' around the paradigm shift, because their aesthetics deal so obviously and directly in the dynamics of coercion, control, cohesion and collective power; in short, about who is empowering whom for what.

In line with the global concerns of this chapter, I will analyse practices that have an international resonance in the explosion of performance beyond theatre. However, the history of totally immersive events in Western experimental performance since the 1960s is somewhat fragmentary, partly because some of the early experiments were greeted with a mixture of bafflement and outrage by established theatre critics. The late-1960s participatory extravagances of New York's Living Theatre were particularly controversial, but there were similar events that enjoyed a quiet success. I will focus first on a contrast between the Living Theatre's famously disruptive *Paradise Now!* and a now forgotten show by the anonymously titled American group, the Company Theatre. Then I will return to *The Labyrinth – Ariadne's Thread* (CPR 1996), the immersive event described in the previous section, one of a series of extraordinary performative mazes created by the Colombian company Taller Investigación de la Imagen Dramatica for the international festival circuit in the last decade of the century. Given that we are searching for the strongest potential of performance to produce collective agency and a sense of community, performative mazes are one of the most unlikely places to look, so we shall once more be entering paradoxical territory in an effort to identify further sources for the radical in performance.

Immersive excesses in *Paradise Now!*

Any effort to create a sense of community through total audience participation in a highly structured performance event is likely to be shot through with contradictions, yet this was a fairly common ambition among the Western experimental theatre companies in the mid-1960s to early-1970s. Shows such as the Performance Group's *Dionysus in 69* (1969) and early People Show extravaganzas at the London Arts Lab (1968), tested the limits of the audience's tolerance (Schechner 1970; Nuttall 1979). But it was the Living Theatre's *Paradise Now!*, first performed in Avignon in July 1968, two months after directors Julian Beck and Judith Malina were in the forefront of the march that took over the Paris Odéon theatre in *les événements de Mai*, that provided the most notorious challenge to virtually all received opinion about what theatre and performance were for. Very similar advanced territory was simultaneously opened up, but in much subtler and creatively suggestive ways, by a group originating in Los Angeles, the Company Theatre. Both companies shared a general commitment to the anarcho-democratic politics of the first counter-culture, but the contrast between their uses of sensuality in performance indicates a crucial dynamic in the successful creation of a sense of empowering community through participatory performance.

Much has been written about *Paradise Now!* already, partly because it was a watershed show for the Living Theatre, but also because it quickly achieved an iconic status for the counter-cultural generation born in the 1940s and 1950s. Theodore Shank reports that the show was supposed to unite audiences 'in non-violent revolutionary action', to produce a new kind of political community (1982: 20). The organising image of the task-based non-narrative performance was that of a ladder, in which the performers metaphorically mount a series of eight 'Rungs' representing a 'vertical ascent to permanent revolution'. The first three Rungs increasingly challenge conventional actor–audience relationships, mainly through a harangue of the spectators by the performers, followed by one-to-one conversations and touching, then by discussion and debate about politics, each action variously dramatising the 'necessity' of revolutionary consciousness. Rung Four, 'The Exorcism of Violence and the Sexual Revolution', ends with 'The Rite of Universal Intercourse' in which the near naked actors lie down on the stage and

Figure 14 The 'love pile' in *Paradise Now!*, Living Theatre, 1968

Note: 'The Rite of Universal Intercourse' in an early stage of development. Note naked audience members preparing for the 'pile' at top of picture

Source: Photograph: Gianfranco Mantegna. Reproduced by kind permission of the Department of Special Collections, University of California, Davis

entwine together to form a 'love pile', caressing and writhing and inviting audience members to join in. When this is finished, actors and spectators together chant the slogan 'Fuck means peace'. Clearly the rite is supposed to create/represent an experience/image of the community united in total revolutionary action for a peaceful world.

Unsurprisingly, it was this scene that generated the greatest reactions from the authorities in both Europe and America. Especially in Europe, performances frequently were heavily policed and clashes between spectators and police in riot gear were quite common. In 1969, following performances in Rome, the company was escorted to the border and expelled from Italy (Tytell 1997: 272). Directors and administrators of theatres were sometimes almost as active in preventing performances, apparently for fear that their stages would collapse under the weight of the bodies in the 'love pile'. Audiences were regularly totally divided in their reactions, with advocates of violent revolution protesting against the company's declared pacifism, or punters arguing that they should not have been made to pay for an event that celebrated money-less societies. But it was the 'love pile' itself that provided the most acute signs of ethical ambivalence in the participatory drama of excess and revolution. Judith Malina recounts how during one performance of 'The Rite of Universal Intercourse' she was hurt 'beyond my capacity to either yield or resist' by four young men with short hair (a significant detail) who held her down while one of them assaulted her. Eventually another company member rescued her, whilst the rest of the pile continued in pleasurable oblivion (Tytell 1997: 244–5).

What was it about this overtly radical performance, a show that shocked so many even in those most permissive of times, that enabled it to carry the seed of such appalling reaction? The American critic Robert Brustein argued in 1969 that its source was in the 'excessive freedom' of *Paradise Now!*, a lack of constraint that could not prevent a 'swerve to fascism' (Tytell 1997: 241). The benefit of hindsight only confirmed this for Brustein, when in 1981 he foreshadowed some common themes of post-modernism in his description of the politics of the Living Theatre:

> Playing on a general sense of emptiness in a world without absolutes...they declared their allegiance to freedom and self-expression – but it was constraint and control that were more in evidence; nobody was ever allowed to break the pattern of manipulated consent.
>
> (1984: 68)

Kenneth Tynan, with typical insouciance, had noted a similar pathology:

> ...the involvement creates a feeling of oppression....The fact that you don't particularly like the smell of the person who's touching you...suddenly becomes unnecessarily important.
>
> (1971: 39–40)

Whereas Eric Bentley identified a strong tendency to intolerance in the company, expressed through the production of a politics of shame as it patronised its audience by accusing them, for example, of passivity in the face of an exploitation that it replicated in its own dramaturgy. At times this offensiveness slipped, for some, into especially objectionable action. When, during a performance of the group's *Antigone*, a woman student at Yale:

> ...launched into a passionate denunciation of the Living Theatre....she was 'hustled offstage by a group of performers who embraced her into silence – unbuttoning her blouse, feeling her legs, and shutting her mouth with theirs.'
>
> (Tytell 1997: 239, 241; see also Croyden 1974: 91)

The totalitarian suppression of difference in the name of 'love', 'peace' and 'freedom' turned the disciplines of theatre inside-out to expose the brutality that can sometimes be nurtured in the search for 'community'.

So the show's contradictory combinations of freedom and oppression were raised to a pitch of impossibility in the potential of the 'love pile' to release both sexual licence *and* libidinous aggression, free love and gang rape. The scene could produce such incommensurable effects because, I think, it dissipated the creative tension between individual expression and community cohesion through a mistaken appeal to unlimited collective ecstasy. It was mistaken because the form of participation proposed a reaching for collective oblivion that was necessarily unreflexive and therefore boundless, not just *in* itself – through orgasmic loss – but also *of* itself. In other words, in predicating that everyone *should have to* participate *in much the same way* in order to achieve a state of 'revolutionary consciousness' through sexual liberation, it denied access in principle to the kinds of reflexivity needed to recognise when a principle – or an assumption or a boundary – has been established. Therefore, as a community-forming process it was an intrinsic non-starter, because, as Anthony Cohen argues, 'community':

...continuously transforms the reality of difference into the appearance of similarity with such efficacy that people can still invest [it] with ideological integrity. It unites them in their opposition, both to each other, and to those 'outside'. It thereby constitutes, and gives reality to, the community's boundaries.

(1985: 21)

In not allowing for negotiation of difference within agreed boundaries, the immersive participation of *Paradise Now!* created a kind of anti-community, thus generating a collective implosion of signification at the very moment it hoped to revolutionise the real through the elimination of the modernist divide between art and life, theatre and the world. In a sense, then, the show as a whole was all false promise, because there was no way in which it could deliver a radical freedom out of a quasi-fascistic injunction that could anyway be easily turned back upon itself.

Given the Living Theatre's appeal to unbridled freedom, many commentators pointed out the obvious irony in the fact that the company, especially in Europe, mostly played in purpose-built theatres. The attack on the traditional disciplines of these buildings through the tropes of participation paradoxically served to expose the Living Theatre's project as enmeshed in a raw struggle for power. As it was axiomatic to the company that Western theatre was not worth saving, this struggle had to be about the 'possession' of the audience, and not only in the sense of ecstatic possession. But it was often an audience in large part *as constituted by that theatre*, an audience that could only exist to begin with through its disciplines. In this context it was inevitable that the ideological battle lines would be drawn up, as it were, between the abstract space of theatre's traditional values and the absolute space created by the Living Theatre's outrageous performances (Lefebvre 1991). Hence, anyone who preferred to stay in the former – the Brusteins, Tynans and Bentleys of that world – would necessarily feel threatened by colonisation; anyone who joined in the latter risked the exploitation that cannot be excluded from a zone that aims ultimately to transcend *all* rules. The desire to completely free the spectator from spectatorship, at least in *Paradise Now!*, seems to have produced a theatrical pathology that played fast and loose with the virus of brute oppression.

The flow of *Liquid Theatre*

There was at least one company working in the late 1960s that may have discovered a more benign ecology of immersion. This group has been largely forgotten because it existed mainly for one show, the curiously titled *The James Joyce Memorial Liquid Theatre*, which was produced in Los Angeles and other major American cities between 1968 and 1971. There is a description of the event in *The Drama Review* that rings with the dated argot of the first counter culture, but which also suggests a participatory resonance of a different order to that achieved by the Living Theatre, even though – or perhaps *because* – it had greater potential for sexual and psychological exploitation than *Paradise Now!*

Most of the *Liquid Theatre* took the form of a maze made from plastic walls that the audience:

> ...had to go through with their eyes closed. They had to trust us. In the maze the people were touched, patted, stroked, fed, hugged, squeezed, rocked and, in the end, kissed by a man and by a woman.
>
> (Larsen 1971: 92)

Inevitably some participants sought to take the sensual liberties that such treatment appeared to invite.

> They tried to hump the men and finger diddle the ladies. When one became intolerable, a hand would reach up and close the offender's nose and mouth, gently, quietly. Then they began to understand.
>
> (1971: 93)

In other words, the maze had a value system built into its sensory excess, a limit to the types of participatory exchange that its makers would tolerate and a structure through which participants could learn of its boundaries. Within this ethic, the commitment required of the participants in placing themselves literally in the hands of the company was greeted with unmistakable care. Apparently, the outcome usually was a 'crazy alien un-American trust in the company and the people in the audience who were once strangers' that fed into a final celebratory vocal orchestration involving everyone. The event would often conclude with a party.

What were the main aesthetic factors that allowed the *Liquid Theatre* to escape the ideological contradictions of immersive participation that wrecked *Paradise Now!* as a vehicle of radical empowerment? And what enabled it to create the performative paradox of unity through difference that is at the heart of any effective community-forming process? There were, I think, three key dimensions to the paradoxical effects of the event. Firstly, its performative use of space was uncompromised by the traditional disciplines of theatre, even when it played in purpose-built theatres, because it created a Temporary Autonomous Zone in which it could construct its own disciplines (Bey 1991). This was achieved by the simple stratagem of making an environment that defined itself as clearly beyond theatre by drawing on the long tradition of labyrinths in Western cultures. Secondly, this spatial organisation created archetypal resonances: 'People were constantly figuring it out for us: "It's the labyrinth," someone said. "It's the archetypal form. It's Theseus and the thread"' (Larsen 1971: 92). Hence the spatiality of the maze could gather various meanings within the general framework of a journey or search: as a zone of dangerous otherness, as a way of encountering self-knowledge, as a focus for a community's fears, and so on. This process of signification gave participants the scope to create a range of different meanings that were all inflected by a more general code. So people in the maze were not, as it were, entirely free-floating from the potential of collective signification. But also obviously the parameters of that poten-tial were far from precise, not least because they were perhaps more implicit in the intimate sensory experience of the participants, in the phenomenology of the maze, than explicit in the event as sign system. Thirdly, compared to the Living Theatre in *Paradise Now!*, which by playing in theatres often positioned itself at the interface between dominant and counter-cultures, the *Liquid Theatre* seems to have been designed to reinforce counter-cultural identities, not as explicitly *against* dominant cultures, but rather through exploration of the limits of the ethics of permissiveness. Obviously, this factor in the politics of the *Liquid Theatre* is difficult to verify without empirical information about the socio-cultural constitution of the participant-audiences. But perhaps we can read something of its significance in this respect off the written report. The abundant counter-cultural slang in the published account – 'freaking out', 'far out', 'crazy' and so on – might thus be interpreted as a kind of counter-signature in the Derridean sense, a signing of the other without which that culture could not have been recognised in the event (Derrida 1992: 315–18).

This last point illustrates the extent to which the *Liquid Theatre* is a complex area for analysis, especially if we want to claim for it the force of a collectively understood event or the principles of a community-forming process. From many perspectives, especially those on the post-modern sides of the paradigm cusp, but also from the neo-conser-vative and possibly the radical democratic corners of the political field, such a claim could easily be seen as preposterous. Surely the *Liquid*

Theatre was little more than a self-indulgent excuse for unfocused wallowing in hippie nostalgia for a vague Utopia of impossible love and peace? To then suggest that there may have been something of the transgressively radical in its sensory design risks projecting us into the realm of the utterly risible. But the rest of this chapter persists with such risks through exploration of a contemporary descendant of the *Liquid Theatre*, particularly in the context of the processes of late twentieth-century globalisation. Again we shall be encountering the paradoxical, for if in *Paradise Now!* the performative ladder that promised total revolution turned out to be wholly misleading, how can a darkened labyrinth throw any light at all on the radical in performance, particularly when it has no centre?

Approaching the labyrinth

The venue is a drama hall on the campus of Bangor Normal College, found by driving up narrow roads fringed by late-Victorian mansions. It is a Welsh Sunday morning in October 1996, bright and breezy, and the town is apparently almost unpopulated. When we arrive at the hall we have to wait outside: there has been an attempted break-in and glass litters part of the foyer. The organisers explain that we must wait, as not the slightest speck of glass must find its way into the maze. So our first direct encounter with *The Labyrinth* is shot through with dislocation: a large group of paying customers, who have travelled over a hundred miles and crossed a national boundary to get to the event, have to stand in the cold and organise ourselves into shifts of small groups that will return at quarter-hour intervals throughout the day in order to enter the 'performance' one at a time. The delay produces acute anticipation and a kind of awkward eagerness, all inflected by the odd convocation of place and event, as if someone had built a secretive funfair in a Sunday shrine, and we had invited ourselves to savour the fun.

But the publicity for *The Labyrinth* spoke nothing of fun. 'Do you Dare?', it said, 'To Make a Journey into the Unknown…To Find the Minotaur in its Lair?', and '…it is not suitable for the faint-hearted'. The *Exposition Columbia* of Bogota talked of a work that is '…complex and defiant…situated between art, performance art and theatre'. Yet we were also promised great rewards: '…it opens the doors to oneself through the perfumes of memory…', and, from *Epifanias* of Madrid, where the show had been an extended smash hit, 'I felt I was present at the birth of a miracle' (CPR 1996). The combination of challenge and mystery, up-front warnings and insinuated seductiveness promised an event that was unclassifiable. Moreover, here is a Colombian company, Taller Investigación de la Imagen Dramatica, dealing with a Greek myth, part of the cradle of modern Europe, in a town on the margins of Britain. The company also lays claim through its name and its base, the University of Colombia, to be engaged in advanced performative research, and yet it has already achieved great popularity on the international festival circuit, in Chile, Portugal, Spain, Italy, Brazil and the USA. In many ways the maze was designed to occupy the kinds of cultural borderland that are paradoxically at the heart of performances that reach beyond national boundaries to position themselves 'globally', as part of 'world theatre' in the late twentieth century (Turner 1982: 20–60).

This is one framework of practice that raises for me a crucial question about contemporary performance on the international scene. Leading theatre anthropologists, such as Victor Turner, Richard Schechner and Eugenio Barba, rightly claim that meaningful intercultural performance is a threshold activity, an exploration of the liminal-liminoid fields that may exist 'betwixt-and-between' different cultures (Barba and Savarese 1991; Turner 1986; Schechner 1988). Yet intercultural theatre is often promoted through the global merry-go-round of high-profile festivals, touring circuits, or 'special events' such as the European City of Culture programme. So at the very moment that such performance tries to confound normative notions of identity and ownership by breaking through to equal exchange or barter, it offers itself up to the hierarchical and divisive ethics of the international cultural market-place.

Hence, intercultural experiments such as Peter Brook's *Mahabharata*, Robert Wilson's *CIVIL warS*, Eugenio Barba's *Kaosmos* and Robert Lepage's *Seven Streams of the River Ota* have cast the participant/audience in the role of secondary producer, as an interpreter of culturally combined aesthetic languages already created by others, usually the master-director of the *mise-en-scène* (Williams 1991; Holmberg 1996; Watson 1993; Wehle 1996). This tendency may be reinforced by the high production values – in terms of visible expenditure embodied in production 'finish' – encouraged by the disciplines of distribution currently operating on the international festival and touring circuits. In addition, given the intense demand often created by high-profile marketing of scarce products, intercultural performance work by 'world leaders' in the field can become, despite its best intentions, just another hot ticket to be snapped up by the jet-setters and globetrotters of the international *cognoscenti*. So wherever they are staged, these events partake of the disciplines of a newly globalised 'theatre'. In this context, how can intercultural performance hope to avoid being turned into a commodity, a hot property with little chance of resisting or displacing, let alone transcending, the forces of consumerism that would turn it into an object to be owned, a piece of cultural capital?

It is, in part, this positioning in the international market-place that has caused leading intercultural shows to become notoriously mired in unpleasant debates about unconscious orientalism, blunt accusations of cultural imperialism and appropriation, and persuasive claims that under the guise of radicalism they are really reinforcing the global systems of surveillance, domination and control (Bharucha 1993; Marranca and Dasgupta 1991; Shevtsova 1993; Williams 1991; Peters 1995; Moody 1995). In contrast, Welfare State International produced democratised performance through people's creative participation in the procession of *Glasgow All Lit Up!*, even as part of the European City of Culture scheme. But how might totally immersive participation in a *ready-made* spectacle, such as *The Labyrinth*, succeed in making a radical breakthrough to isochronous cross-cultural exchange, to a new kind of international community-forming process with a global reach, when large-scale shows by others more famous and financially well-endowed by Western capitalism have so frequently floundered?

Perhaps a view of cross-cultural performance from the perspectives of globalisation might uncover forms of intercultural exchange that are not plagued by inequality or oppression, covert or otherwise. We would then be looking for practices that are not so susceptible to interpretation in terms of the polarities of self and other, source and target, centre and periphery, and so on, which have so far disastrously dogged discussion of intercultural theatre. And we would be looking for an ecology of performance that acknowledged the complex inter-dependencies between performative action and all aspects of its environment. In other words, if globalisation is increasingly placing us all in the same predicament, then it may form the basis of a newly emergent egalitarian politics and ethics through which a new sense of global ecological community might be produced. I suspect that *The Labyrinth* may provide an excellent test case for such precarious contentions.

The labyrinth distanced

The sketch and plan of *The Labyrinth*'s maze were drawn by the show's director, Enrique Vargas (see Figures 15 and 16 on pp. 205 and 207). When I first saw them I was naïvely nervous that they might rob me of some of the resonance of the event itself. They had the opposite effect.

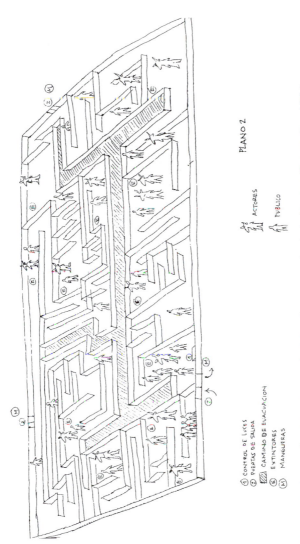

UBICACION DE PUBLICO Y ACTORES EN FUNCION

PLANO 2

① CONTROL DE LUCES
② PUERTAS DE SALIDA
▨ CAMINO DE EVACUACION
Ⓔ EXTINTORES
Ⓜ MANGUERAS

ACTORES

PUBLICO

Figure 15 A sketch of *The Labyrinth*, Taller Investigación de la Imagen Dramatica, 1996

Note: The public enter the maze individually at the door marked 2 at the bottom of the sketch

Source: Reproduced by kind permission of Enrique Vargas

They worked like those pictures of the whole globe taken from space, key semiotic triggers in the globalising process, the astronaut's-eye-view confirming through absence of known detail the amazing richness of life on earth. What I have so far described is about a fifth of the journey through the maze: starting at *Espejos*, passing through *Virgillo* (the mirror beneath the eyes), pausing at *Meandro* (to finger-trace the maze), lingering in *Mnemosyne* (sniffing a dusty book), and moving on to *Tunel*, *Rampa* and *Semillas* (the narrowing tube to rebirth). In each chamber one encounters a single performer from a company of around twenty, whom Vargas significantly calls 'inhabitants' of the maze. The inhabited scenes that follow *Semillas* include a schoolroom and a nursery that you play in, a wardrobe of hung clothes that you have to walk through, a hanging box that you stick your arms and head into to try on wigs and hats in front of a mirror that reflects someone else's face. From there you crawl through a rope-hung cave and on to another chamber where some sleeping beast snores gently – all the time the smells grow earthier, danker, muskier with the fresh and fetid odours of earth and animals. Eventually you arrive in the Minotaur's lair, where there is so little light that you think you see him everywhere, but then suddenly there he is on the other side of a glass screen – huge furry head and horns on the naked body of a man. A brilliant trick of light and he alternately appears to have your head and then your body, a disconcerting effect but soon you find he responds to your every movement and you develop a dance with him, a slow ecstatic dance. Then on to be buried alive, to play with fire on your hands, to put your shoes back on (hardly believing they're yours), to have a warm drink and write down a few thoughts in the 'Decompression' chamber, finally emerging from the maze back where you started.

This bald factual description can give no sense of the full impact of the one-and-a-half to two-hour journey. The long passages of utter darkness, the total disorientation in time and space, the constant state of uncertainty and expectation, the general substitution of the tactile for the visual, the rich array of textures and smells, the close interaction with the performers in their dimly lit chambers, above all perhaps, the constant invisible presence of helping hands in moments of uncertainty, hesitation, fear or even terror: together these seem to have produced for most people a profoundly significant experience, as the comments written in the 'Decompression' chamber indicate. They range from the rare 'Never again. It was hell.' to the high positivity of the majority: 'I have never felt so happy in all my life. I will take this experience with

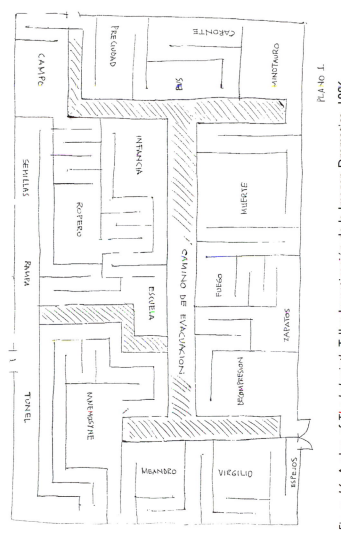

Figure 16 A plan of *The Labyrinth*, Taller Investigación de la Imagen Dramatica, 1996

Note: The maze begins at *Espejos* and ends at *Decompresion*. Note the alternate routes between *Mnemosyne* and *Tunel*, designed to modulate the flow of visitors

Source: Reproduced by kind permission of Enrique Vargas

me everywhere I go. Thank you so much for giving me back my life.'

Such contrasts, and enthusiasm, underscore the elusiveness of live performance when it comes to attempts at translation into words, images or any other discourse (Pavis 1992; de Marinis 1985 and 1993; Tornqvist 1991; McCauley 1994; Melzer 1995). At first sight this may seem to be because they throw us back with a vengeance towards indi- vidual interpretations: what to me was choking fear in a hellishly narrow tube, to another is reassuring comfort in a snugly fitting cradle. From this perspective *The Labyrinth* would seem to conform strongly to Howard Barker's prescriptions for what he calls the catastrophic theatre, 'which insists on the limits of tolerance as its territory [and] inhabits the area of maximum risk...' (1993: 53). Barker's theoretical writings echo over and over with pleas for a totally radical disruption of audience reception that will shock it into a new kind of consciousness. At times this reads like a re-run of Artaud, with its constant emphasis on pain and suffering, its desire for agonisingly sublime release. And as Günter Klotz has pointed out, Barker's whole theatrical stance can be read as a paradigm of post-modernism (Klotz 1991: 20–6). There is no surprise, then, in Barker's radical suspicion of anything that smacks of the collec- tive in performance. Castigating the 'nauseating cheerfulness of socialist realist literature' he offers resounding echoes of post-modernism's doubts about community:

> A similar imperative to enlighten, amuse, and stimulate good thoughts of a collective nature (family, nation, party, community) clings to the carnival mania of the left and the moral crusade of the right. But the banging of the drum is hollow and the rhetoric shallow.
>
> (1993: 53)

In the dramaturgic territory of catastrophic theatre the idea of commu- nity is a fool's illusion; we are all ultimately alone in facing the chasm between self and other, unity and difference, political order and moral chaos, culture and nature.

The Labyrinth encapsulates the problems posed for democratic commu- nity by the catastrophic theatre in a particularly apt way, because each participant goes through the maze alone. Yet out of that solitude was formed, I think, an extraordinary sense of the power of human mutu- ality. While giving great scope for the exploration of individual difference, it also created a performative framework within which people could be together in simple ways that had profound ramifications. I would describe this as the shaping and embodiment of a previously impossible collective. I want to suggest that a sense of embodied virtual community was established by *The Labyrinth* because it touched deeply on the tenor of the times in the late twentieth century, being poised in an especially inspired way on the cusp of the paradigm shift.

Thinking the labyrinth

The key aesthetic tactic of *The Labyrinth* is to subtract and displace. It subtracts sight, and so shifts the locus of perception from the gaze on to hearing, touch and smell. In subtracting sight it displaces the dominant visual economies of Western cultures (Jenks 1995: 10), disrupting the key processes of representation; the world as object of representation is replaced by the self as subject of investigation. In the black maze 'we' become wholly vulnerable because 'we' do not know quite where 'we' are; and so 'one' is thrown back on the instability of the self. Then because this destabilisation of the self as subject is achieved by the switch to relatively under-used channels of communication, especially the tactile and olfactory, new languages of exchange have to be created between 'ourselves' and the unknown other, between participants and inhabitants of the maze. Hence *The Labyrinth* plays off, and on, the undermining of the stable subject figured by post-modernism. Difference becomes alternately highly focused and blurred as the other – both individual inhabitants and the company as a whole – always hovers on the edges of under-used channels of perception. Refusing easy identifications, yet always gently and sensitively supportive, the other produces extremes of fear and empathy, dread and relief, tension and relaxation.

The disruption of everyday perception through the regular deprivation and reinstatement of sight produces an acute awareness that it is impossible to look equally at everything you see, and underlines the key semiotic point that meaning is created in the 'gaps' and 'absences' between the signs and between particular codes, or in Derridean terms, through *differance* and deferral: what exactly was the 'soft gravel' at the bottom of the birthing tube slide? (If you don't later find a few pieces in the creases of your clothes, you may never know that it was coffee beans!) The maze invites the participant, with the inhabitants, to 'fill the gaps' in and between the various senses/codes, an effect that was greatly enhanced by the ways in which the installation drew on several distinct cultures for the creation of its main systems of codes. Three chief sources could be identified: South America, particularly for costumes and objects; Europe, particularly for images deriving from ancient Greek mythology; and Wales, particularly for the kinds of texture and smells encountered.

The net effect of the techniques of perceptual/semiotic disruption was the production of a liminal-liminoid field beyond, or more accurately, between, the sign systems of these particular cultures. Like the maze of the prison in *The Rat Run*, the maze of *The Labyrinth* was a series of thresholds to be negotiated. But whereas the law and the counter-law aimed to shape the primary 'significance' of journeys through the prison-maze in terms of punishment and pain, *The Labyrinth* reversed that performative structure: it created the conditions for the exploration of various forms of autonomy (not all of them immediately pleasurable), through which participants, in collaboration with inhabitants, could construct its 'significance' for themselves. This was its system for the making of individual meanings, its 'catastrophic' dimension in Barker's sense, but how did it generate the potential for collective significance?

Empowerment

The organising principle of *The Labyrinth*'s techniques was not a narrative in any conventional sense; no plot or overt logic of cause and effect could be detected in the sequence of events, partly because the participant could not know what he/she might have missed by being directed along alternative routes. In this respect, as in others, *The Labyrinth* was a *post-modern performative maze*, adding action to the kinds of environmental sculptures, such as Alice Aycock's *Maze* (1972), which occupy hybrid spaces between architecture and landscape, earthworks and functional structures. The hybridity of these sculptures, Rosalind Kraus maintains, creates cultural spaces that can 'no longer be described as modernist' (1985: 39). Yet the sequence of action of *The Labyrinth* had an emotional or imaginative logic or structure to it, because it constituted a journey to and beyond the Minotaur's lair. The participants' comments indicate that this was perceived frequently as venturing to ever deeper psychological depths, or a penetration into the past, or an exploration of memory, or an intensified grappling with fear and self-control. Another way of putting this is that the maze was primarily a carefully constructed phenomenological experience, so that the semiosis of the installation was made to operate as a secondary effect. This is not surprising, given that the usual *distance* between actor and audience, stage and auditorium, which tends to foster a conscious reading of codes (*pace* Brecht), was almost wholly eliminated by immersive participation (Chaim 1984).

The lack of a centre to the maze may be seen as emblematic of this displacement of modernist aesthetics.

In Eugenio Barba's terms *The Labyrinth* may have been working in a zone of pre-expressive barter (Barba 1986: 157; Barba and Savarese 1991: 186–204). It was pre-expressive in that the disruption of everyday perception and processes of communication/interpretation called for exchange between participants and the company that was always exploratory and provisional. This provided potential for action that was 'beyond' what Barba calls the 'colonisation' of both naturalised everyday behaviour (inculturation) *and* the 'second naturalness' of particular performance styles (acculturation) (Watson 1993: 37–8). While this radical shedding of cultural conditioning allowed any meanings construed by participants to be deeply personal or individualised, the barter between participants and company members conformed to the designed phenomenological order. The interactive nature of the maze encouraged participants not simply to submit to that order, to become its object, but to explore its expressive potential *with* its inhabitants, to become an agent in the creation of its 'culture' through barter in Barba's sense: '...not an exchange of equals, but an exchange as the only possibility of finding equality' (1979: 106). This interaction transformed the whole maze into a threshold between all the cultures impinging upon it – Welsh, Colombian, Ancient Greek and others – creating a liminal-liminoid zone in which all cultural markers became potentially subject to a radical suspension of signification. In other words, what was bartered was not the meanings of signs, nor signification itself, but rather the empowerments of individual and collective agency 'beyond' representation, for both participants and inhabitants within that 'culture' *as it was created*. In a crucial sense, empowerment would not depend on mutual trust; rather empowerment (if and when it happened) would become the *source* of the trust so often mentioned by participants in their comments. It is this reversal of the discourses of power in disciplinary systems, where agency and empowerment are an *effect* of signification, that made *The Labyrinth* profoundly radical.

But what was the nature of this 'culture' that enabled it to create a sense of egalitarian communal exchange for such a wide variety of people in many different countries? To theorise this possibility we will turn next to the idea of globalisation.

Globalising the labyrinth

Globalisation, in large part, is an effect of the compression of space and time created by two key international processes in the late twentieth century. First, high-speed travel and instantaneous electronic communications appear to foreshorten or eliminate space. Second, local time tends to become subsumed in global time as space 'shrinks', thus creating an increased awareness of the simultaneity of events: all time zones may be perceived to exist in the same moment (Harvey 1990: 284–307). Hence, globalisation results from the complex *flows* of information, images, materials, people, etc., around the globe in the late twentieth century, creating new diachronic and synchronic intensities of experience (Appadurai 1990: 295–308). Supra-national communications within globalisation are effected by the evolution of universal forms of exchange. Money is the example most frequently cited, though images and sounds, especially music, are equally mobile and ubiquitous (Waters 1995: 65–95).

Two main aspects of this emergent 'world culture' are crucial to the cross-cultural impact of *The Labyrinth*, positioning it partly in the postmodern hyper-real in Baudrillard's sense. First, signifying codes become detached from their originating context and this generates an increased potential for new meanings to be made of them. Second, sign systems may become 'democratised', in the sense that in any particular context of use no one system will inevitably always have privilege over others. Some authorities argue that this may hold in theory, but in practice what is happening is that Western post-industrial societies are imposing their cultural systems across the globe in a new form of capitalist imperialism, albeit with a liberal democratic gloss (Ritzer 1993). In contrast, though, I think that *The Labyrinth* turned an especially neat trick in its creation of a new form of cross-cultural exchange, as already noted. Firstly, by decentring sight it tended to evade a major channel of Western imperial domination, producing a wholly anti-panoptic system of exchange. And secondly, by refusing to privilege any of its main semiotic sources it subverted established hierarchies of signs. Again, the installation appears to have latched on to a crucial element of globalisation, by creating an unusually semiotically democratic system of exchange.

To achieve these effects *The Labyrinth* was grappling with an aspect of globalisation that most commentators agree may be its key ecological feature. The processes of industrial-technological modernisation that have established the conditions through which a new global culture may be being forged have also produced new configurations of human risk and trust (Beck 1992). The risks are endemic, ubiquitous, unavoidable because they have become deeply embedded in the economic, social, political systems and – above all – the eco-systems of the world. Nuclear accidents, acid rain, pollutant threats to the ozone layer: none of these, as we know, respect nationality, race, class, gender or any other forms of difference. In this sense the growth of global risk is a great equaliser. (Again, it may be that the risks are not so equally distributed, that developing countries tend to be the dumping grounds for especially dangerous technologies: consider the Union Carbide disaster in Bhopal, India, or the ecological disputes of the Ogoni in south-east Nigeria, which led to the execution of Ken Saro-Wiwa.) Hence, globalisation implies that to survive people will have to trust others whom they may never actually meet, because the global system is founded on networks of complex interdependencies between nation states, international institutions and organisations, intercultural movements and formations, and so on.

I hope it is by now clear that *The Labyrinth* may be seen as reflexively positioned as a part of those networks in an especially inspired manner. It encouraged participants to take potentially huge risks with themselves, but at the same time it took enormous care to establish the possibility of trust through mutual empowerment with the (mostly) invisible other. The empowerment associated with this trust was *the* major factor in creating the possibility of a common identification that includes difference, a temporary collective that encourages individuality, a virtual community that is created from being alone, and a sense of unity that respects plurality.

So what was radically new, ethically and politically, about *The Labyrinth* as a performance? Maybe it is in the ways it modelled the globalising collapse of universalism and particularism, the global and the local, as implied by 'one world, many peoples'. In the world community everyone should have equal rights to justice and freedom through their common humanity *and* in their local community everyone should be enabled to live their difference as fully as they might wish without harming others. In exploring this collapse so intimately I think the installation may have simultaneously empowered both participants and performers, individually and collectively, in ways that could not be wholly prefigured by either: in other words, paradoxically it had the potential to produce a sense of radical freedom. The underlying factor enabling this potential empowerment was *The Labyrinth*'s encouragement of *reflexivity* in its participants, an acute awareness of the provisional nature of any system of cultural exchange. Such reflexivity derives from 'systems' of cultural production that, through processes of interactive creativity like those produced in *The Labyrinth*, promote the expressive self-constitution of *both* participants and performers, audiences and actors (Lash and Urry 1994). If one were looking for the bed-rock of effective cultural democracy in the late twentieth century, then probably the grounds that produce such far-reaching reflexivity would be as good a place as any to start digging. But in what ways did the maze articulate its processes of radical cultural democracy to global ecological concerns?

An ecology of performance

The immersive quality of the maze also suggests an ecology of performance in its exploration of the relationships between humans and the environment. It proposes a revision of the separation of culture and nature in global society, by implying that the dualisms of modernism that have led to the ecological crisis need to be transcended, particularly those between body and mind, analysis and creativity, thought and action. This was the main 'message' of participation in its immersive aesthetics. There is a paradox in this, because it is an artificial environment that aims to create a healthier relation between the human and the natural world. But it is a paradox of a different order to the one identified by Una Chaudhuri in her challenging essay on ecological theatre, when she writes:

> By making a space on its stage for ongoing acknowledgements of the rupture it participates in – the rupture between nature and culture, forests and books...– the theater can become the site of a much-needed ecological consciousness.
>
> (1994: 28)

But unlike theatre, which shadows the separation between culture and nature in the division between stage and auditorium, actor and audience, representation and reception, the performative maze aims to make the relation between the human and nature *creative* by paradoxically opening up fabulous questions in the close confines of its narrow corridors and small chambers. These questions are not formulated *in* the maze, because it always aims to subvert representation, but *through* the experience it creates, so it aims to side-step the paradox described by Chaudhuri while at the same time dealing with the crucial matters that an ecology of performance must address.

Such matters are fabulous in that they touch on the nature of civilisation and its roots (*sic*), as partly signalled in Chaudhuri's juxtaposition of books and forests. In the Western imaginary that is ultimately the source of the ecological crisis, civilisation and the wilderness, culture and nature are locked in a disastrous opposition, with the former feeding uncontrollably off the latter to offset its fears of the abyss, the totally unknown other. Chaudhuri quotes Robert Harrison on Vico to underline the point:

> To burn out a clearing in the forest and to claim it as the sacred ground of the family – that, according to Vico, was the original deed of appropriation that first opened the space of civil society. It was the first decisive act, which would lead to the founding of cities, nations, and empire.
>
> (1994: 28)

In an important sense, the performative maze reverses that 'decisive act' by returning us to the wilderness, by immersing us in the unknown; or, to be more precise, in the half-known, because it places us constantly on the threshold between civilisation and the wilderness. It achieves this in quite literal ways by bringing us 'back' to the smells of nature (earth, mosses, fungi, in contrast to the odour of the musty book) and by ensuring that as we move deeper into its mysteries we do it animal-like, on all fours. In Harrison's terms it offers to bring the race of sky worshippers, looking up from the forest clearing, down to earth. But at the same time it subverts any sense in this of a nostalgic regression to an entirely pre-human state by making the maze into a metaphorical odyssey in search of the Minotaur, a figure hovering between the animal and the human, nature and culture. In meeting the Minotaur, and then in seeing ourselves in him (or her) through the two-way mirror, we participate in a kind of ecological morality play that invites us to revisit the nature/culture dilemma paradoxically from both sides at once. Moreover, to *dance* with the Minotaur suggests the possibility of a radical transcendence of the current dilemmas in the relationships between nature and culture, because the non-human and the human are re-figured as totally, and complexly, interdependent: how can we tell the dancer from the dance?

What makes this event yet more powerful as an ecology of performance, is that *participation* in the maze implies the possibility of new modes of resolving the global crisis. As Chaudhuri explains, through the figure of the 'greenhouse', Western cultures have commodified the natural world as a kind of compensation for the industrial/technological devastation they have forced on the globe. Hence, from the great glass Winter Palaces of the Victorian age down to the virtual journeys through Wildernesses in today's Disneyland, cultural spectacles have:

...figured forth a new relation of the human and natural worlds, making the latter a privileged sign for the superiority of the former.... [Thus] capitalist exploitation – be it of forests or people – requires that nature be artificially reproduced, preserved, and displayed.

(1994: 29; see also Chaudhuri 1997: 77 passim)

Chaudhuri recognises that attempts to transcend this pathology through 'alternative' metaphors or other types of representation, in the theatre or elsewhere, may serve only to reproduce its structures: the hyper-real as product of the cultural logic of capitalism, for example, has no means for returning us to the ecologically real. But her call for a 'turn towards the literal, a programmatic resistance to the use of nature as metaphor' (1994: 29) as a means to create an ecological *theatre* now sounds plaintively contradictory, because theatre increasingly has produced nothing but metaphor (if it ever did anything else?) as it has succumbed to the disciplines of commodification and the market-place.

As I have argued throughout this book, performance beyond theatre at least may have more of a chance of escaping the virulent encroachment of the commodity form in order to produce pathologies of hope. Moreover, performances beyond theatre that draw on the kinds of participation created by *The Labyrinth* may give access not just to some sense of virtual global community as a source of ecological sanity, but also to a fresh sense of the individual subject as responsible to a nature seen – as I saw the Minotaur – as a senior partner in the dance of culture. The spectacular hubris of the American Biosphere II project – in which man (*sic*) attempts to reproduce a self-sustaining 'nature' for himself inside a huge greenhouse – demonstrates the folly of thinking that everything must adapt itself to the interests of the human (Luke 1995). Starting out as a supposedly scientific experiment in environmental sustainability, it has degenerated into little more than a technological tourist attraction. Such a fall from the illusion of global grace potentially places us closer to an ecologically sound paradigm of the real, beyond the cusp of the paradigms that my argument has figured. But for this to come about, new sources of creativity will have to be found, hopefully even more resonant in their potential for change than those that can be produced by the radical in performance.

Epilogue
The radical in performance

Substance is one of the greatest of our illusions.
Eddington

Dancing to the still bits

In the mid-1970s I was invited by the Devonshire-based community
theatre group Medium Fair to direct a series of rural residencies that
they had dubbed the 'village visit weeks'. The idea was that the
company of four performers and a musical director would live for a
week in each of six villages and run workshops with various community
groupings in order to produce six documentary shows about the histories
of the villages. The shows were to be collectively called *The Doomsday
Show*, a title partly signalling the somewhat pessimistic view that Medium
Fair had of rural life in Devon. All six shows ended up including documentary scenes, but the villagers' enthusiasm for the project ensured
that lots of other types of material were incorporated as well. At their
best the performances became, I think, a kind of anarchic celebration of
the vitality of rural grass roots culture, which proved to be sometimes wild,
unpredictable and distinctly eccentric in character (Kershaw 1978).

One particular example sticks in my memory. In a village called
Kenton, ten miles to the south of Exeter, on the Saturday night that
ended the visit week, the village hall was packed to bursting with over 300
people, including many families with children of all ages. Technically, the
numbers in the hall made this an illegal event, but no one from the
village seemed to mind about that. The programme for the show –
which the villagers had insisted on calling *Kenton Capers* – took a variety
or vaudeville format, and in the second half, towards the end of the bill,
an agricultural labourer called Roy had put his name down for a turn.
When he signed up he refused to tell us what he was going to do!

Now Roy was a big man, not to say fat, and by the time he came onstage the atmosphere in the hall was decidedly hot and steamy. He took off his tweed jacket, rolled up the sleeves and unbuttoned the front of his white shirt, then extracted from his trouser pocket two pairs of 'rickers' – curved bones that when held between the thumb/index and middle/ring fingers can be clacked percussively together. A great cheer went up from the audience, particularly from the children, as he stood full-square facing them and began to play with great verve and vigour – 'The Blue Danube'! His technique was precise and physically extraordinarily expressive: both pairs of rickers playing the same clackity beats, as he swung his arms in wide circles and clenched his big fists on precisely twisting wrists to create a musical calisthenics that had his whole body undulating in rhythmic response to the waltz-time tune. By the time he got to the last bar he was sweating profusely, his shirt ribbed with the tide-marks of enormously controlled effort.

The people gave him a great reception, but mixed in with the adults' loud applause were clear jeers from the large group of children sitting apart from their parents close to the stage. Roy clearly didn't like that kind of reaction, so he played 'The Blue Danube' again, and again, and again, each time with greater concentration, commitment and passion. The performance seemed to have become a battle to win over the younger generations, to seduce them into appreciation, admiration, respect even, for this most uncool of spectacles. And after four attempts he appeared to succeed: as the fourth rendition finished there was absolute silence in the hall for at least twenty seconds – then a pandemonium of whoops, cheers, whistles and shouts from everyone for more as, without bowing and with a broad grin, he walked down into the crowd to be warmly mobbed like a star soccer player.

What had happened? Had anything radical happened?

We could, as you have seen, analyse this performance in terms of carnival and the liminal structures of traditional ritual and through that place it in a modernist frame of reference. Or we could, as you have seen, view it pluralistically and sketch out its relevance to a politics of performance in post-modernity. Then we would be talking about the ways it embodied a political multiplicity. For example, first, there was a politics of the personal, for Roy was a middle-aged, overweight bachelor occupying a marginal position in the tight family networks of the community – but his outstanding performance as precisely such a figure apparently rendered him totally, if only temporarily, acceptable. Second, there was a politics of generation, because initially there was a clear resistance from the young people to the nature of his show – as old-fashioned, or weird, or silly, perhaps – but the resistance evaporated as increasingly he established the integrity of his 'outmoded' talent. Third, there was a (submerged) class politics in play, as Kenton was by then in large part a commuter village for professional and managerial staff, represented in perhaps half of the audience that night, so Roy's triumph implicitly underscored the dignity decreasingly available to the agricultural labouring class. Fourth, there was a politics of community identity that in turn linked into a politics of governance and state, for however we interpret the micro-politics at play in the event there can be little doubt that together they added up to a celebration of the vitality of the people of Kenton as a functioning collective with its own unique dynamics. And so on.

Hence, the argument of this book would mark out Roy's remarkable show as an example of democratised performance, in the sense that here was a community of people constructing a sense of identity through the production of a culture that could potentially enhance their collective agency, self-determination and responsibility to each other. Its eccentricity, its uniqueness, its one-offness indicate an opening up, in that context, of a new domain for democratic empowerment. It achieved this, the argument would run, by being *more* than just resistant to the normative values that may be seen as constraints to democracy – personal, generational, familial, and so on – rather it *transcended* those normative values and, at least for the time it was happening, created a space and time beyond the dominant, a new realm of civil society, in which the crucial values celebrated through creativity were equality, justice and freedom. In this sense it was not just radical, but *coherently* radical.

But how exactly did it manage that – if it did – as Roy's performance was a mass of contradictions?

My memory tells me that he wore an immaculately starched white shirt, and huge muddy boots that were well-worn and scuffed. At over six-feet tall he had a massive and heavy frame, which produced fine music with four tiny bones. His great heaving bulk shed a tide of sweat, yet his face throughout was coolly cherubic. He was obviously just a rural labouring man, yet a great interpreter of a popular classic. Hence, no account that relies only on logic, on rational analysis, could possibly capture the quality of his creative achievement, because somehow his performance had turned its own contradictions into paradoxes; somehow he had transcended the binaries and created something entirely new in its disregard of limitation, even though he was repeating an act he had done many times before. So even when he had stopped, his performance was moving, still.

It was a great caper.

How was it done? What *had* happened?

I like to think that maybe the people of Kenton had danced a wonderful welcome to a grain of radical creative sand. In the figure of Roy maybe they had embraced a pleasurable irritant, an impossible solution, a weird familiar. So the fact that the figure was fat, graceful, sweaty, cool, grotesque, beautiful, bizarre, ordinary, extraordinary, reassuring, dangerous made the encounter all the more potent as a catalyst for change. The performance was way beyond theatre in its engagement with the excessive. And in ways that no one could possibly predict, it opened up new spaces for the politics of performance – people's eyes glinted in the light of freedom; it fostered new senses to the ethics of performance – human rights were re-negotiated through a sweaty passion; it spun out further strands to the genetics of performance – old bones influenced the next generation; and it touched on new environments in the ecology of performance – generating the unique character of the community's nature. Paradoxically, it could encompass so much because its creative reach was modest. So this curious little show, I think, gave the lie to the cusp of the paradigm shift: it got a good dance going between Brecht and Baudrillard, and against all the odds of a commodifying world it resourced the radical in performance.

Bibliography

Absalom, Roger (1971) *France: The May Events 1968*, London: Longman.

Ali, Tariq (1978) *1968 and After: Inside the Revolution*, London: Blond and Briggs.

Althusser, Louis (1971) *Lenin and Philosophy, and Other Essays*, London: Monthly Review Press.

Ansorge, Peter (1975) *Disrupting the Spectacle: Five Years of Experimental and Fringe Theatre in Britain*, London: Pitman.

Appadurai, Arjun (1990) 'Disjuncture and difference in the global cultural economy', in Mike Featherstone (ed.) *Global Culture: Nationalism, Globalisation and Modernity*, London: Sage Publications.

Arts Council of Great Britain (1988) *43rd Annual Report and Accounts*, London: Arts Council of Great Britain.

—— (1986) *A Great British Success Story*, London: Arts Council of Great Britain.

Ashcroft, Bill, Gareth Griffiths and Helen Tiffin (eds) (1995) *The Post-Colonial Studies Reader*, London: Routledge.

Aston, Elaine (1995) *An Introduction to Feminism and Theatre*, London: Routledge.

Auslander, Philip (1997) *From Acting to Performance: Essays in Modernism and Postmodernism*, London: Routledge.

—— (1996) 'Liveness and the anxiety of simulation', in Elin Diamond (ed.) *Performance and Cultural Politics*, London: Routledge.

—— (1995) 'Just be yourself', in Phillip Zarrilli (ed.) *Acting (Re)Considered*, London: Routledge.

—— (1992) *Presence and Resistance: Postmodernism and Cultural Politics in Contemporary Performance*, Ann Arbor: University of Michigan Press.

—— (1987) 'Toward a concept of the political in postmodern theatre', *Theatre Journal* 39.

Bachelard, Gaston (1994) *The Poetics of Space*, trans. Maria Jolas, Boston: Beacon Press.

Bakhtin, Mikhail (1968) *Rabelais and His World*, Cambridge, MA: MIT Press.

—— (1981) *The Dialogic Imagination*, trans. Carly Emerson and Michael Holquist, Austin: University of Texas Press.

Baldwin, James (1964) *The Fire Next Time*, Harmondsworth: Penguin.

Barba, Eugenio (1995) *The Paper Canoe*, London: Routledge.

—— (1986) *Beyond the Floating Islands*, trans. Judy Barba, Richard Fowler, Jerrold C. Rodesch and Saul Shapiro, New York: PAJ Publications.

—— (1979) *The Floating Islands: Reflections with Odin Teatret*, ed. Ferdinando Taviani, trans. Judy Barba, Francis Perdeilhan, Jerrold C. Rodesch and Saul Shapiro, Holsterbro: Odin Teatret.

Barba, Eugenio and Nicola Savarese (1991) *The Secret Art of the Performer: A Dictionary of Theatre Anthropology*, ed. Richard Gough, trans. Richard Fowler, London: Routledge.

Barker, Howard (1993) *Arguments for a Theatre*, Manchester: Manchester University Press.

Barnard, Paul (ed.) (1991) *Drama*, London: National Arts and Media Strategy Unit.

Basting, Anne Davis (1998) *The Stages of Age: Performing Age In Contemporary American Culture*, Ann Arbor: University of Michigan Press.

—— (1995) 'The stages of age: The growth of senior theatre', *The Drama Review* 39(3).

Baudrillard, Jean (1994) *Simulacra and Simulation*, trans. Sheila Farier Glaser, Ann Arbor: University of Michigan Press.

—— (1990) *Fatal Strategies*, ed. Jim Fleming, trans. Philip Beitchman and W.G.J. Niesluchowski, New York: Semiotext(e).

—— (1988) *Selected Writings*, ed. Mark Poster, London: Polity Press.

—— (1983) *Simulations*, trans. Paul Foss, Paul Patton and Philip Beitchman, New York: Semiotext(e).

Baxandall, Lee (ed.) (1972) *Radical Perspectives on the Arts*, Harmondsworth: Penguin.

Beck, Julian (1972) *The Life of the Theatre*, New York: Grove Press.

Beck, Ulrich (1992) *Risk Society: Towards a New Modernity*, trans. Mark Ritter, London: Sage.

Bédarida, François (1979) *A Social History of England, 1851–1975*, trans. A.S. Foster, London: Methuen.

Behr, Edward and Mark Steyn (1991) *The Story of Miss Saigon*, London: Jonathan Cape.

Benjamin, Walter (1992) *Illuminations*, trans. Harry Zohn, London: Fontana/Collins.

Bennett, Susan (1997) *Theatre Audiences: A Theory of Production and Reception*, rev. edn, London: Routledge.

Bennett, Tony (1986a) 'Hegemony, ideology, pleasure: Blackpool,' in Tony Bennett, Colin Mercer and Janet Woollacott (eds) *Popular Culture and Social Relations*, Milton Keynes: Open University Press.

—— (1986b) 'Music in the halls', in J.S. Bratton (ed.) *Music Hall: Performance and Style*, Milton Keynes: Open University Press.

Bentham, Jeremy (1995) *The Panoptic Writings*, ed. Bozovic Miran, London: Verso.

Bey, Hakim (1991) *TAZ: The Temporary Autonomous Zone, Ontological Anarchy, Poetic Terrorism*, Brooklyn: Autonomedia.

Bhabha, Homi K. (1994) *The Location of Culture*, London: Routledge.

Bharucha, Rustom (1993) *Theatre and the World: Performance and the Politics of Culture*, London: Routledge.

Biner, Pierre (1972) *The Living Theatre*, New York: Avon Books.

Blau, Herbert (1990) *The Audience*, Baltimore: Johns Hopkins University Press.

Boal, Augusto (1995) *The Rainbow of Desire*, trans. Adrian Jackson, London: Routledge.

—— (1992) *Games for Actors and Non-Actors*, trans. Adrian Jackson, London: Routledge.

—— (1979) *Theater of the Oppressed*, trans. Charles A. and Maria-Odilia Leal McBride, London: Pluto Press.

Bolt, Christine (1971) *Victorian Attitudes to Race*, London: Routledge and Kegan Paul.

Bond, Howard (1991) *One Hour in the Semi-Open* or *The Rat Run*, unpublished MS.

Bornat, Joanna (ed.) (1994) *Reminiscence Reviewed: Perspectives, Evaluations, Achievements*, Buckingham: Open University Press.

Bottomore, Tom (1984) *The Frankfurt School*, London: Routledge.

Bourdieu, Pierre (1984) *Distinction: A Social Critique of the Judgement of Taste*, trans. Richard Nice, London: Routledge.

Brake, Michael (1985) *Comparative Youth Culture: The Sociology of Youth Culture and Youth Subcultures in America, Britain and Canada*, London: Routledge and Kegan Paul.

Brandes, Donna (1982) *Gamesters' Handbook Two*, London: Hutchinson.

Brandes, Donna and Howard Phillips (1979) *Gamesters' Handbook*, London: Hutchinson.

Bratton, J. S. (ed.) (1986) *Music Hall: Performance and Style*, Milton Keynes: Open University Press.

Bratton, J.S., R.A. Cave, B. Gregory and H.J. Holder (eds) (1991) *Acts of Supremacy: The British Empire and the Stage, 1790–1930*, Manchester: Manchester University Press.

Brecht, Bertolt (1964) *Brecht on Theatre: The Development of an Aesthetic*, ed. and trans. John Willett, London: Eyre Methuen.

Brecht, Stephan (ed.) (1988) *The Bread and Puppet Theatre*, 2 vols, London: Methuen.

Breitinger, Eckhard (ed.) (1994) *Theatre and Performance in Africa: Intercultural Perspectives*, Bayreuth: Bayreuth University.

Bristol, Michael D. (1985) *Carnival and Theatre: Plebeian Culture and the Structure of Authority in Renaissance England*, London: Methuen.

British Pathé News, 1968 – a Year to Remember (1990), London: Ingram (video).

Brook, Peter (1973) 'The politics of sclerosis: Stalin and Lear' (interview), *Theatre Quarterly* III(10).

Brustein, Robert (1984) *Making Scenes: A Personal History of the Turbulent Years at Yale 1966–1979*, New York: Limelight Editions.

Carlson, Marvin (1996) *Performance: A Critical Introduction*, London: Routledge.

—— (1992) 'Theater and dialogism', in Janelle G. Reinelt and Joseph R. Roach (eds) *Critical Theory and Performance*, Ann Arbor: University of Michigan Press.

Case, Sue-Ellen and Janelle Reinelt (eds) (1991) *The Performance of Power: Theatrical Discourse and Politics*, Iowa: University of Iowa Press.

Cavafy, C.P. (1961) *The Complete Poems of Cavafy*, trans. Rae Dalven, London: Hogarth Press.

Cerny, Philip G. (ed.) (1982) *Social Movements and Protest in France*, London: Frances Pinter.

Chaim, Daphna Ben (1984) *Distance in the Theatre: The Aesthetics of Audience Response*, Ann Arbor: UMI Research Press.

Chambers, Iain (1993) 'Cities without maps', in Jon Bird, Barry Curtis, Tim Putam and George Robertson (eds) *Mapping the Futures: Local Cultures, Global Change*, London: Routledge.

Chaney, David (1993) *Fictions of Collective Life: Public Drama in Late Modern Culture*, London: Routledge.

Chapman, Mave and Ben Chapman (1988) *The Pierrots of the Yorkshire Coast*, Beverley: Hutton Press.

Chaudhuri, Una (1997) *Staging Place: The Geography of Modern Drama*, Ann Arbor: University of Michigan Press.

—— (1994) ' "There must be a lot of fish in that lake": Toward an ecological theater', *Theatre* 25.

Cheeseman, Peter (1971) 'A community theatre-in-the-round', *Theatre Quarterly* 1(1).

Chipkowski, Peter (1991) *Revolution in Eastern Europe*, London: John Wiley.

Cockrell, Dale (1997) *Demons of Disorder: Early Blackface Minstrels and Their World*, Cambridge: Cambridge University Press.

Cohen, Anthony P. (1985) *The Symbolic Construction of Community*, Chichester: Ellis Horwood.

Cohen-Cruz, Jan (ed.) (1998) *Radical Street Performance: An International Anthology*, London: Routledge.

Connor, Steven (1989) *Postmodernist Culture: An Introduction to the Theories of the Contemporary*, Oxford: Blackwell.

Conway, Martin A. (1990) *Autobiographical Memory: An Introduction*, Milton Keynes: Open University Press.

Cork, Sir Kenneth (1986) *Theatre Is For All* (The Cork Report), London: Arts Council of Great Britain.

Coult, Tony and Baz Kershaw (eds) (1990) *Engineers of the Imagination: The Welfare State Handbook*, rev. edn, London: Methuen.

CPR (Centre for Performance Research) (1996) Publicity Material for *The Labyrinth – Ariadne's Thread*.

Craig, Sandy (ed.) (1980) *Dreams and Deconstructions: Alternative Theatre in Britain*, Ambergate: Amber Lane.

Crow, Brian and Chris Banfield (1996) *An Introduction to Post-Colonial Theatre*, Cambridge: Cambridge University Press.

Croyden, Margaret (1974) *Lunatics, Lovers and Poets: The Contemporary Experimental Theatre*, New York: Dell Publishing.

Davis, Andrew (1987) *Other Theatres: The Development of Alternative and Experimental Theatre in Britain*, London: Macmillan.

Davis, R.G. (1975) *The San Francisco Mime Troupe: The First Ten Years*, Palo Alto: Ramparts Press.

de Certeau, Michel (1988) *The Practice of Everyday Life*, trans. Stephen Rendall, Berkeley: University of California Press.

de Marinis, Marco (1993) *The Semiotics of Performance*, trans. Áine O'Healy, Bloomington and Indianapolis: Indiana University Press.

—— (1987) 'The dramaturgy of the spectator', *The Drama Review* 31(2).

—— (1985) 'A faithful betrayal of performance: Notes on the use of video in performance', *New Theatre Quarterly* 1(4).

Debord, Guy (1977) *The Society of the Spectacle*, Detroit: Black and Red.

Deleuze, Gilles and Felix Guattari (1984) *Anti-Oedipus: Capitalism and Schizophrenia*, trans. Rod Hurley, Mark Seem and Helen R. Lane, London: The Athlone Press.

Derrida, Jacques (1992) 'From *Psyche* – invention of the other', in Derek Attridge (ed.) *Acts of Literature*, London: Routledge.

—— (1991) *A Derrida Reader: Between the Blinds*, ed. Peggy Kamuf, Hemel Hempstead: Harvester Wheatsheaf.

—— (1982) *Margins of Philosophy*, trans. Alan Bass, Brighton: Harvester Press.

Diamond, Elin (ed.) (1996) *Performance and Cultural Politics*, London: Routledge.

Dolan, Jill (1993) *Presence and Desire: Essays on Gender, Sexuality, Performance*, Ann Arbor: University of Michigan Press.

Dunlop, Rachel and Jeremy Eckstein (eds) (1994) 'The performed arts in London and regional theatres', *Cultural Trends* 22.

Eagleton, Terry (1996) *The Illusions of Postmodernism*, Oxford: Blackwell.

—— (1990) *Ideology: An Introduction*, London: Verso.

Eco, Umberto (1985) *Reflections on 'The Name of the Rose'*, London: Secker & Warburg.

Eddershaw, Margaret (1996) *Performing Brecht: Forty Years of British Performances*, Routledge: London.

EMMA Theatre Company (1981) leaflet.

Epskamp, Kees P. (1989) *Theatre in Search of Social Change*, trans. Corrie Donner, Greet Hooijmans, Jan Jacobs and Carlo Scheldwacht, The Hague: CESO.

Esherick, Joseph W. and Jeffrey N. Wasserstrom (1990) 'Acting out democracy: Political theatre in modern China', *The Journal of Asian Studies* (49)4.

Esslin, Martin (1987) *The Field of Drama*, London: Methuen.

Fanon, Frantz (1986) *Black Skin, White Masks*, trans. Charles Lam Markmann, London: Pluto Press.
—— (1968) *The Wretched of the Earth*, trans. Constance Farrington, New York: Grove Press.
Featherstone, Mike (1991) *Consumer Culture and Postmodernism*, London: Sage.
—— (ed.) (1990) *Global Culture*, London: Sage.
Feigon, Lee (1990) *China Rising: The Meaning of Tienanmen*, Chicago: Ivan Dee.
Feist, Andrew and Robert Hutchison (1990) *Cultural Trends in the Eighties*, London: Policy Studies Institute.
Fiske, John (1993) *Power Plays, Power Works*, London: Verso.
—— (1989) *Understanding Popular Culture*, Boston: Unwin Hyman.
Flax, Jane (1993) *Disputed Subjects: Essays on Psychoanalysis, Politics and Philosophy*, London: Routledge.
Foster, Hal (ed.) (1985) *Postmodern Culture*, London: Pluto Press.
Fotheringham, Richard (ed.) (1987) *Community Theatre in Australia*, Sydney: Currency Press.
Foucault, Michel (1989) *The Order of Things: An Archaeology of the Human Sciences*, London: Routledge.
—— (1977) *Discipline and Punish: The Birth of the Prison*, trans. Alan Sheridan Smith, London: Allen Lane.
—— (1972) *The Archaeology of Knowledge*, trans. Alan Sheridan Smith, London: Tavistock Publications.
—— (1970) *The Order of Things: An Archaeology of the Human Sciences*, trans. Alan Sheridan Smith, London: Tavistock Publications.
Fowler, Catherine (1994) ' "Performing sexualities" at Lancaster', *New Theatre Quarterly* X(38).
Fox, John (1988) 'Between Windscale and Wordsworth' (an interview by Baz Kershaw), *Performance Magazine* 54.
Frith, Simon (1983) *Sound Effects: Youth, Leisure and the Politics of Rock*, London: Constable.
Frow, John (1997) *Time and Commodity Culture: Essays in Cultural Theory and Postmodernity*, Oxford: Clarendon Press.
Fryer, Peter (1984) *Staying Power: The History of Black People in Britain*, London: Pluto Press.
Fuchs, Elinor (1996) *The Death of Character: Perspectives on Theatre After Modernism*, Bloomington and Indianapolis: Indiana University Press.
Garland, Jeffrey (1994) 'What splendour, it all coheres: life-review therapy with older people', in Joanna Bornat (ed.) *Reminiscence Reviewed: Perspectives, Evaluations, Achievements*, Buckingham: Open University Press.
Gash, Anthony (1993) 'Carnival and the poetics of reversal', in Julian Hilton (ed.) *New Directions in Theatre*, London: Macmillan.
Gaynor, J. Ellen (ed.) (1995) *Imperialism and Theatre: Essays on World Theatre*, London: Routledge.

Geertz, Clifford (1993) *Local Knowledge: Further Essays in Interpretive Anthropology*, London: Fontana Press.

George, David E. (1996) 'Performance epistemology', *Performance Research* 1(1).

Giddens, Anthony (1994) *Beyond Left and Right: The Future of Radical Politics*, London: Polity Press.

Gilbert, Helen and Joanne Tomkins (1996) *Post-Colonial Drama: Theory, Practice, Politics*, London: Routledge.

Gleick, James (1988) *Chaos: Making a New Science*, London: Sphere Books.

Goffman, Erving (1959) *The Presentation of Self in Everyday Life*, New York: Doubleday Anchor Books.

Goldberg, RoseLee (1988) *Performance Art: From Futurism to the Present*, rev. edn, London: Thames and Hudson.

Gooch, Steve (1984) *All Together Now: An Alternative View of Theatre and Community*, London: Methuen.

Gordon, Alec (1986) 'Thoughts out of season on counter culture', in David Punter (ed.) *Introduction to Contemporary Cultural Studies*, London: Longman.

Gottlieb, Saul (ed.) (1966) *The Living Theatre in Europe*, Amsterdam: Mickery Books.

Gramsci, Antonio (1971) *Selections for the Prison Notebooks*, ed. and trans. Quintin Hoare and Geoffrey Nowell Smith, London: Lawrence & Wishart.

Gropius, Walter (ed.) (1961) *The Theatre of the Bauhaus*, trans. Arthur S. Wensinger, Middletown: Wesleyan University Press.

Grotowski, Jerzy (1968) *Towards a Poor Theatre*, New York: Simon & Schuster.

Hall, Stuart, Chas Critcher, Tony Jefferson and John Clarke (1978) *Policing the Crisis: Mugging, the State, and Law and Order*, London: Macmillan.

Hall, Stuart and Tony Jefferson (eds) (1976) *Resistance Through Rituals*, London: Hutchinson.

Harvey, David (1990) *The Condition of Postmodernity: An Enquiry into the Origins of Cultural Change*, Oxford: Blackwell.

Hawker, James (1961) *A Victorian Poacher: James Hawker's Journal*, ed. Garth Christian, Oxford: Oxford University Press.

Hebdige, Dick (1993) 'A report on the Western front: postmodernism and the "politics" of style', in Chris Jenks (ed.) *Cultural Reproduction*, London: Routledge.

—— (1979) *Subculture: The Meaning of Style*, London: Methuen.

Held, David (1995) *Democracy and the Global Order: From the Modern State to Cosmopolitan Governance*, London: Polity Press.

—— (1987) *Models of Democracy*, London: Polity Press.

Herns, James/Cooney, Jimmy (n.d.) *The Life of Jimmy Cooney*, privately published.

Hewison, Robert (1988) *The Heritage Industry: Britain in a Climate of Decline*, London: Methuen.

—— (1986) *Too Much: Art and Society in the Sixties, 1960–75*, London: Methuen.

Hoffman, Abbie (1985) 'Museum of the Streets', in Douglas Khan and Diane Naumaier (eds) *Cultures in Contention*, New York: Real Comet Press.
—— (1968) *Revolution for the Hell of It*, New York: Dial Books.
Holderness, Graham (ed.) (1992) *The Politics of Theatre and Drama*, London: Macmillan.
Holmberg, Arthur (1996) *The Theatre of Robert Wilson*, Cambridge: Cambridge University Press.
Horkheimer, Max and Theodor W. Adorno (1972) *Dialectic of Enlightenment*, trans. John Cumming, New York: Seabury Press.
Hughes, Patrick and George Brecht (1978) *Vicious Circles and Infinity: An Anthology of Paradoxes*, Harmondsworth: Penguin.
Hutcheon, Linda (1988) *The Poetics of Postmodernism: History, Theory, Fiction*, London: Routledge.
Hutchison, Robert (1982) *The Politics of the Arts Council*, London: Sinclair Brown.
Hutton, Will (1996) *The State We're In*, rev. edn, London: Vintage.
Illich, Ivan (1985) *Tools for Conviviality*, London: Marion Boyars.
Itzin, Catherine (1980) *Stages in the Revolution: Political Theatre in Britain Since 1968*, London: Eyre Methuen.
Jameson, Fredric (1991) *Postmodernism, or, The Cultural Logic of Late Capitalism*, London: Verso.
Jellicoe, Ann (1987) *Community Plays: How to Put Them On*, London: Methuen.
Jenks, Chris (1995) 'The centrality of the eye in Western culture', in Chris Jenks (ed.) *Visual Culture*, London: Routledge.
Jones, Steve (1997) *In the Blood: God, Genes and Destiny*, London: Flamingo.
Kaye, Nick (1994) *Postmodernism and Performance*, London: Macmillan.
Keat, Russell, Nigel Whiteley and Nicholas Abercrombie (eds) (1994) *The Authority of the Consumer*, London: Routledge.
Kelly, Owen (1984) *Community, Art and the State: Storming the Citadels*, London: Comedia.
Kerr, David (1995) *African Popular Theatre*, Oxford: James Currey.
Kershaw, Baz (1997) 'Fighting in the streets: Dramaturgies of popular protest, 1968–1989', *New Theatre Quarterly* XIII(51).
—— (1996) 'The politics of performance in a postmodern age', in Patrick Campbell (ed.) *Analysing Performance: A Critical Reader*, Manchester: Manchester University Press.
—— (1994) 'Framing the Audience for Theatre', in Russell Keat, Nigel Whiteley and Nicholas Abercrombie (eds) *The Authority of the Consumer*, London: Routledge.
—— (1993) 'Building an unstable pyramid: The fragmentation of British alternative theatre', *New Theatre Quarterly* IX(36).
—— (1992) *The Politics of Performance: Radical Theatre as Cultural Intervention*, London: Routledge.
—— (1978) 'Theatre art and community action: the achievement of Medium Fair', *Theatre Quarterly* VIII(30).

Kiernan, V.G. (1969) *The Lords of Human Kind: European Attitudes Towards the Outside World in the Imperial Age*, London: Weidenfield and Nicholson.

King, Anthony D. (ed.) (1991) *Culture, Globalisation and the World System*, London: Macmillan.

Klotz, Günter (1991) 'Howard Barker: Paradigm of postmodernism', *New Theatre Quarterly* VII(25).

Kraus, Rosalind (1985) 'Sculpture in the expanded field', in Hal Foster (ed.) *Postmodern Culture*, London: Pluto Press.

Kuhn, Thomas S. (1970) *The Structure of Scientific Revolutions*, Chicago: University of Chicago Press.

Laclau, Ernesto and Chantal Mouffe (1986) *Hegemony and Social Strategy: Towards a Radical Democratic Politics*, London: Verso.

Lahr, John and Jonathan Price (1973) *Life Show: How to See Theater in Life and Life in Theater*, New York: Viking Press.

Laing, Dave (1978) *The Marxist Theory of Art: An Introductory Survey*, Brighton: Harvester Press.

Lambley, Dorrian (1992) 'In search of a radical discourse for theatre', *New Theatre Quarterly* VIII(29).

Langley, Gordon and Baz Kershaw (eds) (1982) *Reminiscence Theatre*, Dartington: Dartington Theatre Papers, series 4, no. 6.

Larsen, Lance (1971) 'Liquid Theatre', *The Drama Review* 15(3a) (T51).

Lash, Scott and John Urry (1994) *Economies of Signs and Space*, London: Sage.

Lefebvre, Henri (1991) *The Production of Space*, trans. Donald Nicholson-Smith, Oxford: Blackwell.

—— (1971) *Everyday Life in the Modern World*, trans. Sacha Rabinovich, London: Harper & Row.

Lesnick, Henry (1973) *Guerilla Street Theatre*, New York: Avon Books.

Lewis, Charles N. (1971) 'Reminiscing and self-concept in old age', *Journal of Gerontology* 26(2).

Love, Lauren (1995) 'Resisting the "organic": a feminist actor's approach', in Phillip Zarrilli (ed.) *Acting (Re)Considered: Theories and Practices*, London: Routledge.

Lukács, Georg (1971) *History and Class Consciousness*, trans. R. Livingstone, London: Merlin Press.

Luke, Timothy W. (1995) 'Reproducing planet earth? The hubris of Biosphere 2', *The Ecologist* 25(4).

Lury, Celia (1993) *Cultural Rights: Technology, Legality and Personality*, London: Routledge.

Lyotard, Jean-François (1984) *The Postmodern Condition: A Report on Knowledge*, trans. Geoff Bennington and Brian Massumi, Manchester: Manchester University Press.

McCarthy, Mary (1968) *Vietnam*, Harmondsworth: Penguin Books.

McCauley, Gay (1994) 'The visual documentation of theatrical performance', *New Theatre Quarterly* X(38).

McCluhan, Marshall (1964) *Understanding Media: The Extensions of Man*, New York: Signet.

McCullough, Christopher (1992) 'From Brecht to Brechtian: Estrangement and appropriation', in Graham Holderness (ed.) *The Politics of Theatre and Drama*, London: Macmillan.

McGrath, John (1990) *The Bone Won't Break: On Theatre and Hope in Hard Times*, London: Methuen.

—— (1981) *A Good Night Out – Popular Theatre: Audience, Class and Form*, London: Methuen.

McKay, George (1996) *Senseless Acts of Beauty: Cultures of Resistance Since the Sixties*, London: Verso.

Mackintosh, Iain (1993) *Architecture, Actor and Audience*, London: Routledge.

McMahon, A.W. and P.J. Rhudick (1964) 'Reminiscing: Adaptational significance in the aged', *Archives of General Psychiatry* 10.

Macmillan, Joyce (1990) 'All Lit Up', *Guardian*, 8 October.

Manley, Andrew and Lloyd Johnston (1981) *The Poacher*, unpublished MS.

Marcuse, Herbert (1969) *Eros and Civilisation*, London: Sphere Books.

—— (1968) *One Dimensional Man*, London: Sphere Books.

Marranca, Bonnie and Guatam Dasgupta (eds) (1991) *Interculturalism and Performance: Writings from PAJ*, New York: PAJ.

Martin, Bernice (1981) *A Sociology of Contemporary Cultural Change*, Oxford: Basil Blackwell.

Marwick, Arthur (1982) *British Society Since 1945*, Harmondsworth: Pelican.

Marx, Karl and Frederick Engels (1974) *The German Ideology*, ed. C.J. Arthur, London: Lawrence & Wishart.

—— (1970) *Capital: Vol. 1*, London: Lawrence & Wishart.

Mda, Zakes (1993) *When People Play People*, London: Zed Books.

Mellor, G.J. (1966) *Pom-Poms and Ruffles: The Story of Northern Seaside Entertainment*, Clapham: Daleman Publishing Company.

Melzer, Annabel (1995) ' "Best betrayal": the documentation of performance on video and film, parts one and two', *New Theatre Quarterly* XI(42/43).

Merquior, J.G. (1985) *Foucault*, London: Fontana.

Minzhu, Han (ed.) (1990) *Cries for Democracy: Writing and Speeches from the 1989 Chinese Democracy Movement*, Princeton: Princeton University Press.

Mlama, Penina Muhando (1991) *Culture and Development: The Popular Theatre Approach in Africa*, Uppsala: Nordiska Afrikainstitutet.

Moody, David (1995) 'Peter Brook's heart of light: "primitivism" and intercultural theatre', *New Theatre Quarterly* XI(41).

Morecambe Visitor (1932) 'Obituary: Jimmy Cooney's adventurous life', March 9th.

Morgan, Kenneth O. (1992) *The People's Peace: British History 1945–1990*, Oxford: Oxford University Press.

Morris, Megan (1993) 'Things to do with shopping centres', in Simon During (ed.) *The Cultural Studies Reader*, London: Routledge.

Mouffe, Chantal (ed.) (1992) *Dimensions of Radical Democracy: Pluralism, Citizenship, Democracy*, London: Verso.

Mulgan, Geoff (ed.) (1997) *Life After Politics: New Thinking for the Twenty-first Century*, London: Fontana Press.

—— and Ken Worpole (1986) *Saturday Night or Sunday Morning? From Arts to Industry – New Forms of Cultural Policy*, London: Comedia.

Musgrove, Frank (1974) *Ecstasy and Holiness: Counter Culture and the Open Society*, London: Methuen.

Myerhoff, Barbara (1992) *Remembered Lives: The Work of Ritual, Storytelling and Growing Older*, with Deena Metzger, Jay Ruby and Virginia Tufte, ed. Marc Kaminsky, Ann Arbor: University of Michigan Press.

Myerscough, John (1987) *The Economic Importance of the Arts in Britain*, London: Policy Studies Institute.

—— (1986) *Facts About the Arts II*, London: Policy Studies Institute.

NAMSU (National Arts and Media Strategy Unit) (1992) *Towards a National Arts and Media Strategy*, London: National Arts and Media Strategy Unit.

Nield, Sophie (1996) 'Space and popular theatre', in Ros Merkin (ed.) *Popular Theatres?*, Liverpool: Liverpool John Moores University.

Neville, Richard (1971) *Play Power*, St Albans: Paladin.

Nuttall, Jeff (1979) *Performance Art: Memoirs*, vol. 1, London: Paladin.

Owusu, Kwesi (1986) *The Struggle for Black Arts in Britain: What Can We Consider Better Than Freedom*, London: Comedia.

Parry, Geraint and Michael Moran (eds) (1994) *Democracy and Democratisation*, London: Routledge.

Paskman, Dailey (1976) *'Gentlemen, Be Seated!': A Parade of the American Minstrels*, rev. edn, New York: Clarkson N. Potter.

Pavis, Patrice (1992) *Theatre at the Crossroads of Culture*, trans. Loren Kruger, London: Routledge.

—— (1982) *Languages of the Stage: Essays in the Semiology of Theatre*, trans. Susan Melrose, Susan Bassnett McGuire, Tjaart Potgieter and Marguerite Oerlemans Bunn, New York: PAJ.

Peaker, Anne (ed.) (1996) *Creative Time: The 2nd European Conference On Theatre and Prison*, HM Prison Service Enterprises/TTP International.

Pertwee, Bill (1979) *Promenades and Pierrots: One Hundred Years of Seaside Entertainment*, Newton Abbott: Westbridge Books.

Peters, Julie Stone (1995) 'Intercultural performance, theatre anthropology, and the imperialist critique', in J. Ellen Gaynor (ed.) *Imperialism and Theatre: Essays on World Theatre, Drama and Performance*, London: Routledge.

Phelan, Peggy (1993) *Unmarked: The Politics of Performance*, London: Routledge.

Phillips, Anne (1993) *Democracy and Difference*, London: Polity Press.

Pickering, Michael (1991) 'Mock blacks and racial mockery: the "nigger" minstrel and British imperialism', in J.S. Bratton, R.A. Cave, B. Gregory and H.J. Holder (eds) *Acts of Supremacy – The British Empire and the Stage, 1790–1930*, Manchester: Manchester University Press.

—— (1986) 'White skin, black masks: "nigger" minstrelsy in Victorian Britain', in J.S. Bratton (ed.) *Music Hall – Performance and Style*, Milton Keynes: Open University Press.

Piscator, Irwin (1980) *The Political Theatre*, trans. Hugh Rorrison, London: Eyre Methuen.

Plant, Sadie (1992) *The Most Radical Gesture: The Situationist International in a Postmodern Age*, London: Routledge.

Plastow, Jane (1996) *African Theatre and Politics: The Evolution of Theatre in Ethiopia, Tanzania and Zimbabwe – a Comparative Study*, Amsterdam, Atlanta: Rodopi.

Prentki, Tim (1990) 'Cop-out, cop-in: Carnival as political theatre', *New Theatre Quarterly* VI(24).

Pridham, Geoffrey and Paul G. Lewis (eds) (1996) *Stabilising Fragile Democracies: Comparing New Party Systems in Southern and Eastern Europe*, London: Routledge.

Rabinow, Paul (ed.) (1984) *The Foucault Reader*, Harmondsworth: Penguin.

Read, Alan (1993) *Theatre and Everyday Life: An Ethics of Performance*, London: Routledge.

Reader, Keith A. (1993) *The May 1968 Events in France: Reproductions and Interpretations*, London: St Martin's Press.

Rees, Roland (ed.) (1992) *Fringe Firsts: Pioneers of the Fringe Theatre on Record*, London: Oberon Books.

Rees-Mogg, William (1985) *The Political Economy of Art*, London: Arts Council of Great Britain.

Reinelt, Janelle (ed.) (1996) *Crucibles of Crisis: Performing Social Change*, Ann Arbor: University of Michigan Press.

Reinelt, Janelle and Joseph R. Roach (eds) (1992) *Critical Theory and Performance*, Michigan: University of Michigan Press.

Reynolds, Harry (1928) *Minstrel Memories: The Story of Burnt Cork Minstrelsy in Great Britain from 1836 to 1927*, London: Alston Rivers.

Reynolds, Peter (1992) 'Community theatre: Carnival or camp?' in Graham Holderness (ed.) *The Politics of Theatre and Drama*, London: Macmillan.

Ritzer, George (1993) *The McDonaldization of Society*, Thousand Oaks: Pine Forge Press.

Roach, Joseph (1996a) *Cities of the Dead: Circum-Atlantic Performance*, New York: Columbia University Press.

—— (1996b) 'Kinship, intelligence, and memory as improvisation: Culture and performance in New Orleans', in Elin Diamond (ed.) *Performance and Cultural Politics*, London: Routledge.

—— (1995) 'Culture and performance in the circum-Atlantic world', in Andrew Parker and Eve Kosofsky Sedgwick (eds) *Performativity and Performance*, London: Routledge.

—— (1993) *The Player's Passion: Studies in the Science of Acting*, Ann Arbor: University of Michigan Press.

Robertson, Roland (ed.) (1992) *Globalisation*, London: Sage.

Roose-Evans, James (1984) *Experimental Theatre: From Stanislavski to Peter Brook*, London: Routledge and Kegan Paul.

Rose, Chris (1998) *The Turning of the 'Spar'*, London: Greenpeace.

Rose, Clarkson (1960) *Beside the Seaside*, London: Museum Press.

Roszak, Theodore (1969) *The Making of a Counter Culture: Reflections on the Technocratic Society and its Youthful Opposition*, New York: Doubleday.

Rubin, Jerry (1970) *Do It!*, New York: Simon & Schuster.

Said, Edward (1993) *Culture and Imperialism*, London: Vintage.

—— (1991) *Orientalism: Western Concepts of the Orient*, Harmondsworth: Penguin.

Sainer, Arthur (ed.) (1997) *The New Radical Theatre Notebook*, London: Applause.

—— (ed.) (1975) *The Radical Theatre Notebook*, New York: Avon Books.

Samuel, Raphael (1994) *Theatres of Memory*, London: Verso.

Sands, Stanley (1891) *Turner's Nigger Notions: Book 2*, London: John Alvey Turner.

Savran, David (1986) *Breaking the Rules: The Wooster Group*, New York: Theatre Communications Group.

Sayre, Henry M. (1989) *The Object of Performance: The American Avant-Garde since 1970*, Chicago: University of Chicago Press.

Scarry, Elaine (1985) *The Body in Pain: The Making and Unmaking of the World*, Oxford: Oxford University Press.

Schechner, Richard (1993) *The Future of Ritual: Writings on Culture and Performance*, London: Routledge.

—— (1992) 'A new paradigm for theatre in the academy', *The Drama Review* 36(4).

—— (1988) *Performance Theory*, rev. edn, London: Routledge.

—— (1985) *Between Theatre and Anthropology*, Philadelphia: University of Pennsylvania Press.

—— (1970) *The Performance Group: Dionysus 69*, New York: Farrar, Straus and Giroux.

Schweitzer, Pam (1994a) 'Dramatising reminiscences', in Johanna Bornat (ed.) *Reminiscence Reviewed: Perspectives, Evaluations, Achievements*, Buckingham: Open University Press.

—— (1994b) 'Many happy retirements', in Mady Schultzman and Jan Cohen-Cruz (eds) *Playing Boal: Theatre, Therapy, Activism*, London: Routledge.

Seale, Patrick and Maureen McConville (1968) *French Revolution 1968*, Harmondsworth: Penguin.

Shank, Theodore (ed.) (1996) *Contemporary British Theatre*, London: Macmillan.

—— (1982) *American Alternative Theatre*, London: Macmillan.

Shaw, Roy (1987) *The Arts and the People*, London: Jonathan Cape.

Shevtsova, Maria (1993) *Theatre and Cultural Interaction*, Sydney: Sydney Association for Studies in Society and Culture.

Simpson, J.A. (1976) *Towards Cultural Democracy*, Strasbourg: Council of Europe.

Srampickal, Jacob (1994) *Voice to the Voiceless: The Power of People's Theatre in India*, London: Hust & Company.

Stanislavski, Constantin (1937) *An Actor Prepares*, trans. Elizabeth Reynolds Hapgood, London: Geoffrey Bles.

States, Bert O. (1985) *Great Reckonings in Little Rooms: On the Phenomenology of Theatre*, Berkeley: University of California Press.

Strong, Roy (1984) *Art and Power: Renaissance Festivals, 1650–1850*, Woodbridge: Boydell.

Thompson, James (1998a) 'Out of this sterile space: Notes on pathologies of hope in theatre and drama', *Research in Drama Education* 3(2).

—— (ed.) (1998b) *Prison Theatre: Perspective and Practices*, London: Jessica Kingsley.

Thompson, John B. (1990) *Ideology and Modern Culture*, Cambridge: Polity Press.

Tinker, Anthea (1992) *Elderly People in Modern Society*, third edn, London: Longman.

Toll, Robert C. (1974) *Blacking Up: The Minstrel Show in Nineteenth-Century America*, New York: Oxford University Press.

Tornqvist, Egil (1991) *Transposing Drama: Studies in Representation*, New York: St Martin's Press.

Trend, David (ed.) (1996) *Radical Democracy: Identity, Citizenship and the State*, London: Routledge.

Trotsky, Leon (1964) 'The proletariat and the revolution', in Isaac Deutscher (ed.) *The Age of Permanent Revolution: A Trotsky Anthology*, New York: Dell Publishing.

—— (1935) *The History of the Russian Revolution*, London: Victor Gollancz.

Turner, Victor (1986) *The Anthropology of Performance*, New York: PAJ.

—— (1982) *From Ritual to Theatre: The Human Seriousness of Play*, New York: PAJ.

Tynan, Kenneth (1971) 'The critic comes full circle' (interview), *Theatre Quarterly* 1(2).

Tytell, John (1997) *The Living Theatre: Art, Exile and Outrage*, London: Methuen.

Ubersfeld, Anne (1982) 'The pleasure of the spectator', *Modern Drama* 25(1).

Urry, John (1990) *The Tourist Gaze: Leisure and Travel in Contemporary Societies*, London: Sage.

van Erven, Eugène (1992) *The Playful Revolution: Theatre and Liberation in Asia*, Bloomington and Indianapolis: Indiana University Press.

—— (1988) *Radical People's Theatre*, Bloomington and Indianapolis: Indiana University Press.

Vanhanen, Tatu (1997) *Prospects of Democracy: A Study of 172 Countries*, London: Routledge.

wa Thiongo, Ngũgĩ (1993) *Moving the Centre: The Struggle for Cultural Freedoms*, London: James Currey.

—— (1997) 'The politics of performance space', *The Drama Review* 41(3) (T155).

Wark, McKenzie (1994) *Virtual Geography: Living with Global Media Events*, Bloomington and Indianapolis: Indiana University Press.

Wasserstrom Jeffrey N. and Elizabeth J. Perry (eds) (1994) *Popular Protest and Political Culture in Modern China*, second edn, Oxford: Westview Press.

Waters, Malcolm (1995) *Globalization*, London: Routledge.

Watson, Ian (1993) *Towards a Third Theatre: Eugenio Barba and the Odin Teatret*, London: Routledge.

Wehle, Philippa (1996) 'Robert Lepage's "Seven Streams of the River Ota"', *Theatre Forum* 8.

White, Stephen K. (1991) *Political Theory and Postmodernism*, Cambridge: Cambridge University Press.

Williams, David (ed.) (1991) *Peter Brook and 'The Mahabharata': Critical Perspectives*, London: Routledge.

Williams, Patrick and Laura Chrisman (eds) (1993) *Colonial Discourse and Post-Colonial Theory*, New York: Harvester Wheatsheaf.

Williams, Raymond (1954/1991) *Drama in Performance*, Milton Keynes: Open University Press.

—— (1981) *Culture*, London: Fontana.

—— (1976) *Keywords: A Vocabulary of Culture and Society*, London: Fontana.

Willis, Susan (1991) *A Primer for Daily Life*, London: Routledge.

Wiseman, John (1973) *Guerilla Theatre: Scenarios for Revolution*, New York: Anchor Books.

Woodruff, Graham (1989) 'Community, class and control: a view of community plays', *New Theatre Quarterly* V(20).

Wright, David (n.d.) *The Heat is On: The Making of 'Miss Saigon'*, London: First Night Video.

Wright, Elizabeth (1989) *Postmodern Brecht: A Re-Presentation*, London: Routledge.

Zarrilli, Phillip B. (1995) ' "On the edge of a breath, looking": Disciplining the actor's bodymind through the martial arts in the Asian/experimental theatre programme', in Phillip B. Zarrilli (ed.) *Acting (Re)Considered: Theories and Practices*, London: Routledge.

Name index

Subject index